THE
TYPE 2
DIABETES
SOURCEBOOK
FOR WOMEN

Other Books by M. Sara Rosenthal

The Canadian Type 2 Diabetes Sourcebook (2nd edition, 2005)
The Complete Thyroid Book (2005)
The Thyroid Sourcebook for Women (2nd edition, 2005)
The Skinny on Fat (2004)
The Gynecological Sourcebook (4th edition, 2003)
The Natural Woman's Guide to Hormone Replacement' Therapy
  (2003)
The Thyroid Cancer Book (2nd edition, 2003)
The Fertility Sourcebook (3rd edition, 2002)
The Hypothyroid Sourcebook (2002)
The Natural Woman's Guide to Preventing Diabetes
  Complications (2002)
Women Managing Stress (2002)
Managing PMS Naturally (2001)
Stopping Cancer At the Source (2001)
The Breastfeeding Sourcebook (3rd edition, 2000)
The Thyroid Sourcebook (4th edition, 2000)
Women and Depression (2000)
Women and Passion (2000)
The Breast Sourcebook (2nd edition, 1999)
The Pregnancy Sourcebook (3rd edition, 1999)
The Gastrointestinal Sourcebook (1998)

50 Ways Series

50 Ways to Manage Ulcer, Heartburn and Reflux (2001)
50 Ways to Prevent and Manage Stress (2001)
50 Ways to Prevent Depression Without Drugs (2001)
50 Ways to Prevent Colon Cancer (2000)
50 Ways Women Can Prevent Heart Disease (2000)

Your Health Press titles published by M. Sara Rosenthal

Dr. Rosenthal publishes a line of specialty health books by other authors available only at online bookstores or by calling toll free. Visit www.yourhealthpress.com for more information and a complete catalog.

THE
TYPE 2 DIABETES SOURCEBOOK
FOR WOMEN

M. Sara Rosenthal, Ph.D.

McGraw·Hill

New York   Chicago   San Francisco   Lisbon   London   Madrid   Mexico City
Milan   New Delhi   San Juan   Seoul   Singapore   Sydney   Toronto

The *McGraw-Hill* Companies

Library of Congress Cataloging-in-Publication Data

Rosenthal, M. Sara.
    The type 2 diabetes sourcebook for women / M. Sara Rosenthal.
       p.   cm.
    First ed. published under title: The type 2 diabetic woman. Includes bibliographical
references and index.
    ISBN 0-07-144929-9 (book : alk. paper)
    1. Diabetes in women—Popular works.   2. Diabetes in pregnancy—Popular works.
3. Non-insulin-dependent diabetes—Popular works.   I. Rosenthal, M. Sara. Type 2 diabetic
woman.   II. Title.

RC662.18.R66   2005
616.4′62′0082—dc22   2004026263

1 2 3 4 5 6 7 8 9 0   FGR/FGR   0 9 8 7 6 5

ISBN 0-07-144929-9

McGraw-Hill books are available at special quantity discounts to use as premiums and sales promotions, or for use in corporate training programs. For more information, please write to the Director of Special Sales, Professional Publishing, McGraw-Hill, Two Penn Plaza, New York, NY 10121-2298. Or contact your local bookstore.

The purpose of this book is to educate. It is sold with the understanding that the author and publisher shall have neither liability nor responsibility for any injury caused or alleged to be caused directly or indirectly by the information contained in this book. While every effort has been made to ensure its accuracy, the book's contents should not be construed as medical advice. Each person's health needs are unique. To obtain recommendations appropriate to your particular situation, please consult a qualified health-care provider.

This book is printed on acid-free paper.

Contents

Acknowledgments

FOR THIS REVISED edition, I'd like to thank Dennis G. Karounos, M.D., Director of Diabetes Program and Associate Professor of Internal Medicine, University of Kentucky Medical Center. I'm also grateful to my husband, Kenneth B. Ain, M.D., who gives me love and support, not to mention valuable insights into diabetes management from his perspective as an internist and endocrinologist.

Finally, I wish to thank the following colleagues (listed alphabetically) for their commitment, hard work, and guidance on earlier works I've written on type 2 diabetes, which helped to frame so much of the content of this book: Irwin Antone, M.D., C.C.F.P.; Brenda Cook, R.D.; Tasha Hamilton, Ba.Sc., R.D.; Stuart Harris, M.D., M.P.H., C.C.F.P., A.B.P.M.; Anne Kenshol, M.D.; Barbara McIntosh, R.N., B.Sc.N., C.D.E.; James McSherry, M.B., Ch.B., F.C.F.P., F.R.C.G.P., F.A.A.F.P., F.A.B.M.P.; David Michaels, D.D.S.; Mark and Judy Nesbitt (patient advocates); Robert Panchyson, B.Sc.N., R.N.; Diana Phayre; Robert Silver, M.D., F.R.C.P.C.; Gary May, M.D., F.R.C.P.; William Warren Rudd, M.D.

Introduction

All in the Family

LET ME TELL you a little about my family, which will explain why I'm interested in the subject of type 2 diabetes.

In 1978, my grandmother, obese and physically inactive, who had type 2 diabetes, died of a massive heart attack at the age of sixty-two. She was survived by her own mother by a full decade. I have still never quite recovered from the loss because it was such an untimely death. My grandfather, a family physician who died in 1989, used to say that my grandmother "ate herself to death." And the more I research type 2 diabetes, the more I understand what he meant by this comment.

Roughly 85 percent of those diagnosed with type 2 diabetes are obese. My grandmother was a textbook case. In her midforties, she developed type 2 diabetes. She had poor blood sugar control, but outlived her baby sister, who was also obese and also died from complications of type 2 diabetes. Despite her sister's death, my grandmother never made any effort to adjust her own eating habits. My mother, who has spent most of her adult life battling obesity, used to be coaxed into eating rich desserts by my grandmother with comments such as, "It's a *sin* not to eat it."

My grandmother could never pass up rich and tasty foods, possibly as a consequence of the hard times she experienced coming of age in the prairies during the Depression. She developed heart disease and spent most of her forties and fifties continuously plagued with one health problem after another. Given this information, you are probably not surprised that she died. The odd thing is, everyone who loved her was shocked by her death. My great-grandmother bore the terrible fate of outliving almost all of her children, who were all obese; most of them died from complications related to type 2 diabetes.

This is the book I wish my grandmother and her siblings had read. I want to give you the information my grandmother should have had, and might have used if it had been available to her.

Today, one in four people over the age of forty-five has been diagnosed with type 2 diabetes, and the prevalence is greater in women than in men. In 2003, diabetes experts recommended that all people over forty be screened for type 2 diabetes. We now know, too, that there are special risks for women with type 2 diabetes; they have a higher risk of heart disease, tend to have high blood pressure, and also suffer from urinary and vaginal infections more frequently. Throughout the life cycle, women with diabetes also have special challenges with hormonal contraception, pregnancy, and menopause.

My grandmother was a collector of Inuit (Eskimo) art. The irony is that she did not know how much she had in common with aboriginal cultures, whose rates of type 2 diabetes have been soaring out of control since the 1940s. Today the rate of diabetes among Native Americans, Pacific Islanders, and Alaskan Natives is five times that of those in the general population. In fact, the artists my grandmother loved probably suffered from the same diseases she did.

Type 2 diabetes is now being seen as a complication of a larger epidemic: obesity. This sourcebook contains chapters on the role of obesity and lowering fat consumption in your diet. Women are also more vulnerable to the complications of diabetes, which can be prevented through better blood sugar control. This book includes information on heart disease, nerve damage, diabetes eye disease, gum disease, and kidney disease.

As obesity becomes more of an epidemic in the United States, more women than ever before can benefit from the information in this book, which outlines how to manage diabetes, prevent complications, and for some, how to stop diabetes before it starts.

THE
TYPE 2
DIABETES
SOURCEBOOK
FOR WOMEN

1

What Is Type 2 Diabetes, and Who's at Risk?

You've just come home from your doctor's office. You can't remember anything he or she said other than those three horrible words, "You have diabetes." What does this mean? How will your life change? You've never been any good at diets, meal plans, or exercising. And since you can't stand the sight of blood, how can you be expected to prick your finger every day to monitor your blood sugar? Today, one in four Americans over the age of forty-five has been diagnosed with type 2 diabetes. Currently, eighteen million Americans, or 63 percent of the total United States population, have type 2 diabetes. Between 1990 and 1998 a 70 percent increase in type 2 diabetes has been seen in women ages thirty to thirty-nine. As of this writing, roughly 1.8 million premenopausal women have type 2 diabetes, and 30 percent of these remain undiagnosed.

Name Changes and Definitions

Over the years, the names for different types of diabetes have changed, creating a lot of confusion for people who are newly diagnosed with type 2 diabetes. Other names for this disease were used when our parents or grandparents were diagnosed, and a lot of people over forty still remember them. When Dr. Frederick G. Banting first had the idea for developing a therapy for diabetes in 1921, diabetes, like the World War, wasn't yet numbered. It was long known, however, that there was a milder form of diabetes as well as a more severe form, but diabetes wasn't officially labeled *type 1* and *type 2* until 1979.

When you see the word *diabetes*, it refers to *diabetes mellitus*, which is a condition in which the body either cannot produce insulin or cannot effectively use the insulin it produces, causing high blood sugar (hyperglycemia). But the literal meaning of the word *diabetes* is from the Greek *siphon*. The word *mellitus* is Latin for "sweet." That doesn't mean much today, but it does make sense: in ancient Greece, diabetes used to be diagnosed by "urine tasters" because the urine becomes sweet when blood sugar is dangerously high. The Greeks noticed that when people with sweet urine drank fluids, the fluids came out in the form of urine immediately—like a siphon. Hence the term *diabetes mellitus* was coined and has stuck to this day.

Confusing Type 2 with Type 1

Many people confuse type 2 diabetes with type 1 diabetes, a misunderstanding that interferes with getting accurate information about type 2 diabetes, so here's what you need to understand: type 2 diabetes can be managed, reversed, or even prevented by modifying your lifestyle; managing type 2 diabetes does not necessarily require insulin. Most diabetes experts agree that poor diet combined with a sedentary lifestyle triggers the type 2 gene for those of us who are genetically predisposed to it. In other words, a combination of environment and genes is at work with type 2 diabetes.

Type 1 diabetes is completely different. It cannot be reversed or prevented through lifestyle modification. The working theory, believed by most diabetes experts, is that type 1 diabetes is an autoimmune disease that just strikes without warning. Here, the immune system attacks the beta cells in the pancreas, effectively destroying them. The result is that no insulin is produced by the pancreas. Type 1 diabetes is usually diagnosed before age thirty, often in childhood. For this reason, type 1 diabetes was once known as *juvenile diabetes* or *juvenile-onset diabetes*. Because of organizations such as the Juvenile Diabetes Foundation, we still see *juvenile diabetes* widely used in the literature on diabetes, even though it is technically an outdated term. It is also misleading since we are now diagnosing type 2 diabetes in children, especially in indigenous groups or children who are obese.

Because people with type 1 diabetes depend on insulin injections to live, it was also once called *insulin-dependent diabetes mellitus (IDDM)*. Only 10 percent of all people with diabetes have type 1 diabetes.

The Many Names for Type 2 Diabetes

Ninety percent of all people with diabetes have type 2 diabetes. Since type 2 diabetes is a disease of resistance to, rather than an absence of, insulin, it often can be managed through diet and exercise, without insulin injections. For this reason, type 2 diabetes was once called *non-insulin-dependent diabetes mellitus (NIDDM)*. But since many people with type 2 diabetes may require insulin down the road, NIDDM is an inaccurate and misleading name and is not used anymore. In fact, about one-third of all people with type 2 diabetes will eventually need insulin therapy.

When people with type 2 diabetes require insulin, they can mistakenly believe that their diabetes has "turned into" type 1 diabetes. But this isn't so; in the same way that an apple cannot turn into a banana, type 2 diabetes cannot turn into type 1 diabetes. For reasons I will discuss later in this book, type 2 diabetes can progress and become more severe over the years, requiring insulin therapy. That's why the terms *NIDDM* and *IDDM* were dropped; they are both inaccurate and misleading. Nonetheless, you may still see these terms widely used in diabetes literature.

Since type 2 diabetes doesn't usually develop until after age forty-five, before it was named NIDDM it had even earlier names: *mature-onset diabetes* or *adult-onset diabetes*. *Mature-onset diabetes in the young (MODY)* referred to type 2 diabetes in people under thirty years old. None of these terms are used anymore.

Type I and Type II Versus Type 1 and Type 2

In 1979, when the types of diabetes were numbered, most literature used Roman numerals (*I* and *II*) instead of Arabic numerals (*1* and *2*).

As a result, many people remain confused over whether *type I* and *type II* diabetes are the same as *type 1* and *type 2* diabetes. Yes, they are. In the late 1990s, consensus was reached in the diabetes medical community over finally dropping the Roman numerals and using only Arabic *1* and *2* in the literature to distinguish between the two types of diabetes. The term *latent autoimmune diabetes* (*LADA*) has been used to describe the small number of people who are diagnosed with type 2 diabetes, but who actually have type 1 diabetes—the autoimmune form of diabetes.

What Happens in Type 2 Diabetes?

If you have type 2 diabetes, your pancreas is functioning. You are making plenty of insulin. In fact, you are probably making too much insulin, a condition called *hyperinsulinemia*. Insulin is a hormone made by your *beta cells*, the insulin-producing cells within the *islets of Langerhans*—small islands of cells afloat in your pancreas. The *pancreas* is a bird beak–shaped gland located behind the stomach.

Insulin is a major player in our bodies. One of its most important functions is to regulate blood sugar levels. It does this by "knocking" on your cells' door and announcing, "Sugar's here; come and get it!" Your cells then open the door to let sugar in from your bloodstream. That sugar is absolutely vital to your health and provides your cells with the energy they need to function.

Insulin Resistance

When the cells don't answer the door, it is called *insulin resistance*: the cells are resisting insulin. Two things happen when the cells resist insulin. First, the sugar will accumulate in your bloodstream because it has nowhere to go. (It's the kind of situation that develops when your newspapers pile up outside your door when you're away.) This results in high blood sugar. Second, your pancreas will keep sending out more insulin to try to get your cells to open that door. This causes too much sugar and too much insulin to pile up. This is a bad combination of problems, which can lead to high blood pressure (also called *hypertension*) and high cholesterol, and a host of other complications.

It wasn't until the 1960s that researchers discovered that most people with type 2 diabetes suffered from a *resistance* to insulin, not necessarily a *lack* of insulin. If insulin resistance goes on for too long, the pancreas can become overworked and eventually may not make enough, or any, insulin. In effect, it's like a strike. This is why some people with type 2 diabetes may require insulin injections one day. (I discuss this in more detail later on.)

When the body uses insulin properly, it not only lowers blood sugar but also assists in the distribution of fat and protein. Therefore, when your body doesn't use insulin properly, obesity can be the by-product. Insulin also increases appetite, which can also lead to obesity. Some diabetes experts I've interviewed believe that insulin resistance may be what actually causes obesity, not the other way around.

High Blood Sugar

The high blood sugar that results from insulin resistance can lead to a number of other diseases, including cardiovascular disease (heart disease and stroke) and peripheral vascular disease (PVD), a condition in which the blood doesn't flow properly to parts of your body. This can create a number of problems, discussed in later chapters. Many people who suffer a heart attack or stroke have type 2 diabetes.

High blood sugar can also become aggravated by glycogen, a form of glucose that is stored in the liver and muscles, which is released when you need energy. Insulin enables your cells to store glucose as glycogen. But when your cells are resisting insulin, glycogen can be released in a confused response because it appears to the cells that there is no sugar in the blood.

When You Have Type 2 Diabetes and Require Insulin

Insulin resistance, characterized by the body's inability to use insulin, sometimes leads to a condition in which the pancreas stops making insulin altogether. The cells' resistance to insulin causes the pancreas to work harder, causing too much insulin in the system (hyperinsulinemia) until it just wears itself out. Your pancreas makes the insulin and knocks on the door, but the cells don't answer. Your pancreas will eventually say, "Okay, fine! I'll shut down production since you obviously aren't using what I'm making."

But this isn't always the reason that you may need insulin. Often the problem is that your body becomes increasingly more resistant to the insulin your pancreas is producing. This is sometimes exacerbated by medications or the disease over time. Controlling your blood sugar becomes harder and harder until, ultimately, you need to inject insulin.

You may also require insulin if you go for long periods with high blood sugar levels. In this case, the high blood sugar can put you at very high risk for other health complications. It is not unusual to be diagnosed with type 2 diabetes in a later stage and prescribed insulin.

Conditions That Can Lead to Type 2 Diabetes

There are a variety of risk factors for type 2 diabetes, such as high cholesterol or obesity, which I discuss in Chapter 2. The following conditions, however, are definite precursors to type 2 diabetes, meaning that if you have any of the following conditions, you are at very high risk of developing type 2 diabetes.

Prediabetes: Impaired Fasting Glucose and Impaired Glucose Tolerance

Normal fasting blood glucose levels (meaning what your blood glucose levels are eight hours after your last meal), also called *fasting plasma glucose*, are between 72 and 108 mg/dl. A fasting blood sugar level between 110 and 126 mg/dl is classified as *impaired fasting glucose (IFG)*. Anyone with symptoms of diabetes and with a fasting blood sugar level of 126 mg/dl or more in one test is considered to have type 2 diabetes. People with no symptoms who have a fasting blood sugar level greater than 126 mg/dl on two occasions are also considered to have diabetes. Readings higher than 126 mg/dl on a *casual blood glucose test*, which refers to a test taken any time of day, should be repeated with a fasting blood glucose test.

Some doctors still recommend an oral glucose tolerance test, which means that you ingest about seventy-five grams of a very sweet cola-like drink (known as *glucola*) first thing in the morning, before eating (meaning after about twelve hours of fasting), and then have your blood glucose tested two hours later. (In the past, your blood was tested immediately after the drink and then every thirty minutes until the three-hour mark. Today most centers will just test you two hours later.) The term *impaired glucose tolerance (IGT)* is used to classify people with a blood glucose level between 140 and 200 mg/dl at the two-hour mark after drinking the glucose. Some women's health experts believe that the oral glucose tolerance test is the most accurate test in diagnosing type 2 diabetes in women. The more convenient fasting plasma glucose test, widely recommended by the American Diabetes Association, can result in a missed diagnosis in many women.

Metabolic Syndrome or Syndrome X

Metabolic syndrome (also called *Syndrome X*) describes a group of people with insulin resistance and impaired fasting glucose levels and a distinct collection of other health problems that include abdominal obesity, hypertension, and dyslipidemia (abnormal lipids). People with metabolic syndrome do not yet have type 2 diabetes but are at a much higher risk of developing it, along with cardiovascular disease. Essentially, if you have three or more of the following health conditions in addition to insulin resistance (demonstrated by impaired fasting glucose—see Table 1.1), then you have metabolic syndrome:

- High blood pressure (blood pressure reading of 130/85)
- High fasting triglycerides, or "blood fats" (a reading of 150 mg/dl or more)
- Too low a level of good cholesterol (an HDL reading of less than 50 mg/dl)
- Abdominal obesity (a waist circumference of more than thirty-five inches for women)
- Polycystic ovarian syndrome (PCOS) (see Chapter 3)
- Fasting blood glucose of between 110 and 126 mg/dl

Gestational Diabetes Mellitus (GDM)

Gestational diabetes mellitus refers to diabetes first recognized or diagnosed during any stage of pregnancy. If you develop gestational dia-

Table 1.1 What Your Readings Mean

Fasting Plasma Glucose Test (after fasting for eight hours)

Normal	Impaired Fasting Glucose (IFG)	Diabetes
Below 110 mg/dl	110 to 126 mg/dl	>126 mg/dl or higher

Oral Glucose Tolerance Test (two hours after drinking a special sweet drink)

Normal	Impaired Glucose Tolerance (IGT)	Diabetes
Below 140 mg/dl	140 to 200 mg/dl	Over 200 mg/dl

Suggested screening age: forty or over

betes during pregnancy, consider yourself put on alert. Approximately 20 percent of all women with gestational diabetes develop type 2 diabetes, presuming no other risk factors. If you are genetically predisposed to type 2 diabetes, a history of gestational diabetes can raise your risk of eventually developing the disease. Gestational diabetes develops more often in women who were overweight prior to pregnancy and women who are over thirty-five; the risk increases with maternal age. If your mother had gestational diabetes, you are also more likely to develop it. (For a more detailed discussion, see Chapter 3.)

If you had diabetes prior to your pregnancy (type 1 or type 2), it is known in the medical literature as *preexisting diabetes*, which is a completely different story and not at all the same thing as gestational diabetes.

Pancreatitis

Diabetes can be caused by a condition known as *pancreatitis*, which means "inflammation of the pancreas." This occurs when the pancreas's digestive enzymes attack the pancreas itself. This can cause the gland to bleed, as well as serious tissue damage, infection, and cysts. (Other organs, such as the heart, lungs, and kidneys, could be affected in severe cases.) Pancreatitis is most often chronic, as opposed to acute (sudden), and it is usually caused by years of alcohol abuse. Ninety percent of all chronic pancreatitis affects men between thirty and forty years of age. In rare cases, chronic pancreatitis is inherited, but experts are not sure why this is. People with chronic pancreatitis tend to have three main symptoms: pain, weight loss (due to poor food absorption and digestion), and diabetes (the type of diabetes depends on how much damage has been done to the islet or insulin-producing cells of the pancreas).

The treatment usually is to first stop drinking. Then the resulting diabetes is managed like that of any other diabetes patient: using blood glucose monitoring, meal planning, and possibly insulin injections.

Side-Effect Diabetes

Side-effect diabetes is a term I've coined to describe what's more commonly known as *secondary diabetes*. This occurs when your diabetes is a side effect of a particular drug or surgical procedure.

A number of prescription medications, including steroids or Dilantin, can raise your blood sugar levels, which would affect the outcome of a blood sugar test, for example. Make sure you tell your doctor about all medications you're on prior to having your blood sugar checked.

If you've had your pancreas removed (a pancreatectomy), diabetes will definitely result because the pancreas is no longer present to produce insulin. Diabetes may also develop if you've experienced severe injury to your pancreas, liver disease, or iron overload.

Who Gets Type 2 Diabetes?

Screening studies show that type 2 diabetes is prevalent all over the world, particularly in Westernized countries. Type 2 diabetes is increasing in the developed world at an annual rate of about 6 percent, while the number of people with type 2 diabetes doubles every fifteen years. Roughly 6 percent of all Caucasian adults have type 2 diabetes, but the disease affects North Americans of African descent at a rate of 12 to 15 percent, Hispanics at a rate of 20 percent, and Native North Americans at a rate exceeding 30 percent. In some Native North American communities, up to 70 percent of adults have type 2 diabetes.

Many people don't realize they have type 2 diabetes until they develop a complication such as eye problems, nerve problems, cardio-vascular disease, or peripheral vascular disease—all discussed in later chapters. People with type 2 diabetes are four times more likely to develop heart disease and five times more likely to suffer a stroke than people without type 2 diabetes.

If you consume a diet higher in fat than carbohydrates and low in fiber, you increase your risk for type 2 diabetes if you are genetically predisposed to the disease. If you weigh at least 20 percent more than you should for your height and age, are sedentary, and are over the age of forty-five, you are considered at high risk for type 2 diabetes. Your risk further increases if you:

- Are of indigenous descent (this is true for indigenous peoples all over the world, from Australia to North America; in the United States, American Indians and Pacific Islanders are at highest risk)
- Are of African, Hispanic, or South Asian (for example, Indian or Pakistani) descent
- Have a family history of type 2 diabetes
- Are obese and female (73 percent of all women with diabetes are obese)
- Are pregnant (one in twenty women will develop gestational diabetes by the third trimester; this number increases with age, while gestational diabetes can predispose you to type 2 diabetes later in life)
- Have abdominal obesity (a waist circumference of more than thirty-five inches for women)
- Have been diagnosed with polycystic ovarian syndrome
- Have given birth to a baby over nine pounds
- Have been diagnosed with acanthosis nigricans (a skin disorder)
- Have been diagnosed with schizophrenia

As you can see, many factors contribute to your risk profile and can affect your level of risk. The purpose of this section is to give you a clear idea of where you fit into the risk puzzle. That way, you'll be more aware of early warning signs of the disease, which will make it easier for you to get an accurate diagnosis. If you've already been diagnosed with type 2 diabetes, this section will help you understand *why* you developed the disease, and what you can do today to eliminate some of the factors that may be aggravating your condition.

Risk Factors You Can Change

Type 2 diabetes more than meets the requirements to be called an epidemic. In 2002, it was estimated that 18.2 million Americans had diabetes, with type 2 diabetes accounting for 90 to 95 percent of all diagnosed cases. An estimated 5.2 million cases of diabetes remain undiagnosed. As the U.S. population ages, the numbers will grow; by 2030, the number of older Americans with diabetes is projected to double to 70 million, or one in every five Americans.

Thirty-two percent of people who have at least three of the risk factors can *double* their risk of developing type 2 diabetes, while 89 percent of people with the disease have at least one modifiable risk factor. That means you can lower your risk of developing diabetes by changing your lifestyle or diet.

There are two categories of risk: modifiable risk factors—risk factors you can change; and risk markers—risk factors you cannot change, such as your age or genes. It's crucial to understand that risk estimates are only guesses that are not based on you personally, but on people *like* you, who share your physical characteristics or lifestyle patterns. It's like betting on a horse. You look at the age of the horse, its vigor and shape, its breeding, its training, and where the race is being run. Then you come up with odds. If you own the horse, you can't change your horse's color or breeding, but you can change its training, its diet, its jockey, and where it's being raced, when and how often. Chance, of course, plays a role in horse racing. You can't control acts of God. But you can decide whether you're going to tempt fate by racing your horse during a thunderstorm. In the same way, even though there are some risk factors you cannot change, by changing the factors you can, you can improve your likelihood of having good health.

The following are modifiable risk factors. You can reduce the risk if you make the change.

High Cholesterol

Cholesterol is a whitish, waxy fat made in vast quantities by the liver. (That's why liver and other organ meats are high in cholesterol!) Cholesterol is also known as a *lipid*, the umbrella name for the many different fats found in the body. Cholesterol is needed to make hormones as well as cell membranes. Dietary cholesterol is found only in foods from animals and fish. The daily maximum amount of dietary cholesterol recommended by nutrition experts is 300 milligrams (mg). If you have high cholesterol, the excess cholesterol in your blood can lead to narrowed arteries, which in turn can lead to a heart attack. Saturated fat, discussed in detail in Chapter 5, is often a culprit when it comes to high cholesterol, but the highest levels of cholesterol are due to a genetic defect in the liver. Since people with diabetes are four times more likely to develop heart disease and five times more likely to suffer a stroke, lowering your cholesterol, especially if you're already at risk for type 2 diabetes, is a good idea.

Insulin's Role in Cholesterol

Insulin not only keeps blood sugar in check, it also keeps the levels of good cholesterol (HDL, or high-density lipoproteins), bad cholesterol (LDL, or low-density lipoproteins), and triglycerides in check. When you're not making enough insulin or your body isn't using insulin efficiently, your LDL levels and your triglycerides rise, but more important, *your HDL levels fall*, which can lead to heart disease. When diabetes is in control, cholesterol levels will return to normal, which will cut your risk of heart disease and stroke as well. The usual pattern in type 2 diabetes is to have high triglycerides, lower than optimal levels of good cholesterol or HDL, and normal levels of bad cholesterol or LDL.

Checking Your Cholesterol

If you're over thirty, a total cholesterol level of less than 200 mg/dl is considered healthy. If your total cholesterol levels are higher than 200 mg/dl, discuss with your doctor lifestyle changes that can lower cholesterol levels. Your doctor may recommend cholesterol-lowering drugs if your lifestyle changes are not successful.

High cholesterol is also called *hypercholesterolemia*. Another term used in conjunction with high cholesterol is *hyperlipidemia*, which refers to an elevation of lipids (fats) in the bloodstream; lipids include cholesterol and triglycerides (the most common form of fat from food sources in our bodies). For adults with type 2 diabetes, diabetes experts advise that a triglyceride level of less than 150 mg/dl is optimal.

Total blood cholesterol levels are guidelines only. You also have to look at the relative proportion of high-density lipoprotein (HDL) or good cholesterol to low-density lipoprotein (LDL) or bad cholesterol in the blood. If you have diabetes, an HDL reading of less than 50 mg/dl for women is too low (in men below 40 mg/dl is too low), and an HDL reading of 60 mg/dl or greater is considered healthy and heart-protective. Meanwhile, an LDL reading of less than 100 mg/dl is optimal if you have type 2 diabetes. If your LDL is 130 mg/dl or higher, you may be a candidate for cholesterol-lowering medication. *Weight loss of roughly 20 pounds can reduce LDL levels by 15 percent, reduce triglyceride levels by 30 percent, increase HDL levels by 8 percent, and reduce your total cholesterol levels by 10 percent.*

Cholesterol-Lowering Drugs

For many, losing weight and modifying fat intake simply aren't enough to bring cholesterol levels down to optimal levels. You may be a candidate for one of the numerous cholesterol-lowering drugs. These medications, when combined with a low-fat, low-cholesterol diet, target the intestine, blocking food absorption, and/or the liver, where they interfere with the processing of cholesterol. These are strong drugs, however, and they ought to be a last resort after really giving a low-fat, low-cholesterol diet a chance. You might be given a combination of cholesterol-lowering medications to try with a low-cholesterol diet. It's important to ask about all side effects accompanying your medication because they can include gastrointestinal problems, allergic reactions, blood disorders, and depression. One study looking at male patients taking cholesterol-lowering drugs found an unusually high rate of suicide and accidental trauma. There have not been enough studies on women taking these drugs to know for certain how they interact with women's health conditions. At any rate, here's what's available as of this writing. Please note that only the generic drug names are listed.

Statins

Statins hinder the liver's ability to produce cholesterol, keeping LDL levels to a minimum while increasing levels of HDL. Statins are used to lower LDL levels higher than 130 mg/dl. When combined with the proper diet, statins can reduce your risk of death from heart disease by as much as 40 percent. However, certain statins have been known to cause liver damage, muscle pain, and weakness. The official drug category for statins is HMG (hydroxymethylgluteryl) CoA reductase inhibitors.

Fibrates

These lower cholesterol and triglyceride levels in the blood. In a Finnish study, the rate of coronary artery disease among four thousand men with high cholesterol dropped 34 percent when they took fibrates. Fibrates are usually recommended when the HDL levels are optimal but the LDL levels are between 100 and 129 mg/dl.

Niacin

Niacin, a water-soluble B vitamin, can lower LDL by 30 percent and triglyceride levels by as much as 55 percent. It also increases HDL by about 35 percent. Recent studies suggest that niacin, also known as nicotinic acid, should be taken at a dose ranging between 750 and 2,000 milligrams per day. Many patients experience itching, flushing, and panic attacks when taking these doses of niacin, however. Switching to slow-release capsules, taking an aspirin thirty minutes before taking the medication, or taking it on a full stomach might help alleviate some of these symptoms. The trouble with niacin is that it can increase blood sugar, and therefore aggravate diabetes as well as stomach ulcers. If your HDL levels are too low and you are at risk of cardiovascular problems, niacin may be worth taking if you cannot adjust your diet appropriately.

Resins

Resins, technically called *bile acid sequestrants*, these drugs, such as cholestyramine, help the body eliminate cholesterol through the gut.

Cholestyramine is considered the safest of cholesterol-lowering drugs; it has also been around the longest. A National Institutes of Health study in the early 1980s demonstrated that cholestyramine decreases heart attack deaths by lowering cholesterol levels. In fact, for each 1 percent drop in the cholesterol levels of participants, there was a 2 percent drop in death rates, which is pretty impressive when you consider that the average decline in blood cholesterol was 25 percent. Although cholestyramine reduces LDL, or bad cholesterol, it can sometimes raise triglyceride levels. It can also trigger a host of side effects, the most unpleasant of which is really bad gas. Cholestyramine interferes with the effectiveness of digitalis, diuretics, warfarin, thyroxine (thyroid hormone), fat-soluble vitamins, and beta-blockers. It can also lead to gallstones. Cholestyramine should be taken in the morning and at bedtime.

There are other cholesterol-lowering agents reported in both the medical and alternative medicine literature, including trials using coenzyme Q_{10}, but the agents discussed in this book are based on what diabetes experts are prescribing to people with type 2 diabetes.

Hypertension (High Blood Pressure)

To understand high blood pressure, it's useful to explain what blood pressure is. The blood flows from the heart into the arteries (blood vessels), pressing against the artery walls. The simplest way to explain this is to think about the streets of a small city. During the evening rush hour everybody drives home using the same major streets that head to the suburbs. Normally, all of the traffic is easily handled by the multi-lane streets and roads, or the "arteries" of the city; however, as the city ages, and more people move there, roads develop potholes and areas of disrepair. This results in lane closures, and the traffic backs up as the diminished road capacity is forced to accept the same flow of cars returning home. The increased "pressure," manifested by elevated tempers and rapid, jerky accelerations of cars trying to get through intersections, reflects the constricted roadways.

This is much like the constricted blood vessels, some partially blocked by fatty deposits of atherosclerotic cardiovascular disease (ASCVD), attempting to handle the full flow of blood needed by your body. Over time, the left ventricle enlarges and thickens as it works harder than normal to squeeze the blood through the constricted and narrowed arteries. The thickened heart muscle is more difficult to feed through its own coronary arteries and demands greater sustenance from these coronary arteries, placing it at greater risk of a heart attack (death of a section of the heart muscle) should the coronary arteries have fatty narrowing or blood clots.

Since each pumping chamber of the heart, the two ventricles and their respective atria, have one-way heart valves that only let blood flow in the proper forward direction, the increased pressure of the blood places greater strain on the heart valves. Any leaking of blood backward through any of the valves, worsened by hypertension, adds to the backward congestion of blood in the body regions feeding that side of the heart (lungs feeding the left side and the rest of the body feeding the right side). This shows itself as worsening congestive heart failure.

The term *hypertension* refers to the tension or force exerted on your artery walls. (*Hyper* means "too much," as in "too much tension.") Blood pressure is measured in two readings: X over Y. The X is the *systolic pressure*, which is the pressure that occurs during the heart's contraction. The Y is the *diastolic pressure*, which is the pressure that occurs when the heart rests between contractions.

It's known that obesity, smoking, and a high-sodium diet can put you at risk for hypertension. Genetic factors are very important as well, so that your risks for hypertension are much higher if it runs in your family, and there are certain ethnic groups with greater risks. High blood pressure can also be caused by kidney disorders (prevalent in people with diabetes) or during pregnancy (known as *pregnancy-induced hypertension*).

In the general population, target blood pressure readings are less than 130 over 80 (130/80). Readings greater than 130/80 are considered by diabetes educators to be too high for people with diabetes, but in the general population, readings of 140/90 or higher are generally considered borderline, although for some people this is still considered a normal reading. For the general population, 140/90 is lecture time, when your doctor will begin to counsel you about dietary and lifestyle habits. By 160/100, many people are prescribed a hypertensive drug, which is designed to lower blood pressure.

Medications are also common culprits in causing high blood pressure. Estrogen-containing medications (such as oral contraceptives), nonsteroidal anti-inflammatory drugs (NSAIDs)—such as ibuprofen, nasal decongestants, cold remedies, appetite suppressants, certain antidepressants, and other drugs—can all increase blood pressure. Be sure to check with your pharmacist.

How to Lower Your Blood Pressure Without Drugs

To lower your blood pressure without drugs, change your diet and begin exercising (see Chapter 5). Specifically, the DASH diet is recommended. DASH stands for "Dietary Approaches to Stop Hypertension," an eating plan known to lower blood pressure. This diet involves limiting sodium intake to 1,500 milligrams per day; lowering saturated fat, cholesterol, and total fat (mainly by reducing red meat, sweets, and sugar-containing beverages); increasing intake of whole-grain products, fish, poultry, and nuts; and increasing intake of fruits, vegetables, and low-fat dairy foods. In addition:

- Limit alcohol consumption to no more than two ounces of liquor, eight ounces of wine, or twenty-four ounces of beer per day, and even less for liver health.
- Increase your intake of potassium (bananas are a good source). Some still-inconclusive studies suggest that people with hypertension are calcium- and potassium-deficient.
- Lower your stress levels. Studies show that lowering stress leads to a decrease in blood pressure.

Blood Pressure–Lowering Drugs

If you can't lower your blood pressure through lifestyle changes, you may be a candidate for one of the following blood pressure–lowering drugs, listed alphabetically.

ACE Inhibitors
ACE inhibitors lower blood pressure by preventing the formation of a hormone called angiotensin II, which causes the blood vessels to nar-

row. ACE inhibitors are also used to treat heart failure. Possible side effects include a cough and swelling of the face and tongue.

Alpha-Blocking Agents
Alpha-blocking agents block the effects of noradrenaline, a stress hormone, allowing the blood vessels to relax. Blood pressure and cholesterol decrease with treatment. You may also notice an increase in HDL, or good cholesterol. A possible side effect is blood pressure variation when standing versus reclining.

Angiotensin Receptor Blockers (ARBs)
Similar to ACE inhibitors, ARBs block the effects of angiotensin II on the cells of the blood vessel wall. Essentially ARBs act further down the angiotensin pathway. They're popular because they tend to have fewer side effects than ACE inhibitors, but appear to be equally effective in terms of blood pressure control.

Beta-Blockers
Beta-blockers alter the way hormones like adrenaline control blood pressure. They slow the heart rate by decreasing the strength of the heart's contractions. Beta-blockers are most often used by young people and/or people with coronary artery disease. Possible side effects include fatigue and an increase in blood sugar and cholesterol levels. Another major problem with beta-blockers is that because they block adrenaline, they can mask signs of hypoglycemia (see Chapter 8), which could be dangerous if your blood sugar levels are not well controlled.

Calcium Channel Blockers
Calcium channel blockers limit the amount of calcium entering the cells, allowing the muscles in the blood vessels to relax. Possible side effects include ankle swelling, flushing, constipation, and indigestion.

Centrally Acting Agents
These drugs act through centers in the brain to slow the heart rate and relax the blood vessels. Possible side effects include stuffy nose, dry mouth, and drowsiness.

Diuretics
Diuretics are the most commonly used blood pressure medication. Also known as *water pills*, diuretics work by flushing excess water and

salt—often two to four pounds' worth!—out of your system. But diuretics may actually increase the risk of heart attack by leaching potassium salts needed by the heart, and the heart may respond to blocked nerve signals by trying harder and harder until it fails. Another common side effect of diuretic therapy is low potassium. Levels of potassium tend to drop when diuretics replace the low-fat diet you've worked so hard to maintain. If you make sure not to substitute one therapy for another, diuretics will not affect your potassium levels. Other side effects include increased blood sugar and cholesterol levels.

Vasodilators
Vasodilators dilate, or relax, the blood vessels, thereby reducing blood pressure.

Obesity

Chapter 2 covers the important risk factor of obesity, and Chapter 5 discusses lowering fat and healthy eating.

Smoking

Smoking and diabetes are a toxic combination. You already know that smoking leads to heart attacks. But what you might not know is that if you have type 2 diabetes and do not smoke, you are *already* four times more likely to have a heart attack than a person without diabetes. If you smoke *and* have type 2 diabetes, you have an even greater risk of having a heart attack. In spite of these well-known statistics on the dangers of smoking and diabetes, however, only half of North American smokers with diabetes are advised to quit by their doctors.

Women and Smoking

Women tend to begin smoking in their teens as a way to control their weight. The idea of controlling weight with cigarettes emerged in the 1920s when a tobacco company wife was told by her doctor to smoke to relax; not only did smoking relax her, but it actually helped to curb her appetite. Thus the luring of women to cigarettes as a food replacement began. In fact, medical journals and the medical profession at that time actually recommended smoking to women as a way to calm them. Even in the absence of diabetes, smoking-related diseases kill more women than any other health or social problem. The number one killer of women is smoking-related heart disease. Next come smoking-related lung cancer, smoking-related stroke, and smoking-related chronic lung diseases, which are very common, yet underreported. And did you know that early menopause and osteoporosis are more common among smokers? All studies show that women who smoke "get sicker quicker." And that is doubly so in women with type 2 diabetes.

Risk Factors You Can't Change

By reducing any of the modifiable risk factors above, you can help to offset your risk of developing type 2 diabetes. While you can't change your genetic makeup, medical history, or age, you can significantly reduce the odds of these factors predisposing you to type 2 diabetes.

Age

The risk of developing type 2 diabetes increases with age. Screening by age forty is the current recommendation. Perhaps at no other time in history has the population included so many people over age forty. This may, in part, account for the increase we're seeing in type 2 diabetes, as well as other age-related diseases. However, the lifestyle and dietary habits you practice before age forty count—either against you or for you. So, by changing your diet and becoming more active before age forty, you may not necessarily be able to prevent your genetic fate, but you may certainly be able to delay it. And in the event that you develop type 2 diabetes, a healthy diet and active lifestyle will go a long way in controlling the disease.

Genes

Most diabetes experts believe that type 2 diabetes is a genetic disease, which means you have the "wiring" installed for type 2 diabetes at birth. Fortunately, we do understand some of the outside factors that can trip the type 2 "switch." Body shape (the "apple" shape, in which excess fat is located in the abdomen, is associated with health risk more than the "pear" shape, which carries excess weight around the hips), diet, and activity level are strong switch-trippers. On the other hand, if you don't have any type 2 diabetes genes (you're not "wired" for this disease), these outside factors cannot, by themselves, cause you to develop type 2 diabetes. For example, being obese or sedentary doesn't mean you have type 2 diabetes or will develop it in the future.

When underdeveloped populations become urbanized and adopt a Western lifestyle, there is an explosion in type 2 diabetes. But the genes must be present in order to allow for the disease in the first place. This is more proof that there is a genetic-environmental combination at work when it comes to this disease. What aspect of westernization triggers type 2 diabetes? *Western* means many things, including a higher-fat diet and less physical activity, as well as more access to medical care, which means people live longer.

And what role does earlier screening and better detection of type 2 diabetes play in the perceived global increase of the disease? One doctor said to me, "When you don't look for it, you don't find it." More and more evidence points to the fact that type 2 diabetes has been around for a long time.

What Are the Odds?

Type 2 diabetes is caused by multiple factors. The odds of developing it have to do with some genes interacting with some environmental factors. Obesity, excess calories, deficient calorie expenditure, and aging can all lead to a resistance to insulin. If you remove the environmental risks, however, you can probably modify the risk of type 2 diabetes.

Your Ethnic Background

As discussed earlier, indigenous cultures (for example, Native Americans, such as Pima and Navaho; Pacific Islanders) develop type 2 diabetes at far higher rates than the general population. Roughly 13 percent of Native American adults have diabetes, meaning that they are affected by this disease at three times the rate of nonnative adults. We also see two to five times more new cases in native populations than nonnative populations. On some reserves, type 2 diabetes is present in 70 percent of the adult population. Approximately 15 percent of

African–North American adults have type 2 diabetes, while about 20 percent of all Hispanic North Americans have type 2 diabetes.

The "thrifty gene" is so named because it is believed to have evolved out of biological efficiency, or thriftiness. It is thought to be responsible for the higher rates of type 2 diabetes in indigenous populations. This means that the more recently your culture has lived indigenously or nomadically (that is, living off the land you came from and eating seasonally), the more efficient your metabolism is. Unfortunately, it is also more sensitive to nutrient excess. If you're a Native American, for example, only about one hundred years have passed since your ancestors lived indigenously. This is an exceedingly short amount of time for thousands of years of hunter-gatherer genes to adjust to a Western diet. If you're African-American, your ancestors did not live here any longer than about four hundred years; prior to that, they were living a tribal, nomadic lifestyle. Again, four hundred years is *not* a long time.

Some immigrant populations come from families who have spent generations in poverty. Their metabolisms adjusted to long periods of famine and are often overloaded by Western foods. Poverty itself may also be a risk factor. People with very low incomes may eat cheaper, lower-quality food, which, when introduced to the "thrifty gene," can trigger type 2 diabetes.

Type 2 diabetes seems to occur in Southeast Asian populations at Western rates even when the diet is Eastern. East Indians, in particular, have very high rates of heart disease. In fact, India has the largest type 2 population in the world. Urbanization is cited as a major factor.

Your risk of developing type 2 diabetes depends on your mix of genes and your current and past lifestyle and diet. If you are part Native American and part European, for example, you will probably need to be more conscientious about your diet than if you are part Asian and part European. Studying your family tree and family history of type 2 diabetes is the best way to assess your risk and make the necessary changes in your own diet and lifestyle to fight it.

Other Medical Conditions

There are genetic diseases, endocrine diseases, medical conditions, and medications that affect insulin action and lead to insulin resistance and/or type 2 diabetes. Any disease affecting the pancreas, such as cystic fibrosis and pancreatic cancer, also lead to diabetes. See the sidebar "Rare Diseases or Conditions Affecting Insulin Production or Action" for more information.

Signs and Symptoms of Type 2 Diabetes

These are the signs of type 2 diabetes:

- Weight gain. When you're not using your insulin properly, you may suffer from excess insulin, which can increase your appetite.
- Blurred vision or any change in sight
- Drowsiness or extreme fatigue at times when you shouldn't be drowsy or tired
- Frequent infections that are slow to heal. (Women should be on alert for recurring vaginal yeast infections.)
- Tingling or numbness in the hands and feet
- Gum disease. High blood sugar affects the blood vessels in your mouth, causing inflamed gums; the sugar content can get into your saliva, causing cavities in your teeth.

These are the particular risk factors for type 2 diabetes in women:

- Obesity (see Chapter 2)
- Two features of Syndrome X (described earlier in this chapter)
- Minority ethnicity or of Native American descent (including Pacific Islander and Alaskan native)
- Sedentary lifestyle
- Family history of type 2 diabetes
- History of gestational diabetes
- Having given birth to a baby too big or too small
- History of preeclampsia in pregnancy
- Smoking
- High saturated fat diet
- Polycystic ovary syndrome (see Chapter 3)

Rare Diseases or Conditions Affecting Insulin Production or Action

The following groups list extremely unusual or rare diseases that could affect insulin production, result in insulin resistance, or affect insulin action in the body. These are the most commonly cited in the medical literature and exclude pediatric disorders. For more information about any of the diseases listed in this table, contact the National Organization for Rare Disorders.

Genetic Disorders

The following genetic disorders are associated with diabetes:

- Alstrom syndrome
- Lipotrophic diabetes
- Type A insulin resistance
- Cystic fibrosis affects the pancreas and is sometimes listed as a disease of the pancreas
- Chromosomal defects leading to type 2 diabetes in young adults (formerly labeled MODY1, MODY2, MODY3, MODY4, MODY5, and MODY6; *MODY* stands for mature-onset diabetes in the young)

The following genetic disorders are sometimes, but not always, associated with diabetes:

- Down syndrome
- Friedreich's ataxia
- Huntington's chorea
- Klinefelter's syndrome
- Laurence-Moon-Bardet-Beidl syndrome
- Myotonic dystrophy
- Porphyria
- Prader-Willi syndrome

- Turner's syndrome
- Wolfram's syndrome

Endocrine Disorders or Diseases Antagonizing Insulin Production or Action

- Acromegaly
- Aldosteronoma
- Cushing's syndrome or Cushing's disease
- Gluconoma
- Hyperthyroidism
- Pheochromocytoma
- Somatostatinoma

Sources: American Diabetes Association, "Clinical Practice Recommendations 2004," *Diabetes Care* 27, Supplement 1, January 2004; Canadian Diabetes Association, *2003 Clinical Practice Guidelines.*

2

Women, Obesity, and
Type 2 Diabetes

IF YOU'RE STRUGGLING with obesity and have type 2 diabetes, take
heart: you're not alone. The majority of women with type 2 diabetes
(80 percent) struggle with obesity. As women age, their metabolism
changes, which can lead to weight gain even without changes in diet
or exercise. Many women begin to struggle with weight gain in their
forties. Many women have a pre-existing weight problem from earlier
pregnancies that gets aggravated with age and more sedentary living.
Some women struggle with the genetic tendency to gain weight, due
to thrifty genes, which are discussed later in this chapter. In most cases
type 2 diabetes develops as a complication of obesity. Heart disease,
circulation and digestive problems, and a higher risk of certain cancers
are other complications obese women face.

At one time, anyone who weighed 20 percent more than the ideal
weight for their age and height was defined as obese. A more accurate
indicator, the body mass index (BMI), is now the best measurement of
obesity. The BMI is calculated by dividing your weight (in kilograms)
by your height (in meters) squared. According to cdc.gov, the formula
converted to pounds and inches is:

$$\text{BMI} = \left(\frac{\text{Weight in Pounds}}{(\text{Height in inches}) \times (\text{Height in inches})} \right) \times 703$$

BMI charts abound on the Internet, on the backs of cereal boxes,
and in numerous health magazines. You can find BMI converters on

the Internet, where you type in your weight in pounds and your height in inches to arrive at your BMI. As of this writing, a BMI calculator can be found at consumer.gov/weightloss/bmi.htm.

Currently, a BMI of 18.5 or less indicates that you are underweight. A BMI between 18.5 and 24.9 is normal. People with a BMI between 25 and 29.9 are considered overweight, and those with a BMI between 30 and 34.9 are mildly to moderately obese. A BMI between 35 and 39.9 indicates severe obesity; people with a BMI of 40 or greater are considered morbidly obese. Obesity is not an eating disorder, but it can be the result of compulsive overeating, known as *binge eating disorder (BED)*, discussed later in this chapter. Roughly 20 to 46 percent of obese people suffer from BED.

Obesity rates in children and teens are calculated through BMIs that are at or above sex- and age-specific weights within the ninety-fifth percentiles. This is a more conservative approach than was previously used to account for growing spurts.

When you are obese with type 2 diabetes, you are instructed by your doctor to lose weight. For many women, the key to losing weight is to understand *why* they got fat to begin with. What are the external factors that you should take into account?

Obesity experts consider the Western lifestyle to be the single largest contributing factor to obesity. Although social, behavioral, metabolic, cellular, and molecular factors all contribute to obesity, obesity genes are "turned on" only when they are exposed to an environment conducive to weight gain.

North Americans have the highest obesity rates in the world. More than half of North American adults and about 25 percent of North American children are now obese. These figures reflect a doubling of adult obesity rates since the 1960s, and a doubling of the childhood obesity rate since the late 1970s—a staggering increase when you think about it in raw numbers. Obese children will most likely grow up to become obese adults, according to the most recent research.

Waist circumference is another factor in calculating obesity—particularly abdominal obesity. Women with a waist circumference of thirty-five inches or more are at increased risk of obesity-related health problems.

Amazingly, diabetes experts have noted that when their patients lose just five pounds, the body begins to use insulin more effectively.

But "Eat sensibly and exercise" just doesn't hold any weight for most people battling theirs.

This chapter will help you understand *why* Westerners eat so much, and why we're getting fatter in spite of a low-fat and low-carb culture. Where did the modern diet come from? The root word of *diet* comes from the Greek *diatta*, meaning "way of life." Since controlling your diet and weight are the tools to managing type 2 diabetes, let's start with how diet and lifestyle became linked to type 2 diabetes to begin with.

The "Good Times Disease"

Type 2 diabetes is referred to as the "good times disease," partly because of the work of Dr. Bouchardat, a French physician in the 1870s, who noticed that his diabetic patients seemed to do rather well in war. When their food was rationed, the sugar disappeared from the urine of Dr. Bouchardat's diabetic patients. It was at this point that a connection between food quantity and diabetes was made. This observation paved the way for special low-carbohydrate diets as a treatment for diabetes, but it seemed to be effective only in eliminating sugar from the urine in "milder" diabetes, which was what type 2 diabetes was called before the disease was better understood.

Economies and Scales

Bouchardat's observations were confirmed throughout Europe a few decades later. During the two World Wars, many European countries experienced a significant drop not only in "mild" diabetes but also in other obesity-related diseases when meat, dairy food, and eggs became scarce in large populations. Wartime rations forced people to survive on brown bread, oats, barley meal, and home-grown produce.

Had it not been for the Depression, we in North America might have seen an increase in type 2 diabetes much earlier than we did. The seeds of sedentary life were already planted in the 1920s, as consumer comforts, mainly the automobile and radio, led to more driving, less walking, and more sedentary recreation. The Depression interrupted what was supposed to be prosperous times for everyone. It also intercepted obesity and all diseases related to obesity, as the people in most industrialized nations ate barely enough to survive.

The Depression years, combined with six long years of war, led to an unprecedented yearning for consumer goods such as cars, refrigerators, stoves, radios, and washing machines. The return of the veterans led to an unprecedented baby boom, driving the candy, sweets, and junk-food markets for decades to come. Opportunities from U.S. government programs, such as the G.I. Bill, led to advancement in education and wealth. Never before had North Americans had so much money.

Manufacturers and packaged-goods companies were looking for better ways to compete and sell their products. The answer to their prayers arrived in the late 1940s with the cathode ray tube: television. In the end, television would become the appliance most responsible for dietary decline and sedentary lifestyle as it turned into a babysitter that mesmerized the baby boom generation for hours.

The Diet of Leisure

Naturally, after the war, people wanted to celebrate. They gave parties, drank wine, smoked, and went to restaurants. Their diets included more high-fat items, refined carbohydrates, sugar, alcohol, and chemical additives. And as people began to manage large families, easy-fix meals in boxes and cans were manufactured in abundance and sold on television to millions.

The demand for the diet of leisure radically changed agriculture, too. Today, 80 percent of our grain harvest feeds livestock. The rest of our arable land is used for other cash crops such as tomatoes, sugar, coffee, and bananas. Ultimately, these changes have helped to create the modern Western diet: huge amounts of meat, eggs, dairy products, sugar, and refined flour.

Since 1940, chemical additives and preservatives in food have risen by 995 percent. In 1959, the Flavor and Extract Manufacturers Association of the United States (FEMA) established a panel of experts to determine the safety status of food flavorings to deal with the overwhelming number of chemicals that companies wanted to add to our foods.

One of the most popular food additives is monosodium glutamate (MSG), the sodium salt of glutamic acid, an amino acid that occurs naturally in protein-containing foods such as meat, fish, milk, and many vegetables. MSG is a flavor enhancer that researchers believe contributes a "fifth taste" to savory foods such as meats, stews, tomatoes, and cheese. It was originally extracted from seaweed and other plant sources to function in foods the same way as other spices or extracts. Today, MSG is made from starch, corn sugar, or molasses from sugarcane or sugar beets. MSG is produced by a fermentation process similar to that used for making beer, vinegar, and yogurt. While MSG is labeled "generally recommended as safe" (GRAS) by the United States Food and Drug Administration (FDA), questions about the safety of ingesting MSG have been raised because food sensitivities to the substance have been reported. This fact notwithstanding, the main problem with MSG is that it arouses our appetites even more. MSG, widespread in our food supply, makes food taste better. And the better food tastes, the more we eat.

Hydrolyzed proteins are also used as flavor enhancers. These are made by using enzymes to chemically digest proteins from soy meal, wheat gluten, corn gluten, edible strains of yeast, or other food sources. This process, known as *hydrolysis*, breaks down proteins into their component amino acids. Today, several hundred additive substances like these are used in our food, in addition to standard additives such as sugar, baking soda, and vitamins.

Of course, one of the key functions of food additives is to preserve foods for transport. The problem is, once we begin to eat foods that are not indigenous to our country, the food loses many of its nutrient properties. Refrigerators make it possible for us to eat tropical foods in cold climates and Texas-raised beef in Japan. As a result, few industrialized countries eat indigenously anymore.

Fast-Food Culture

The 1970s and beyond have moved us from a diet of leisure into a *Fast Food Nation* (the title of Eric Schlosser's book on the legacy of fast food on our health). Other changes in our society, such as dual working parents, have contributed to obesity, too. In a nutshell, we have become dependent on fast food. Schlosser notes that in 1960, the typical North American ate only four pounds of frozen french fries per year; today the typical North American consumes roughly forty-nine pounds of frozen fries per year—90 percent of which are purchased at fast-food restaurants.

We are more sedentary due to long commutes, bigger and better televisions, cable television, "strip mall" living that makes it harder to do errands on foot (endemic in the suburbs), as well as time spent on the computer and Internet. Our children are no longer encouraged to walk to school or play outside in many neighborhoods because of safety considerations. Many parents are opting for indoor, safer activities. In many communities, budget cuts have led schools to cut their physical education programs and facilities. In urban communities, there is less green space and fewer parks, replaced by malls (always with food courts) and parking lots.

People are working harder to make the same wages, and two-income families are more stretched and stressed each year. Alongside these changes, the fast-food industry has experienced enormous growth, making more high-fat, inexpensive meals widely available to all. Thus, convenience food, as it is also called, has become the standard North American diet. Even when we consciously try to select what we think are more nutritious foods, we frequently wind up consuming hidden calories because of hidden ingredients in fast food.

Why We Like Our Fat

Fat tastes good. Fat also *feels* good in our mouths. Foods that have the particular texture and taste of fat are more palatable to us than foods that don't. This is why packaged-goods manufacturers describe their products as "smooth, creamy, moist, tender, and rich." All the foods that boast these qualities—from ice cream to chocolate to cheese— give us that unique feeling of satiety and satisfaction that makes us feel good.

Eating is a sensual experience. When we enjoy our food, our brains produce endorphins, "feel good" hormones that are, ironically, also produced when we exercise. To many of us, eating is an empty experience when food doesn't have the taste and texture of fat. And when we're in emotional pain or need, the texture and taste of fat become even more important. Bingeing or falling off the diet wagon is not only due to losing control, but is an attempt to regain good feelings. Food, as millions of overeaters will tell you, is our friend. It's always there; it never lets us down.

The Impact of Low-Fat Products

Since the late 1970s, North Americans have been deluged with low-fat products. In 1990, the United States government launched Healthy People 2000, a campaign to urge manufacturers to double their output of low-fat products by the year 2000. Since 1990, more than one thousand new fat-free or low-fat products have been introduced into North American supermarkets annually.

Current guidelines tell us that we should consume less than 30 percent of calories from fat, while no more than one-third of fat calories should come from saturated fat. According to U.S. estimates, the average person gets between 34 and 37 percent of his or her calories from fat and roughly 12 percent of all his or her calories from saturated fat. Data shows that with regard to "absolute fat" (all types of fat), the intake increased from eighty-one grams per day in 1980 to about 3,800 calories today. In fact, the only reason that data shows a drop in the percentage of calories from fat is because of the huge increase in calories per day. The result is that as a population we weigh more today than in 1980, despite the fact that roughly ten thousand more low-fat foods are available to us now than in 1980.

Most of these low-fat products, however, actually encourage us to eat more. For example, if a bag of regular chips has nine grams of fat per serving (one serving usually equals five or six chips or one handful), we will more likely stick to that one handful. However, if we find a low-fat brand of chips that boasts "50 percent less fat" per serving, we're more likely to eat the whole bag (feeling good about eating "low-fat" chips), which can easily triple our fat intake.

Low-fat or fat-free foods trick our bodies with ingredients that mimic the functions of fat in foods. This is often achieved by using modified fats that are only partially metabolized, if at all. While some foods have the fat reduced by removing the fat (skim milk, lean cuts of meat), most low fat-foods require a variety of "fat copycats" to preserve the taste and texture of the food. Water, for example, is often combined with carbohydrates and protein to mimic a particular texture or taste, as is the case with a variety of baked goods or cake mixes. In general, the low-fat copycats are carbohydrate-based, protein-based, or fat-based.

Carbohydrate-based fat replacers are starches and gums that are often used as thickening agents to create the texture of fat. You'll find them in abundance in low-fat salad dressings, sauces, gravies, frozen desserts, and baked goods. Compared to natural fats, which contain about nine calories per gram, carbohydrate-based fat replacers run anywhere from zero to four calories per gram.

Protein-based low-fat ingredients are created by doing things to the proteins that make them behave differently. For example, by taking proteins such as whey or egg white and heating or blending them at high speeds, you can create the look and feel of "creamy." Soy and corn proteins are often used in these cases. You'll find these ingredients in low-fat cheese, butter, mayonnaise, salad dressings, frozen dairy desserts, sour cream, and baked goods. They run between one and four calories per gram.

Low-fat foods that use fat-based ingredients tailor the fat in some way so that we do not absorb or metabolize it fully. These ingredients are found in chocolate, chocolate coatings, margarine, spreads, sour cream, and cheese. You can also use these ingredients as low-fat substitutes for frying foods (you do this when you fry eggs in margarine, for example). Olestra, the new fat substitute approved by the United States Food and Drug Administration (FDA) in recent years, is an example of a fat substitute that is not absorbed by our bodies, providing no calories. Caprenin and salatrim are examples of partially absorbed fats (they contain more long-chain fatty acids) and are the more traditional fat-based low-fat ingredients. They contain roughly five calories per gram.

Low-fat foods are designed to give you more freedom of choice with your diet, allowing you to cut fat without compromising your taste buds. Studies show that taste outperforms nutrition in your brain. Yet many experts believe that in the long term low-fat products create a barrier to weight loss.

The good news about low-fat or fat-free products is that they are, in fact, lower in fat and are created to substitute for the higher-fat foods you know you shouldn't have but don't want to live without. The phrase "everything in moderation" applies to low-fat products, too. Balancing these products with "good stuff" is the key. A low-fat treat should still be treated like its high-fat original. In other words, don't have double the amount because it's low fat. Instead, have the same amount as you would of the original.

Studies and surveys show that we are actually eating about 500 calories more each day than we did in the 1970s. The addition of frequent snacking that has resulted from the development and marketing of more innovative and tempting snack foods by the food industry has been cited as one of the most apparent changes in our eating patterns over the last thirty years. In fact, the practice of snacking doubled from the mid-eighties to mid-nineties. The fast-food invasion, of course, has contributed to the increase as well.

Chronic Dieting

The road to obesity is also paved with chronic dieting. It is estimated that at least 50 percent of all North Americans are dieting at any given time, while one-third of North American dieters initiate a diet at least once a month. The very act of dieting in your teens and twenties can predispose you to obesity in your thirties, forties, and beyond. This occurs because most people "crash and burn" instead of eating sensibly. In other words, they're chronic dieters. Because of unrealistic beauty standards, women are particularly vulnerable to chronic dieting.

The crash-and-burn approach to diet is what we do when we want to lose a specific amount of weight for a particular occasion or to be able to wear a particular outfit. The pattern is to starve for a few days and then eat what we normally do. Or we eat only certain foods (such as celery and grapefruit) for a number of days and then eat normally after we've lost the weight. Most of these diets do not incorporate exercise, which means that we burn up some of our muscle as well as fat. Then, when we eat normally, we gain only fat. And over the years, that fat simply grows fatter. The bottom line is that when there is more fat on your body than muscle, you cannot burn calories as efficiently. It is the muscle that makes it possible to burn calories. Diet it away, and you diet away your ability to burn fat.

If starvation is involved in our trying to lose weight, our bodies become more efficient at getting fat. Starvation triggers an intelligence in the metabolism; our body suddenly thinks we're living in a war zone and goes into "super-efficient nomadic mode," not realizing that we're living in an environment that has an abundance of food. So, when we return to our normal caloric intake, or even a lower-than-normal caloric intake, after we've starved ourselves, we gain more weight. Our bodies say, "Oh look—food! Better store that as fat for the next famine." Some researchers believe that starvation diets slow our metabolic rates far below normal so that weight gain becomes more rapid after each starvation episode.

This cycle of crash or starvation dieting is known as the *yo-yo diet* syndrome, the subject of thousands of articles in women's magazines throughout the last twenty years. Breaking the pattern sounds easy: combine exercise with a sensible diet. But it's not that easy if you've led a sedentary life most of your adult years. Ninety-five percent of the people who go on a diet gain back the weight they lost, as well as extra weight, within two years. As discussed further on, the failure often lies in psychological and behavioral factors. We have to understand why we eat too much before we can eat less. Experts say that unless you are significantly overweight or have a medical condition, *don't diet*. Just eat well. The best way to break the yo-yo diet pattern for children is to educate your children early about food habits and appropriate body weight.

Eating Disorders and Compulsive Eating

The two most common eating disorders involve starvation. They are *anorexia nervosa* (a pathological fear of weight gain leading to faulty eating patterns, malnutrition, and excessive weight loss) and bingeing followed by purging, known as *bulimia nervosa*. People will purge after a bingeing episode by inducing vomiting and abusing laxatives, diuretics, and thyroid hormones. Eating disorders are most common in women, but men are also succumbing to impractical body standards and are prone to purging behaviors in particular.

A Healthier Approach to a Diet

If you're contemplating a diet, you should also consider the following:

- What is a reasonable weight for you, given your genetic makeup, family history, age, and culture? A smaller weight loss in some people can produce dramatic effects. A lot of people want to lose beyond what is a healthy weight, according to their ideal BMI.
- Aim to lose weight at a slower rate. Too much too fast will probably lead to gaining it all back.
- Incorporate exercise into your routine, particularly activities that build muscle mass.
- Take your vitamins. Make sure you're meeting basic nutritional requirements (see Chapter 5).

Perhaps the most accepted weight-control behavior is *overexercising*. Today, rigorous, strenuous exercise is used as a method of "purging" after overeating and has become one of the tenets of socially accepted behavior. A healthier alternative is to combine balanced eating with a reasonable amount of exercise.

Binge Eating

When we hear the term *eating disorder*, we usually think about anorexia or bulimia. Many people, however, binge without purging. This practice is also known as *binge eating disorder* (also known as compulsive overeating), which is a common cause of obesity, and consequently can lead to obesity-related conditions such as type 2 diabetes. In this case, the bingeing is an announcement to the world that something is bothering you emotionally. Someone who purges after bingeing is usually thought to be hiding his or her problem, whether it's depression, anxiety, or another problem. Someone who binges and never purges is *advertising* his or her problems, according to some research. The theory is that the purger is passively asking for help; the binger who doesn't purge is aggressively asking for help. It's the same disease with a different result. But there is one more layer when it comes to compulsive overeating that is controversial and is often rejected by the overeater: the desire to get fat may be behind the compulsion. Many people who overeat insist that fat is a consequence of eating food, not a goal. But many therapists who deal with overeating disagree and believe that if a woman admits that she has an emotional interest in being large, she may be much closer to stopping her compulsion to eat, for example, women recovering from sexual abuse often have a desire to de-sexualize their body shape.

Furthermore, many women who eat compulsively do not recognize that they are doing so. The following is a typical profile of a compulsive eater:

- Eating when you're not hungry
- Feeling out of control when you're around food, either trying to resist it or gorging on it
- Spending a lot of time thinking or worrying about food and your weight
- Always desperate to try another diet that promises results
- Having feelings of self-loathing and shame
- Hating your own body
- Obsessing with what you can or will eat, or have eaten
- Eating in secret or with "eating friends"
- Appearing in public to be a professional dieter who's in control
- Buying cakes or pies as "gifts" and having them wrapped to hide the fact that they're for you
- Having a pristine kitchen with only the "right" foods
- Feeling either out of control with food (compulsive eating) or imprisoned by it (dieting)
- Feeling temporary relief by not eating
- Looking forward with pleasure and anticipation to the time when you can eat alone
- Feeling unhappy because of your eating behavior

The Issue of Hunger

Most people eat when they're hungry. But if you're a compulsive eater, hunger cues have nothing to do with when you eat. You may eat for any of the following reasons:

- As a social event: this includes family meals or meeting friends at restaurants. The point is that you plan food as the social entertainment. Most people do this now and then, but it is a problem when we do it when we're not even hungry.
- To satisfy "mouth hunger," the need to have something in your mouth even though you are not hungry
- To prevent *future* hunger: "Better eat now because later I may not get a chance."
- As a reward for a bad day or bad experience or to reward yourself for a *good* day or good experience
- Because "it's the only pleasure I can count on!"
- To quell nerves
- Boredom
- You're "going on a diet" tomorrow; hence, the eating is done now out of a real fear that you will be deprived later.
- Because food is your friend

Biological Causes of Obesity

The physiological cause of obesity is eating more calories than you burn. People gain weight for two reasons: they may eat excessively (often excessive amounts of nutritious foods), which results in daily consumption of just too many calories; or they may eat moderately, but simply be too inactive for the calories they *do* ingest. Genetic makeup can predispose some body types to obesity earlier in life because of "thrifty genes" (see next section). Our genetic makeup combined with a more sedentary lifestyle and an overabundance of food are to blame for the rise in obesity. Furthermore, as we age, our metabolism slows down, which means that unless we decrease our calories or increase activity levels to compensate, we will probably gain weight. Other hormonal problems can also contribute to obesity, such as an underactive thyroid gland (called *hypothyroidism*), which is very common in women.

Thrifty Genes

Just as genetics plays a role in the risk of type 2 diabetes, it also plays a role in obesity, which is also the most noted risk factor for type 2 diabetes. The "thrifty gene" (see Chapter 1) is the gene thought to be responsible for the higher rates of obesity and obesity-related conditions in indigenous and non-European populations.

Asian populations generally have the lowest rates of obesity, but that is in part because they frequently maintain their traditional dietary habits with the help of an abundance of Asian markets and restaurants in many Western cities. In fact, people of other ethnic groups tend to benefit when they adopt the same diets as Asians. That said, when Asian and Southeast Asian populations begin eating the Western way—pizzas, hamburgers, fries, sweet drinks, and snack foods, their thrifty genes are responsible for soaring obesity rates and quicker progression to type 2 diabetes. Thrifty genes are also evident when you look at obesity patterns in the United States. Obesity is more prevalent in African-Americans, Hispanics, Native Americans, Hawaiians, and Samoans; these groups have higher incidences of diabetes and cardiovascular disease as well.

Diets of poverty may also be a factor in obesity rates in lower socioeconomic groups. Diets of poverty typically rely on calories from high-fat, low-nutrient foods instead of fresher foods, fruits, and vegetables. When epidemiologists look at "thrifty gene" groups in higher income levels, the obesity rates are lower.

Leptin and Other Hormones

The most promising antiobesity treatment once involved the "antifat hormone" leptin; its discovery led to a surge of obesity drug research. Leptin, discovered in 1994, seemed promising because it was the first antifat hormone that surfaced. The leptin hormone receptor was found in 1997. Leptin was discovered when a mutant strain of extremely obese mice (lacking the gene to make leptin) were able to shed their weight when given leptin. On leptin, the mice's appetite decreased while their metabolic rates increased. Although it led researchers to wonder whether all obese people would lose weight on leptin, this did not occur. It turns out that like the mutant obese mice, there are only a few rare cases of human obesity caused by leptin deficiency. The leptin discovery led to a successful treatment for these rare cases of obesity in leptin-deficient individuals, however, who in the past would not have been able to lose weight.

Most people who are obese actually have higher than normal blood levels of leptin, which is produced by fat cells, but are resistant to its actions. In fact, obesity researchers now believe that leptin has more to do with protecting against weight *loss* in times of famine, than protecting against weight gain in times of plenty. When fat stores increase, so does leptin; when fat stores shrink, so does leptin. Appetite increases and metabolism decreases when leptin levels shrink, but the opposite does not occur when leptin levels rise; appetite is not suppressed when leptin increases, nor is metabolism increased. Leptin, it seems, is one of those evolutionary hormones designed to keep our species alive by protecting us from starvation. Finding leptin has led obesity researchers into finding out more about how appetite, fat stores, and famine-protection mechanisms work in the body.

On the Horizon

In the wake of leptin research, a host of antiobesity drugs are now in clinical trials. One such drug is Axokine, which works by activating a set of brain cells that produce appetite-dampening peptides, which normally rise during meals and signal satiety. Axokine could limit calorie intake by boosting these peptides. Again, because Axokine works with brain chemistry, endocrinologists are skeptical about long-term effects.

Drug research is also revolving around the hormone ghrelin, which peaks before meals and triggers appetite. Ghrelin is produced in the gastrointestinal tract; researchers describe it as "your stomach's way of telling your brain you're hungry." Drugs can be made to block ghrelin, which would kill hunger. Again, through calorie intake reduction, such a drug could cause weight loss.

One of the most exciting finds in obesity research, presented at the 2003 Endocrine Society Meeting in Philadelphia, is the discovery of a brand-new hormone known as PYY. While looking at the effects of bariatric surgery on appetite and the hormones secreted that make us feel full or satisfied, a British research team found that levels of PYY surged in people who had undergone bariatric surgery. This research team suspects that PYY is responsible for a person's loss of the desire to overeat. PYY research may lead to an effective obesity drug.

Insulin Resistance and Obesity

An important theory about why we get fat concerns insulin resistance. It's believed that when the body produces too much insulin, we eat more to try to maintain a balance. This is why weight gain is often the first symptom of type 2 diabetes. But then we have to ask what causes insulin resistance to begin with; many researchers believe that it is triggered by obesity, so it becomes a "Which came first, the chicken or the egg?" puzzle.

Drug Treatment for Obesity

Drug treatment for obesity has a shady history. Women have been especially abused by the medical system. Throughout the 1950s, 1960s, and even 1970s, women were prescribed thyroxine, which is a thyroid hormone, to speed up their metabolisms. Unless a person has an underactive thyroid gland or no thyroid gland (it may have been surgically removed), this is a very dangerous medication that can cause heart failure. Request a thyroid function test before you accept this medication.

Amphetamines or "speed" were often widely peddled to women by doctors throughout the 1930s right up until the 1980s, but these drugs, too, are dangerous and can put your health at risk. One of the most controversial antiobesity therapies was the use of fenfluramine and phentermine (fen-phen) in the 1990s. Both drugs were approved for use individually more than twenty years ago, but in 1992, doctors began to prescribe them together for long-term management of obesity. In 1996, U.S. doctors wrote a total of eighteen million monthly prescriptions for fen-phen. And many of the prescriptions were issued to people who were not obese. (This practice is known as "off-label" prescribing.) In July 1997, the United States Food and Drug Administration and researchers at the Mayo Clinic and the Mayo Foundation made a joint announcement warning doctors that fen-phen can cause heart disease. On September 15, 1997, fenfluramine was taken off the market. More bad news has since surfaced about fen-phen wreaking havoc on serotonin levels. The fen-phen lesson: diet and lifestyle modification are still considered the best approach to wellness.

Approved Antiobesity Pills

In 1999, an antiobesity pill that blocks the absorption of almost one-third of the fat people eat was approved. One of the side effects of this new prescription drug, called orlistat (Xenical), is rather embarrassing diarrhea when the fat content in your meal exceeds 20 percent. To avoid the drug's side effects, simply avoid fat! The pill can also decrease absorption of vitamin D and other important nutrients, however.

Orlistat is the first drug to fight obesity through the intestine instead of the brain. Taken with each meal, it binds to certain pancreatic enzymes to block the digestion of 30 percent of the fat you ingest. When combined with a sensible diet, people on orlistat lost more weight than those not on orlistat. This drug is not intended for people who need to lose a few pounds; it is designed for medically obese people. The safety of orlistat for people with diabetes is under debate. Although in studies orlistat was found to lower cholesterol, blood pressure, and blood sugar levels (as a result of weight loss), it can lead to pancreatitis (see Chapter 1) and inflammation of the gallbladder.

Another obesity drug, sibutramine, was approved for use as well. Sibutramine is meant for people whose body mass index (BMI) registers at 27 or higher. This is generally people who weigh more than 20 percent above their ideal weight. However, sibutramine's safety for people with type 2 diabetes is debatable, and anyone with high blood pressure should be cautioned against taking sibutramine, because it can significantly raise your blood pressure.

If you're taking medications for depression, thyroid problems, seizures, glaucoma, osteoporosis, gallbladder disease, liver disease, heart disease or stroke prevention, kidney disease, migraines, or Parkinson's disease, you should consult with your doctore before taking sibutramine. Many nutritional supplements, such as tryptophan, also are not recommended with sibutramine. Make sure your doctor knows about all nonprescription, over-the-counter medications as well as all herbal and nutritional substances you're taking before you start sibutramine.

Childhood Obesity

Health-care practitioners bemoan the rise of type 2 diabetes in obese children in certain high-risk groups (including Native American, Pacific Islander, African-American, and Hispanic), a trend now starting to be seen in children of other cultures. Any child who is obese is prone to type 2 diabetes.

Children today spend about twenty-two hours per week in front of the television, consuming high-fat snacks while they're watching the advertising of more high-fat snacks. If you count computer time, videos, and Nintendo, children spend thirty-eight hours a week in front of some type of screen; that almost equals the hours spent on the average full-time job. Children watch more than thirty thousand commercials per year, and roughly 25 percent of North American children between the ages of two and five have a TV in their bedroom.

Since improving a child's diet often means altering the entire family's eating patterns, changing poor dietary habits is difficult. Many children come from families with terrible patterns: they skip breakfast, snack all day, and have huge dinners with desserts. This is the diet that paves the way to childhood obesity and type 2 diabetes.

One of the largest contributors to childhood obesity is the soft drink industry. Soft drink manufacturers have spent a lot of money to increase the amount of soft drinks children consume. They have even forged relationships with schools, providing them with logoed school supplies in exchange for exclusive rights as the brand carried in the school district; in the United States, these are known as "pouring rights" contracts. There is no nutritional value to soft drinks, which makes it the perfect junk food, or what the Center for Science in the Public Interest refers to as "liquid candy." Nutritionists advise that any other beverage would be better than a regular soft drink, including sweet juices, which at least have vitamins. Between 1985 and 1997, schools purchased 30 percent less milk, while increasing their purchasing of soft drinks by 1,100 percent.

Preventing Childhood Obesity

North American children are considered the worst examples of childhood obesity. Children are also developing other obesity-related diseases once diagnosed only in adults, like high cholesterol. Between the late 1970s and the early 1990s, the prevalence of childhood obesity doubled (from 8 to 14 percent in children ages six to eleven and from 6 to 12 percent in teens). In 1992, Sweden banned all television advertising directed at children under twelve. Similarly, ads have been banned from children's television programming in Norway, Belgium, Ireland, and Holland. Most countries look at North American children as the example of "what not to become."

In 1995 the American Academy of Pediatrics stated that advertising to children under eight was exploitative. Although companies doing the advertising assert that banning their ads would interfere with their freedoms, child health experts compare the peddling of junk food and fat to our children to peddling tobacco and alcohol to them. Preventing obesity in children means limiting their exposure to these ads.

3

Fertility, Pregnancy, and the Role of Estrogen

THIS CHAPTER IS designed for two specific groups of women: The first group is women who have been diagnosed with type 2 diabetes and have delayed having children, but nevertheless are planning a pregnancy or are already pregnant. A good many of the women in this group may also have been dealing with infertility or may be undergoing assisted reproductive technology. Many women in their mid- to late forties, for example, have more options regarding pregnancy as a result of egg donation. Therefore, the old belief that women with type 2 diabetes and over forty are too old to have babies and don't need this information is being radically revised. In fact, there has been an upsurge in what is called *postmenopausal pregnancy* as a direct result of new fertility treatments. What you need to know about fertility treatments and diabetes is therefore discussed, as well as how type 2 diabetes often affects fertility. And of course, everything you need to know about managing type 2 diabetes *during* pregnancy is discussed, too.

The second group of women reading this chapter will not have been diagnosed at all with type 2 diabetes, but instead have been diagnosed with *gestational diabetes*, which means diabetes during pregnancy. Gestational diabetes is not the same disease as type 2 diabetes, even though it usually behaves the same way. It is a condition that occurs during pregnancy when your body is resistant to the insulin it makes, but it can often be managed through dietary changes and meal planning. And it often disappears after pregnancy. Gestational diabetes, however, is often a warning that unless lifestyle and dietary habits change between pregnancies or after childbirth, type 2 diabetes may be in the cards after all. If this is the reason you're reading this chapter, go directly to the section "Gestational Diabetes Mellitus (GDM)."

Finally, if you have type 1 diabetes, this is *not* the book for you, although you may find certain sections of this chapter helpful.

Getting Pregnant

You have type 2 diabetes, and you want to get pregnant. What do you need to do in order to have a healthy baby, while staying healthy yourself?

The first step is to *plan ahead*! Get yourself under tight blood sugar control through diet, exercise, and frequent blood sugar monitoring. If you are taking oral medication for your diabetes, you must stop; these medications cannot be taken during pregnancy. You must either discuss with your doctor managing your diabetes through diet and exercise alone, or must go on insulin during your conception phase and pregnancy. If you have to go on temporary insulin, see Chapter 7 for some "getting started" information, as well as an explanation of what kinds of insulin are available. However, be forewarned: you must be able to handle taking insulin and going through a fairly radical change in your lifestyle habits, as well as being able to handle another huge lifestyle change—having a baby! Please have a frank discussion with your partner and doctor prior to making this decision.

Experts recommend that you should ideally plan your pregnancy three to six months in advance of conception, so that you can make sure that your glycosylated hemoglobin levels (known as A1C levels—see Chapter 7) are within normal ranges during this period. A normal level means that your diabetes is well managed; therefore, the risk of birth defects is low. (This is a risk in the early stages of pregnancy if you have high blood sugar.) The following tests prior to getting pregnant are also recommended:

- Eye exam (to rule out diabetes eye disease)
- Blood pressure and urine test to check your kidney function
- A gynecological exam (this should include a pelvic exam, breast exam, Pap test, and screening for vaginal infections or sexually transmitted diseases)
- A general checkup to rule out heart disease or other circulatory problems

Obesity

If you are obese prior to pregnancy, it's important to try to get to a normal weight before you conceive. Women who are obese during their pregnancy are far more likely to develop gestational diabetes and type 2 diabetes beyond their pregnancy.

Having Sex

Getting pregnant means having sex (usually!). But if you're a woman with diabetes, the act of having sex can interfere with blood sugar levels since it is, after all, an *activity*. Therefore, many experts recommend that you treat sexual activity as any other activity and plan for it accordingly as a physical exercise of sorts. The risk of developing low blood sugar, or hypoglycemia, is actually not uncommon with sexual activity and diabetes. You may need to eat after sex, or eat something beforehand to ward off low blood sugar.

There is also the opposite problem: no desire for sex. This can occur because of vaginal infections (see Chapter 10), or because of changing hormones if you are approaching menopause. Studies that looked specifically at the effect diabetes has on women and sexuality found that loss of libido was often caused by high blood sugar, vaginal infections and the resulting pain or itching during intercourse, or nerve damage, which affects blood flow to the female genitalia and hence can interfere with pleasure, sensation, and orgasm.

Many women with diabetes also report that they feel more unattractive as a result of their diabetes. They are concerned with not just their own performance, but their ability to please their partners. Fears of a "low blood sugar attack in the sack" are particularly common. The only way to avoid feelings of unattractiveness or fears is openness with your partner. Discussing these issues with a sex therapist or counselor may also be a valuable experience.

Who Should Not Get Pregnant?

If your diabetes has affected your kidneys (see Chapter 12), talk to your health-care professional about your risks. There could be serious ramifications that could even be fatal. If you have kidney disease, please discuss all of the risks of pregnancy with your heath-care provider. By controlling your diabetes during pregnancy, it is, however, possible to give birth to a healthy child even when you have kidney disease.

Infertility and Diabetes: Women with Polycystic Ovarian Syndrome (PCOS)

This section may shed some light on a common problem affecting many women with type 2 diabetes. It is a condition known as *polycystic ovarian syndrome* (PCOS), which is also a classic female infertility problem in the general population. Women with PCOS are considered at high risk for type 2 diabetes because between 50 to 80 percent of these women are obese (the common shape is abdominal obesity or the apple shape) with insulin resistance.

What happens in PCOS is that your body secretes far too much androgen, the male hormone, which counteracts your ovaries' ability to make enough progesterone for a normal menstrual cycle. Androgen levels interfere with your FSH (follicle-stimulating hormone), which you need to trigger progesterone. So your follicles never develop but turn into small, pea-sized cysts on your ovaries. Your ovaries can then enlarge. Because your androgen levels are out of whack, you can develop male characteristics: facial hair, hair on other parts of your body (this happens in 70 percent of the cases and is called *hirsutism*), or even a balding problem. Acne is another typical symptom because of the increase in androgen, as is obesity (although women who have a normal weight or are thin can also have this syndrome).

Your periods will also be irregular and, as result, you might be at greater risk for developing *endometrial hyperplasia*, a condition in which your uterine lining thickens to the point of becoming precancerous. (If you have endometrial hyperplasia, either progesterone supplements will be given to you to induce a period, or a dilatation and curettage may be required to get rid of the lining.) Because of your high levels of androgen, you may also be at an increased risk of cardiovascular disease. Diet can help reduce the onset of heart problems. You can treat PCOS with natural progesterone therapy or oral contraceptives. Sometimes, women with normal cycles for many years may develop PCOS later in life. In this case, they will suddenly develop irregular cycles (called *secondary amenorrhea*) out of the blue.

Insulin Resistance and PCOS

Roughly 30 percent of women with PCOS either have type 2 diabetes or impaired glucose tolerance by age thirty-five. Weight loss can improve PCOS, and can improve insulin resistance and lower the risk of type 2 diabetes.

Improving the body's ability to use insulin in women with polycystic ovarian syndrome seems to help restore menstrual cycles and lower male hormone levels. Insulin-sensitizing drugs used to treat type 2 diabetes (see Chapter 7) are now being used to treat PCOS, although these agents must be stopped once you become pregnant. Before you're placed on an insulin-lowering drug, ask your doctor about how diet and exercise can help your body use insulin more efficiently.

In general, PCOS is hereditary and is more common among women of Mediterranean descent. It's also uncommon to develop PCOS later in life, although it can happen. Generally, a woman with PCOS will begin to experience menstrual irregularities within three or four years after her menarche (first period). About 4 percent of the general female population suffers from this, which accounts for half of all hormonal disorders affecting female fertility.

Reversing Infertility

To reverse infertility in women with PCOS, the fertility drug clomiphene citrate in tablet form is the most common route. You'll start clomiphene citrate around day five of your cycle, and then go off the tablet at about day ten. If you've had long bouts of amenorrhea, your period will first be induced via a progesterone supplement before starting on clomiphene citrate. An average dosage of clomiphene citrate in this case ranges between 25 and 50 milligrams. Roughly 70 to 90 percent of all PCOS women on clomiphene will ovulate, but pregnancy rates really vary; 30 to 70 percent of PCOS women on clomiphene will conceive.

If you're still not ovulating after taking clomiphene citrate, stronger fertility drugs can be used. A general gynecological workup may also find other problems that are structural, such as blocked fallopian tubes.

I urge any woman with diabetes, however, to consult her diabetes specialist prior to going on *any* fertility drugs. Estrogen can raise blood sugar levels, and you need to know how these drugs will affect your *blood sugar*, not just your ovaries.

Other Treatments for PCOS

In many women with PCOS, weight loss is considered the cure, just as it often is for insulin resistance. However, when infertility is a concern and your birthdays are coming fast and furious, weight loss alone may not be a realistic short-term treatment because it's a slow, time-consuming process. If you have PCOS and are being treated with fertility drugs, you may be able to reverse your infertility through natural weight loss for future pregnancies. Your diabetes educator or a dietitian can help you with meal planning, which will not only help you control your diabetes, but may help you get pregnant.

In some women with PCOS, androgens are also produced in the adrenal glands. Under these circumstances, your doctor may want to put you on a corticosteroid to suppress the adrenal gland, lowering the production of androgens. This will help induce ovulation as well.

Bromocriptine, which suppresses prolactin, will be given to 15 to 20 percent of all PCOS women. The high levels of estrogen associated with PCOS commonly cause *hyperprolactinemia*, meaning "too much prolactin," which can interfere with fertility.

Hirsutism (Unwanted Hair)

Women with PCOS are typically plagued with hirsutism: unwanted hair in culturally unacceptable places for women, such as on the face.

Other Causes of Infertility

There are many other causes of female-factor and male-factor infertility that are completely unrelated to blood sugar. For the record, roughly 80 percent of all female-factor infertility is caused by structural problems in which the fallopian tubes become blocked. This could be due to pelvic inflammatory disease, a condition that erupts when bacterial infections (from a sexually transmitted disease or from bacteria entering during pelvic surgery or previous childbirth) travel up the reproductive tract, causing tubal scarring and inflammation. Endometriosis is another cause of tubal blockage.

Being Pregnant

If you were diagnosed with type 2 diabetes *prior* to becoming pregnant, this section is for you. This means you have what's known as *pre-existing diabetes* (diabetes before pregnancy). If you have developed diabetes *during* pregnancy, see the section on gestational diabetes (diabetes during pregnancy).

So long as your blood glucose levels are normal throughout your pregnancy and you have normal blood pressure, you can expect as normal a pregnancy as anyone else in your age group. Nevertheless, there are some concerns unique to women with type 2 diabetes. The rate of birth defects is 8 to 13 percent among pregnant women with diabetes compared to 2 to 4 percent in the general population. Most of these defects occur before the seventh week, so preconception planning is important (such as getting down to a normal weight prior to pregnancy). The general risks of pregnancy in women with type 2 diabetes include:

- Miscarriage
- Stillbirth
- Birth weight over nine pounds (macrosomia)
- Infant disorders (breathing difficulties, jaundice, heart problems)

- Traumatic delivery (usually due to large size), leading to C-sections
- Hypertension or preeclampsia

If you have type 2 diabetes and were taking oral hypoglycemic agents prior to your pregnancy, you may not have learned to be as strict with your diet as you should be—something you cannot afford during pregnancy. But since these pills cannot be taken during pregnancy (they cause birth defects), your doctor will switch you over to insulin before you conceive. The danger of taking oral hypoglycemic agents during pregnancy is that the drug crosses the placenta and gets into the baby's bloodstream, which can cause very low blood sugar in the fetus. Insulin, however, does not cross the placenta and is safe during pregnancy.

Unfortunately, unless you became an expert on your diabetes prior to conceiving, you may have more difficulty controlling your blood sugar. You're in for a bumpy ride. In fact, the early weeks in pregnancy are so critical that if your blood sugar levels were not under control *three to six months prior to your pregnancy*, have a frank discussion with your health-care team about your options.

During the first three months of pregnancy the fetus is developing its brain, nervous system, and other body organs. It's also during this time that your blood sugar levels are most vulnerable because of hormonal changes, fatigue, and/or vomiting as a result of morning sickness.

Staying in Control

No matter what type of diabetes you have, every diabetes book will tell you that a healthy pregnancy depends on how well you manage your disease. If you can keep your blood sugar levels as close to normal as possible throughout your pregnancy, then your chances of a healthy baby are as good as a nondiabetic woman's. To do this, you must carefully plan out your meals, exercise, and insulin requirements with your doctor. If you do require insulin during your pregnancy, your insulin requirements will continue to increase as your pregnancy progresses. Keep in mind that the state of pregnancy means that your blood sugar levels are usually lower than they are for women who are not pregnant. Therefore, what's considered to be in the normal range for nonpregnant women will be different than what is considered normal for pregnant women. Consult your doctor about what the normal range should be for you.

When You Lose Control

If you lose control of your blood sugar levels in the first eight weeks of pregnancy, your baby is at risk for birth defects. High blood sugar levels may interfere with the formation of your baby's organs, causing heart defects or spina bifida (open spine). Once your baby's organs are formed, the risk of birth defects from high blood sugar levels disappears, but new problems may surface.

High blood sugar levels will cross the placenta and feed the baby too much glucose, causing the baby to make extra fat and therefore grow too big and fat for its gestational age. This condition is called *macrosomia*, which is defined as birth weight greater than nine pounds or greater than the ninetieth percentile for all babies.

In addition, the baby is at risk for becoming lethargic and developing a malfunctioning metabolism in utero, which can lead to stillbirth. You can solve this problem when you regain control of your blood sugar levels. Babies with macrosomia are usually not able to fit through the birth canal; they often sustain damage to their shoulders during a vaginal birth (the shoulders get stuck). So, if your baby is too big, you will need a Caesarean section.

The extra glucose that gets into the baby also causes the baby's pancreas to make extra insulin. Then, after birth, the baby's body needs time to adjust to normal glucose levels, and this can cause the baby to suffer from hypoglycemia, or low blood glucose levels. These babies are also at higher risk for breathing problems and are at a higher risk for obesity and developing type 2 diabetes later in life.

Your baby may also develop jaundice after birth, which is very common for all newborns, but is more frequently found in babies born to diabetic mothers. Newborn jaundice is caused by a buildup of old red blood cells that aren't clearing out of the body fast enough. Breastfeeding is the best cure for newborn jaundice.

Five Steps to Good Glucose

1. Use a home blood glucose monitor to test your blood sugar levels. Pregnancy can mask the symptoms of low blood glucose, so do not rely on how well you feel. Your goal is to get your blood glucose levels to copy those of a nondiabetic pregnant woman, which would be lower than in a nondiabetic, nonpregnant woman.
2. Ask your doctor when you should test your blood glucose levels. During pregnancy, it's common to test up to eight times per day, especially after eating.
3. Record your results in a journal you keep handy. Take the journal with you when you go out, especially to restaurants.
4. In a separate journal, keep track of when you're exercising and what you're eating.
5. Check with your doctor or diabetes educator before you make *any* changes to your diet or insulin plan. Midwives and doulas are *not* the appropriate practitioners to rely on for this information.

Gestational Diabetes Mellitus (GDM)

Gestational diabetes mellitus refers to diabetes that is first recognized or diagnosed at any stage during pregnancy. If you had diabetes prior to your pregnancy (type 1 or type 2), see the previous section.

Technically, *gestational diabetes* means high blood sugar (hyperglycemia) first recognized during pregnancy. Three to 12 percent of all pregnant women will develop gestational diabetes between weeks twenty-four and twenty-eight of their pregnancies. The symptoms of gestational diabetes are extreme thirst, hunger, or fatigue, but many women do not notice these symptoms. GDM complicates about 4 percent of pregnancies in the United States, and it's also a risk factor for type 2 diabetes after delivery.

What Is GDM?

During pregnancy, hormones made by the placenta can block the insulin the pancreas normally makes. This forces the pancreas to work harder to manufacture three times as much insulin as usual. In many cases, the pancreas isn't able to keep up, and blood sugar levels rise. Gestational diabetes is a common pregnancy-related health problem and is in the same league as other pregnancy-related conditions that develop during the second or third trimesters, such as high blood pres-

Your Diabetes Prenatal Team

A healthy pregnancy also depends on a good prenatal team that can help you stay in control. In the same way that you would hand-pick various skill sets for a baseball team, you must do the same for this team. Here are the specialists to look for:

- An endocrinologist or internist who specializes in diabetes and diabetic pregnancies.
- An obstetrician who specializes in high-risk pregnancies, particularly diabetic pregnancies. You may wish to use a *perinatologist*, a doctor who exclusively specializes in high-risk pregnancies.
- A neonatologist (a specialist for newborns) or a pediatrician who is trained to manage babies of diabetic moms.
- A nutritionist or registered dietitian who can help you create a realistic diet and insulin plan during your pregnancy.
- A diabetes educator who is available to answer questions throughout your pregnancy.
- A midwife or doula for additional support for the mother.

sure. Gestational diabetes develops more often in women who were overweight prior to pregnancy, and women who are over thirty-five.

Since pregnancy is also a time in your life when you're gaining weight, some experts believe that it is the sheer weight gain that contributes to insulin resistance, as the pancreas cannot keep up with the new weight *and* new demand for insulin. It's akin to a small restaurant with only ten tables suddenly being presented with triple the number of customers. It will be understaffed and unable to accommodate the new demand for tables.

GDM, a form of type 2 diabetes, can be managed through diet and blood sugar monitoring. However, recent research on California women with gestational diabetes showed that only one-third were able to control their condition through diet and blood sugar monitoring alone. Therefore, insulin may be necessary. GDM will usually disappear once you deliver, but it recurs two out of three times in future pregnancies. In some cases, GDM is really the unveiling of type 2 or even type 1 diabetes during pregnancy.

If you are genetically predisposed to type 2 diabetes, you are more likely to develop type 2 diabetes in the future if you develop gestational diabetes. Moreover, if you have GDM, you're more at risk for other pregnancy-related conditions, such as hypertension (high blood pressure), preeclampsia, and polyhydramnios (too much amniotic fluid). And if you're carrying more than one fetus, your pregnancy may be even more at risk. Therefore, it's wise to seek out an obstetrician if you have GDM. In very high-risk situations, a perinatologist (an obstetrician who specializes in high-risk pregnancies) may also have to be consulted.

Diagnosing GDM

GDM is diagnosed through a test known as *glucose screening*. Obviously, if you've already been diagnosed with type 2 diabetes, you will not need to be screened for diabetes during pregnancy. Candidates for glucose screening are women who are worried about developing diabetes during pregnancy because they have risk factors (see Chapter 1), a family history of gestational diabetes, or a personal history of gestational diabetes from a previous pregnancy.

Who Should Be Screened?

The symptoms of gestational diabetes are extreme thirst, hunger, or fatigue, all of which can be masked by the normal discomforts of pregnancy. Therefore, all women should be screened for GDM during weeks twenty-four to twenty-eight of their pregnancy (see Chapter 1 and Table 1.1). This is particularly crucial if:

- You are of Native American, African, or Hispanic descent
- Your mother had GDM
- You previously gave birth to a baby with a birth weight of more than nine pounds
- You've miscarried or had a stillbirth
- You're over twenty-five years of age
- You're overweight or obese (20 percent above your ideal weight)
- You have high blood pressure

Some doctors believe it isn't necessary to screen a woman for GDM if she has no symptoms and none of the risk factors; the attitude is that universal screening can create unnecessary anxiety. However, U.S. studies show that almost half of all gestational diabetes is missed by screening only women with risk factors. Some doctors wonder if even selective screening (screening only women with risk factors) reduces the problem of macrosomic babies.

Jelly Beans Versus Cola

The good news is that a jelly bean glucose test is being made available in some areas instead of the cola-like beverage traditionally used, which can cause nausea, vomiting, abdominal pain, bloating, and profuse sweating. By eating eighteen jelly beans and having blood glucose tested an hour later, gestational diabetes is just as accurately detected as it is with the old, horrid cola. Furthermore, the jelly beans do not cause any side effects other than a mild headache or nausea in a tiny percentage of women. If you are going to have your blood glucose tested, show your doctor this passage and ask for the jelly beans!

Treating GDM

The treatment for GDM is controlling blood sugar levels through diet, exercise, insulin, if necessary, and blood sugar monitoring. To do this, you must be under the care of a pregnancy practitioner (obstetrician, midwife), a diabetes specialist, and a dietician. Guidelines for nutrition and weight gain during a diabetic pregnancy depend on your current health, the fetal size, and your weight.

At least 80 percent of the time, gestational diabetes disappears after delivery. Unfortunately, it has been known to come back in subsequent pregnancies 80 to 90 percent of the time unless you get yourself in good physical shape between pregnancies. Experts report that sometimes each subsequent bout of gestational diabetes is more severe than the previous one.

Many women may be worried that a history of gestational diabetes means they will eventually develop type 2 diabetes. If you develop gestational diabetes during pregnancy, be alert. Approximately 20 percent of all women with gestational diabetes develop type 2 diabetes, presuming no other risk factors. If you are genetically predisposed to type 2 diabetes, a history of gestational diabetes can raise your risk of eventually developing the disease.

Treating Low Blood Sugar in Pregnancy

Many women with gestational diabetes will find they have episodes of low blood sugar, which is not harmful to the fetus, but very unpleasant for the mother. The thinking is that it's better to risk low blood sugar (hypoglycemia) in pregnancy to avoid high blood sugar (hyperglycemia), which is damaging to the fetus. Treating low blood sugar is the same in pregnancy as at any other time. (See Chapter 8.)

Special Delivery: The C-Section

About one in four babies is delivered by Caesarean section, which is a surgical procedure that is essentially abdominal delivery. The procedure dates back to Julius Caesar, who, as legend tells us, was born in this manner. Whether Caesar's truly was a Caesarean birth is hotly debated among historians, but what historians *do* know is that the abdominal delivery dates back to ancient Rome. In fact, Roman law made it legal to perform a Caesarean section only if the mother died in the last four weeks of pregnancy. The procedure therefore originated only as a means to save the child. Using the procedure to save the *mother* was not even considered until the nineteenth century, under the influence of two prominent obstetricians, Max Sanger and Eduardo Porro.

Women who have diabetes during pregnancy (preexisting or gestational) are at a higher risk of requiring a Caesarean section than the general pregnant population. That's because they can give birth to very large babies, who may not be able to fit through the birth canal. Prior to your due date discuss with your pregnancy health-care provider the situations that would warrant a Caesarean section.

This procedure is considered major pelvic surgery that usually involves either a spinal or epidural anesthetic (a type of local anesthetic). A vertical or horizontal incision is made just above your pubic hairline. Then the surgeon (usually) cuts horizontally through the uterine muscle and eases out the baby. Sometimes, this second cut is vertical, known as the *classic incision*. It is this second cut, into the uterine muscle, that will affect whether you can have a vaginal birth after Caesarean (VBAC) or not. With a horizontal cut, women have gone on to have normal second vaginal births.

In some instances, you'll know in advance whether you need to have a Caesarean section. Your pelvis may be clearly too small; you may have scarring on your cervix from previous pelvic surgery that will prevent dilation; or an emergency may arise that requires the fetus to be taken out immediately.

A Dozen Good Reasons to Have a C-Section

Here are twelve legitimate reasons why a Caesarean section may be performed.

1. When a vaginal delivery, even with intervention, is risky. You may fall into this category if your baby is large.
2. A prolonged labor caused by failure to dilate, failure for the labor to progress, too large a head, and several other reasons

3. A failed induction attempt. Labor induction sometimes fails, and when the baby is overdue, a Caesarean is the next alternative.
4. When the baby is in a breech position
5. Placental problems
6. Fetal distress
7. Health problems that prevent normal vaginal delivery
8. A history of difficult deliveries or stillbirth
9. When the baby is in a transverse lie, or horizontal, position
10. When the mother has primary genital herpes or other sexually transmitted diseases, such as genital warts, chlamydia, or gonorrhea, which are in danger of being passed on to the newborn via vaginal delivery
11. When the mother is HIV positive
12. A multiple birth

Unnecessary Versus Necessary Caesareans

Many unnecessary Caesarean sections are performed. Most second Caesareans are not necessary, for instance, if the uterine cut was horizontal. Another common practice is to perform a C-section when a woman fails to go into labor after being induced. Reasons for being induced usually have to do with progressing past the due date. In this case, if the fetus isn't in distress, you may want to wait or get a second opinion regarding a C-section. In a U.S. study, situations in which a C-section was performed depended more on the *doctor* than on any other single factor; the rate of C-sections varied from 19 to 42 percent according to the individual doctor's preference. This is a huge discrepancy. What it boils down to is the *doctor's* definition of what constitutes an emergency. No competent doctor will delay a C-section if he or she thinks that the labor is endangering the baby's or the mother's health.

Again, to avoid an unnecessary procedure, consult with your practitioner and midwife before the third trimester. Find out what situations truly warrant a C-section, and whether you're a vaginal birth after cesarean, or VBAC (pronounced "vee-back"), candidate. If you're experiencing a difficult or high-risk pregnancy or will be having a multiple birth, you may be more likely to have the procedure than a woman with a low-risk pregnancy.

After the Baby Is Born

The question that may be at the top of your mind after you give birth is whether your diabetes is gone. This is a valid question only for women who have had gestational diabetes. In this case, the only way to tell is to have another glucose tolerance test when you get your first postpartum menstrual period (if you're breast-feeding), or alternatively, six weeks after childbirth. If the test results are normal, then your diabetes is, indeed, gone—but should not be forgotten. It's a warning to you that you better "shape up" between pregnancies, or forever after; otherwise, future bouts of gestational diabetes or type 2 diabetes in later years could occur. In addition, there are some other issues that will surface for mothers who experience gestational diabetes, such as lifestyle habits.

If your test results show continuing high blood sugar, you may have type 2 diabetes that has just revealed itself during your pregnancy. In this case, your diabetes is a permanent health condition that was simply diagnosed during pregnancy or was triggered by it.

Breast-Feeding and GDM

If you've been told you can't breast-feed because you have or had gestational diabetes you may be surprised to find out that *this is completely false*! If your diabetes is controlled and you've given birth to a healthy baby, breast-feeding is the normal way to feed your baby and does not place your baby at risk for the numerous undisputed and well-documented health problems associated with babies fed with cow's milk. Stick to your "pregnancy rules" and keep self-monitoring your blood sugar levels so you can adjust your diet and exercise routine to your new levels of hormones. Estrogen levels affect blood sugar levels; when they rise, your blood sugar rises. When they drop—which is what happens during breast-feeding as a result of the hormone prolactin—blood sugar levels may drop, which could mean you need to eat more while breast-feeding to keep up your levels. If you had gestational diabetes, this natural drop in blood sugar levels is nature's way of helping you bounce back to health faster if you breast-feed. If you need to take insulin to control high blood sugar after childbirth, your baby doesn't care! Insulin cannot be ingested, so even if it crosses into the breast milk, it will have zero effect on the baby. Remember, if insulin could be ingested, you wouldn't need to inject it in the first place! Furthermore, several studies show that breast-fed babies have lower incidences of both type 1 diabetes and type 2 diabetes later in life.

If you have high blood sugar in the days and/or weeks following childbirth, your milk will be much sweeter than usual. That's not dangerous per se to the baby; the baby has his or her own functioning pancreas, which can produce the insulin she or he needs to handle the sweetness, but the baby could begin to put on too much weight and get fat. There may also be cases when the sweetness is a "turnoff" to the baby and she or he may not be as receptive to the milk, which will cause problems with your milk supply. Sweet milk may cause engorgement, which is painful and can put you at risk for mastitis (inflammation in the breast, usually due to bacterial infection). In general, the main danger of high blood sugar during breast-feeding is to *you*; you'll want to control your diabetes so you can be as healthy and fit as possible. And it's important for every woman to take care of herself—whether or not she has children or she is breast-feeding.

Postpartum Blues and Diabetes

Many women find the enormous lifestyle adjustment after childbirth tiring. They may be fatigued, stressed, and overwhelmed and have all the other normal feelings that accompany the event of giving birth. Unfortunately, some women may also suffer from postpartum depression, which is characterized by a loss of interest in formerly pleasurable activities, changes in appetite, changes in sleep patterns (which happens after childbirth anyway), sadness, and a host of other emotional and physical symptoms.

Just because you have diabetes does not mean that you can't develop another condition on top of it, such as postpartum depression. But keeping your blood sugar in check after childbirth will help to avoid high or low blood sugar levels, and their associated mood swings, which may mask postpartum depression or vice versa. It's also recommended that you have your thyroid checked after childbirth to make sure that you are not also suffering from postpartum thyroid disease, which affects about 18 percent of the postpartum population and also can be misdiagnosed as postpartum depression.

The Role of Estrogen

Estrogen definitely influences your blood sugar levels and insulin requirements. There is also evidence that estrogen-containing products can even trigger insulin resistance in women who have a family history of or genetic predisposition to type 2 diabetes. Estrogen usually raises blood sugar levels, which interferes with medication or insulin doses. This is why estrogen-containing medications, such as oral contraceptives or hormone replacement therapy after menopause, were once considered "no-nos" for women with diabetes. It is also why diabetes is still considered a *contraindication*, a condition that is not compatible with a given therapy or medication, for many estrogen-containing products. In recent years, however, the thinking surrounding estrogen and diabetes has been changing, and guidelines for women with diabetes are being revised to reflect, in part, more knowledge about the health benefits of various therapies, as well as the lower doses of estrogen contained in newer generations of medications. As for hormone replacement therapy, there are clear benefits and risks, discussed in Chapter 4.

Unfortunately, there is no surefire mathematical equation you can use to calculate how severely your own blood sugar levels will be affected by the estrogen your ovaries naturally produce or by the external estrogen that may be prescribed for you. Much of the risk has to do with how well controlled your blood sugar is. Therefore, the message of this chapter is a simple one: You may need to adjust your diabetes medication, insulin, or blood sugar monitoring habits to accommodate the estrogen that is affecting your system. That estrogen can be from your own ovaries (some women find that they need to adjust their blood sugar monitoring habits or medication at certain times in their monthly cycles), or synthetic sources, in the form of pills and patches. If taking estrogen from external sources is too high a risk for you (something you must determine in consultation with your health-care practitioner), you need to investigate alternative forms of birth control or hormonal therapy (see Chapter 4).

Periods with Diabetes

When estrogen levels are naturally high in the cycle, your body may be more resistant to its own insulin or to medications or the insulin you inject. Most women find that their blood sugar levels will be high for about three to five days before, during, or after their periods. Every woman is different, so the only way to manage your blood sugar levels is to test your levels and chart them along with your cycle. Many experts advise that you check your blood sugar levels two to four times a day the week before, during, and after your period for two to three months. (See Chapter 7 for details on blood sugar monitoring.) This will help you establish an accurate chart so you can find your pattern.

PMS and High Blood Sugar

Most women will experience premenstrual symptoms seven to ten days before their periods. Some evidence points to the fact that high blood sugar can exacerbate these symptoms, meaning that instead of feeling blue or sad or moody, you would feel intensely blue, sad, or moody. This creates a vicious cycle because these feelings of anxiety and moodiness can raise your blood sugar even higher, making blood sugar control more difficult. The only way to prevent severe PMS is to keep your blood sugar as controlled as possible around this time in your cycle. Charting your cycles and keeping track of when in the cycle your PMS strikes will help to pinpoint when you need to more frequently monitor your blood sugar.

If you are approaching menopause, you may be experiencing changes in your cycles as a result of your station in life rather than high blood sugar. You may wish to ask your doctor to test your levels of follicle-stimulating hormone (FSH) to see if they are high, which is an indication that you're approaching menopause. This will help sort out whether severe PMS is related to sugar or your age. In many cases, it is related to both.

Food Cravings, PMS, and Diabetes

Food cravings are a classic symptom of PMS but can be especially problematic for women trying to manage diabetes. The cravings are caused by an increase in progesterone at this time in your cycle, and affect all women equally—regardless of whether they have diabetes. These cravings, like all PMS symptoms, will diminish after menopause. Most often, these desires point women in the direction of chocolate or sweet foods. The advice from many experts is to simply allow yourself the food you are craving in perhaps a sugar-free or fat-free format, such as fat-free chocolate pudding. If you deprive yourself of the particular food you're longing for, you may wind up bingeing, which can be far more destructive. Bear in mind, however, that the food you eat during this craving period may, alone, be responsible for a rise in your blood sugar. Charting the foods you eat during your cycle may help to pinpoint when to anticipate a change in blood sugar levels. It's also important to note that many women have less energy as a result of PMS or because of the period itself. This can interfere with daily activities or exercise routines, also causing your blood sugar levels to rise.

Hormonal Contraception and Diabetes

Many women in their late thirties and forties find hormonal contraceptives the best method of preventing unwanted pregnancy. This is particularly the case with the advent of new studies showing that women who stay on hormonal contraception beyond age thirty-five, right up until menopause, have greater protection from ovarian cancer, ovarian cysts, and endometrial cancer. Since type 2 diabetes often strikes women prior to menopause, women need to know how diabetes will affect this method of contraception.

Any hormonal contraceptive can affect women who have diabetes or high cholesterol (also called lipid or blood fat disorders). The synthetic progesterone that is used in many hormonal contraceptives—called *progestin*—can decrease your glucose tolerance by increasing insulin resistance, while estrogen has the opposite effect; you may need to adjust your meal and exercise routine, insulin dosage, or diabetes medication while taking an estrogen-containing contraceptive. Women who go on low-dose oral contraceptives have fewer problems with balancing blood sugar than women on high-dose pills. In the general population, low-dose oral contraceptives have fewer side effects, too. There are only a small number of situations where a high-dose oral contraceptive may be clinically necessary, which may be the case where heavy bleeding needs to be controlled.

When it comes to cholesterol, progestin (the synthetic progesterone) can exacerbate high cholesterol because it reduces high-density lipoprotein (HDL), or good cholesterol, and raises low-density lipoprotein (LDL), or bad cholesterol. If your cholesterol levels are normal, progestin can put you at risk for a cholesterol problem, which aggravates type 2 diabetes. Therefore, a progestin-only contraceptive, such as the minipill, would not be as good a choice as a combination hormonal contraceptive, which contains estrogen; estrogen can help to counteract the lipid effect of the progestin. The amount of estrogen in your combination oral contraceptive will influence how severely your cholesterol is affected.

Who Can Be on Combination Oral Contraceptives (OCs)?

If you don't smoke and your diabetes is controlled, you may be a candidate for a combination OC. There are a number of fringe health benefits, known by clinicians as *noncontraceptive benefits*, to taking OCs. Because OCs prevent ovulation, they also help prevent diseases associated with the ovaries, such as ovarian cancer, ovarian cysts, and endometrial cancer. In fact, if you have no children, or have no plans to get pregnant and breast-feed, staying on an OC will have the same therapeutic effect on your ovaries as pregnancy and breast-feeding because it will give your ovaries a break. The following are considered clear, undisputed benefits of OCs:

- OCs reduce the incidence of endometrial cancer and ovarian cancer.
- OCs reduce the likelihood of developing fibrocystic breast conditions.
- OCs reduce the likelihood of developing ovarian cysts.

- OC users have less menstrual blood loss and have more regular cycles, which reduces the chance of developing iron deficiency anemia.
- OCs help reduce the severity of cramps and other symptoms of PMS.
- OCs reduce the symptoms of PCOS (such as unwanted hair).

Will I Get a Blood Clot?

Women with type 2 diabetes should be alert to the risk of blood clots, because their risks increase when taking an OC. The rule for the gen-

When Your Glucose Readings Say GDM

A fasting plasma glucose test (also called a fasting blood sugar test, see Chapter 1) can be used to screen for gestational diabetes mellitus (GDM). In this case, the readings outlined in Table 1.1 will indicate normal blood sugar levels or impaired fasting glucose (IFG) or if high, diabetes. If you have IFG, you may be diagnosed with GDM, or you may have an oral glucose tolerance test to confirm it.

Suggested GDM After an Oral Glucose Tolerance Test
    One hour after 100 grams of glucose: 180 mg/dl;
      after 75 grams: 200 mg/dl
    Two hours after 100 grams of glucose: 155 mg/dl;
      after 75 grams: 140–200 mg/dl
    Three hours after 100 or 75 grams of glucose:
      140 mg/dl
    Eight hours after 100 or 75 grams: 95 mg/dl

These readings are based on no other food intake following the ingestion of a glucose drink.

eral population is that if you're healthy and don't smoke, serious cardiovascular problems linked to OCs are rare in women taking low-dose pills. Nevertheless, it's important to make sure that you're not already at risk for blood clots. If you have a history of thrombophlebitis, pulmonary emboli, and other cardiovascular diseases, you should not be encouraged to take OCs. Your risk of blood clots also increases if you:

- Smoke
- Don't exercise
- Are overweight
- Are over age fifty
- Are hypertensive
- Have high cholesterol

Unfortunately, many women with type 2 diabetes will check off all the risk factors above. So if you decide, despite warnings to the contrary, to opt for an oral contraceptive, you must discuss your choice with your doctor and have your cholesterol and blood pressure checked regularly while on OCs. If you currently have high blood pressure, you should also note that OCs can aggravate diabetes eye disease or kidney disease (see Chapters 11 and 12).

4

Type 2 Diabetes, Menopause, and Aging

TYPE 2 DIABETES is generally diagnosed beyond age forty. However, as women age beyond forty, other health conditions can complicate a diagnosis of type 2 diabetes. This chapter looks at specific conditions associated with aging and type 2 diabetes, such as menopause, osteoporosis, and management goals for women over seventy-five. In women seventy-five and older, type 2 diabetes is expected to increase by 271 percent over the next forty-five years.

Menopause

When it comes to menopause, women with type 2 diabetes have a little more to be concerned about than women without type 2 diabetes. Estrogen loss increases *all* women's risk of heart disease, which is the major cause of death for postmenopausal women. But in postmenopausal women with diabetes, the risk of heart disease is two to three times higher than in the general female population. Furthermore, as estrogen and progesterone levels drop, women with diabetes can expect fluctuations in their blood sugar levels and possibly more episodes of low blood sugar (see Chapter 8). After menopause, women taking insulin may find that their insulin requirements have dropped by as much as 20 percent. In light of the 2002 studies on hormone replacement therapy (HRT) and heart disease, which are discussed in the section "HRT and Type 2 Diabetes" later in this chapter, managing type 2 diabetes postmenopause is a challenge.

Natural Menopause

When menopause occurs naturally, it tends to take place anywhere between the ages of forty-eight and fifty-two, but it can occur as early as your late thirties or as late as your mid-fifties. When menopause occurs before age forty-five, it is considered *early menopause*, but just as menarche is genetically predetermined, so is menopause. For an average woman with an unremarkable medical history, what she eats or the activities she engages in will not influence the timing of her menopause. However, women who have had chemotherapy or who have been exposed to high levels of radiation (such as radiation therapy in the pelvic area for cancer treatment) may go into earlier menopause. In any event, the average age of menopause is fifty to fifty-one.

Other causes that have been cited to trigger an early menopause include mumps (in small groups of women, the infection causing the mumps has been known to spread to the ovaries, prematurely shutting them down) and specific autoimmune diseases, such as lupus or rheumatoid arthritis (some women with these diseases find that their bodies develop antibodies that attack their own ovaries).

Perimenopause refers to women who are in the thick of menopause—their cycles are wildly erratic, and they are experiencing hot flashes and vaginal dryness. This label is applicable for about four years, covering the two years prior to the official "last" period to the two years following the last menstrual period.

Menopause refers to your final menstrual period. You will not be able to pinpoint your final period until you've been completely free from periods for one year. Then you count back to the last period you charted, and that date is the date of your menopause.

Postmenopause refers to the last third of most women's lives and includes women who have been free of menstrual periods for at least four years to women celebrating their one hundredth birthday.

Signs of Natural Menopause

There are just three classic short-term symptoms of menopause: erratic periods, hot flashes, and vaginal dryness. All three of these symptoms are caused by a decrease in estrogen. As for the emotional symptoms of menopause, such as irritability, mood swings, and melancholy, they are actually caused by a rise in follicle-stimulating hormone, or FSH. As the cycle changes and the ovaries' egg supply dwindles, FSH is secreted in very high amounts and reaches a lifetime peak—as much as fifteen times higher; it's the body's way of trying to "jump-start" the ovarian engine.

Decreased levels of estrogen can make you more vulnerable to stress, depression, and anxiety because estrogen loss affects REM sleep. When we're not rested, we're not able to cope with stresses that normally may not affect us. Stress can also increase blood sugar.

Every woman entering menopause will experience a change in her menstrual cycle. However, not all women will experience hot flashes or even notice vaginal changes. This is particularly true if a woman is overweight. Estrogen is stored in fat cells, which is why overweight women also tend to be more at risk for estrogen-dependent cancers. In menopause the fat cells release their stored estrogen, creating an estrogen reserve that the body will use during menopause and that can reduce the severity of estrogen loss symptoms.

Cycles may become longer or shorter with long bouts of amenorrhea. There will also be flow changes, where periods may suddenly become light and scanty, or very heavy and crampy.

Roughly 85 percent of all pre- and perimenopausal women experience *hot flashes*. Hot flashes can begin when periods are either still regular or have just started to become irregular. They usually stop between one and two years after your final menstrual period. A hot flash can feel different for each woman. Some women experience a feeling of warmth in their face and upper body, while others experience hot flashes as a simultaneous sweating with chills. Some women feel anxious, tense, dizzy, or nauseous just before the hot flash; others feel tingling in their fingers or heart palpitations just before. Some women will experience their hot flashes during the day; others will experience them at night and may wake up so wet from perspiration that they need to change their bed sheets and/or nightclothes.

A hot flash is not the same as being overheated. Although the skin temperature often rises between four and eight degrees, the internal body temperature drops, creating this odd sensation. Certain groups of women will experience more severe hot flashes than others:

- Women who are in surgical menopause (discussed later in this chapter).
- Women who are thin. When there's less fat on the body to store estrogen reserves, estrogen loss symptoms are more severe.
- Women who don't sweat easily. An ability to sweat makes extreme temperatures easier to tolerate. Women who have trouble sweating may experience more severe hot flashes that are difficult to adjust to.

You can lessen your discomfort by adjusting your lifestyle to cope with the hot flashes. The more comfortable you are, the less intense your flashes will feel. Once you establish a pattern by charting the flashes, you can do a few things around the time of day your flashes occur. Some suggestions:

- Avoid synthetic clothing, such as polyester, because it traps perspiration.
- Use only 100 percent cotton bedding if you have night sweats.
- Avoid clothing with high necks and long sleeves.
- Dress in layers.
- Keep cold drinks handy.
- Quit smoking. This is particularly important if you have diabetes. Smoking constricts blood vessels and can intensify and prolong a flash. It also leads to severe complications from diabetes, discussed in Chapter 1.
- Avoid trigger foods such as caffeine, alcohol, spicy foods, sugars, and large meals. Substitute herbal teas for coffee or regular tea.
- Discuss with your doctor the benefits of taking vitamin E supplements. Evidence suggests that vitamin E is essential for proper circulation and the production of sex hormones.

- Exercise to improve your circulation.
- Reduce your exposure to the sun; sunburn will aggravate your hot flashes because burnt skin cannot regulate heat as effectively.

Other Changes

Estrogen loss will also cause vaginal changes. Since it is the production of estrogen that causes the vagina to continuously stay moist and elastic through its natural secretions, the loss of estrogen will cause the vagina to become drier, thinner, and less elastic. This may also cause the vagina to shrink slightly in width and length. In addition, the reduction in vaginal secretions causes the vagina to be less acidic. This can put you at risk for more vaginal infections, particularly if you have high blood sugar. As a result of these vaginal changes, you'll notice a change in your sexual activity. Your vagina may take longer to become lubricated, or you may have to depend on lubricants to have comfortable intercourse.

Estrogen loss can affect other parts of your sex life as well. Your libido may actually increase because testosterone levels can rise when estrogen levels drop. (The general rule is that your levels of testosterone will either stay the same or increase.) However, women who *do* experience an increase in sexual desire may also be frustrated that their vaginas are not accommodating their needs. First, there is the lubrication problem: more stimulation is required to lubricate the vagina naturally, and you still may need to use synthetic lubricants. Second, a decrease in estrogen means that less blood flows to the vagina and clitoris, which means that orgasm may be more difficult to achieve or may not last as long as it normally has in the past. Other changes involve the breasts. Normally, estrogen causes blood to flow into the breasts during arousal, which makes the nipples more erect, sensitive, and responsive. Estrogen loss causes less blood to flow to the breasts, which makes them less sensitive. And finally, since the vagina shrinks as estrogen decreases, it doesn't expand as much during intercourse, which may make intercourse less comfortable, particularly since the vagina is less lubricated.

Mood Swings

Mood swings can be an especially tricky symptom of both menopause and fluctuating blood sugar levels. Many women with diabetes struggle with severe mood swings, which can make controlling blood sugar more difficult. While anger and depression can be symptoms of low blood sugar, anxiety and irritability can be symptoms of high blood sugar. Factor in hormonal changes during menopause, and your moods can be severely affected. Unfortunately, depression and irritability can lead women to poor control of their diabetes. Frequent monitoring of your blood sugar levels and sticking to your meal plan can help to prevent drastic mood swings.

Menopause and Blood Sugar

As you approach menopause, you'll want to revisit your blood sugar monitoring habits. That's because menopause often masks the symptoms of low or high blood sugar and vice versa. For example, hot flashes (or sweating), moodiness, and short-term memory loss are also associated with low blood sugar. Experts recommend that before you decide that you're "low" and bite into that chocolate bar, you may want to test your blood sugar first to see if your symptoms are caused by sugar or hormones. Otherwise, ingesting more sugar than you need could cause high blood sugar unnecessarily.

That said many women find that because estrogen and progesterone levels are dropping, they experience more frequent and severe episodes of low blood sugar. As mentioned previously, estrogen can trigger insulin resistance; the loss of estrogen will therefore have the opposite effect, causing insulin to be taken up more quickly by the body, which could result in low blood sugar. An easy way to remember how estrogen levels affect blood sugar is to simply note that when estrogen is up, so is blood sugar; when estrogen is down, so is blood sugar. Therefore, high estrogen levels equal high blood sugar; low estrogen levels equal low blood sugar.

The only way to cope with these fluctuations is to try to eliminate other causes of blood sugar fluctuations, such as stress, deviating from meal and exercise plans, and so on. If you're on oral hypoglycemic agents, you may need to adjust your dosages around the time of menopause to compensate for less resistance to insulin as your hormone levels drop. (And if you go on hormone replacement therapy you may need to readjust your dosages again.)

Women who have persistent high blood sugar levels may find the normal menopausal symptoms, such as vaginal dryness, for example, exacerbated. In this case, by gaining more control over blood sugar levels, they may find their menopausal symptoms are less severe.

Surgical Menopause or Premature Menopause

Surgical menopause occurs when you've had your ovaries surgically removed, or chemically shut down as a result of certain medications, such as chemotherapy for cancer. In this case, you will likely experience all of the symptoms of natural menopause but in the extreme. Most women in surgical menopause report far more severe symptoms because the process of estrogen loss has been sudden rather than gradual. Surgical menopause or premature menopause (before the age of forty-five) are best managed using traditional hormone replacement therapy until the natural age of menopause. In this case, HRT simply replaces what your body should have been making naturally, were it not for illness or premature ovarian failure. Once you reach the natural age of menopause (fifty to fifty-five), you can decide whether it is risky for you to continue HRT in light of the heart disease risks and your blood sugar control. The 2002 Women's Health Initiative (WHI) study looked at the long-term use of HRT in women over fifty-five, and the results do not affect women on HRT to correct premature menopause due to surgery, chemotherapy, or premature ovarian failure caused by other factors.

HRT and Type 2 Diabetes

The average American woman will live until age seventy-eight, meaning that she will live one-third of her life after her menopause. Since heart disease is a major complication of type 2 diabetes, and women are more prone to heart disease as a result of estrogen loss after menopause, in the 1980s and 1990s, women with type 2 diabetes were encouraged to seriously consider hormone replacement therapy after menopause, because it was believed that long-term HRT protected women from heart disease. *That's all changed.*

In July 2002, a study by the U.S. National Heart, Lung and Blood Institute, part of a huge research program called the WHI, suggested that HRT should not be recommended for long-term use; in fact, the results were so alarming, the study was halted before its completion date. It was found that Prempro, a combination of estrogen and progestin, which was a "standard issue" HRT formulation for post-menopausal women, increased the risk of invasive breast cancer, heart disease, stroke, and pulmonary embolisms (blood clots). However, Prempro *did* reduce the incidence of bone fractures from osteoporosis and colon cancer. The study participants were informed in a letter that they should stop taking their pills. Among women in good health, without type 2 diabetes, HRT in the short term to relieve menopausal symptoms is still considered a good option, and there was no evidence to suggest that short-term use of HRT was harmful. The study only has implications for women on HRT for long-term use—something that was recommended to millions of women over the past twenty years because of perceived protection against heart disease.

In 1998, an earlier trial known as the Heart and Estrogen/Progestin Replacement Study (HERS), looked at whether HRT reduced risk in women who already had heart disease. HRT was not found to have any beneficial effect. Women who were at risk for breast cancer were never advised to go on HRT; similarly, women who had suffered a stroke or were considered at risk for blood clots were also never considered good candidates for HRT. It had long been known that breast cancer was a risk of long-term HRT, as well as stroke and blood clots. However, many women made the HRT decision based on the perceived heart disease protection. Today, the only thing the experts can agree on is that the HRT decision is highly individual and must be an informed decision, where all of the possible risks and benefits of taking—or not taking—HRT are disclosed.

The Components of HRT

Hormone replacement therapy (HRT) refers to estrogen and progestin, which is a factory-made progesterone, given to women after menopause who still have their uterus to prevent the lining from overgrowing and becoming cancerous (known as *endometrial hyperplasia*). Estrogen replacement therapy (ERT), sometimes called ET, refers to estrogen only, which is given to women after surgical menopause who no longer have a uterus. Both HRT and ERT are designed to replace the estrogen lost after menopause, and hence:

• Prevent or even reverse the long-term consequences of estrogen loss. The only proven long-term benefit of HRT is that it can help to prevent bone loss and reduce the incidence of fractures. Until July 2002, it was believed that HRT protected women from cardiovascular disease, but this is no longer considered true. In women who are at higher risk of breast cancer, HRT was always believed to be risky; now it is believed that it may trigger breast cancer in low-risk women.

• Treat the short-term discomforts of menopause such as hot flashes and vaginal dryness. This is all still true for women in otherwise good health. You must discuss with your doctor whether this is true for you, if your blood sugar is well controlled.

You can take estrogen in a number of ways. The most common estrogen product uses a synthesis of various estrogens that are derived from the urine of pregnant horses. That way the estrogen mimics nature more accurately. Estrogen replacement comes in pills, patches (transdermal), or vaginal creams. Other common synthetic forms of estrogen include micronized estradiol, ethinyl estradiol, esterified estrogen, and quinestrol.

The most common progestins include: Provera, Amen, Curretab, and Cycrin (all brand names of medroxyprogesterone acetate); Duralutin, Gesterol LA, Hylutin, Hyprogest 250 (all brand names of hydroxyprogesterone caproate); and Aygestin, Norlutate, and Norgestrel (all brand names for norethindrone acetate). Progestins are taken in separate tablets along with estrogen. Together, the estrogen and progestin you take is called HRT.

If you are suffering from great discomfort during perimenopause, and your blood sugar levels are well controlled, discuss with your health-care provider whether short-term HRT is an option. Because of the high risk for heart disease and macrovascular complications associated with diabetes, HRT involves far more risks to women with diabetes in light of the 2002 study results. There are also numerous natural methods to control symptoms; for more information, consult my book: *The Natural Woman's Guide to Hormone Replacement Therapy* (2003).

Blood Sugar Levels During Menopause

As stated previously, decreasing levels of estrogen and progesterone in your bloodstream lead to decreased blood sugar levels as your body's responsiveness to insulin improves. As a result, you may need to adjust your diabetes medication or insulin.

You may also need to adjust your meal and exercise plan because menopause slows down your metabolism. That means it will be easier to gain weight on fewer calories. The only way around this is to increase activity or decrease your calorie intake.

Women who have high blood sugar levels may find that their skin is drier and more scaly, while vaginal dryness may be more severe, than women with lower blood sugar levels. They may also notice that their nails are deteriorating more rapidly. Controlling blood sugar can reverse these effects.

Osteoporosis

Postmenopausal women are at highest risk of developing osteoporosis, which can complicate type 2 diabetes, particularly with respect to meal planning and exercise. Eighty percent of all osteoporosis sufferers are women as a direct result of estrogen loss. Maintaining bone mass and good bone health is your best defense against bone loss. Although osteoporosis can be disfiguring, it is a relatively silent disease in that there are often no immediate symptoms, pain, or suffering that occur with it. The problem is not osteoporosis in itself, but the risk of fractures. One out of two women over fifty will have an osteoporosis-related fracture in her lifetime. If you have osteoporosis and fall down, a fracture can dramatically affect your quality of life. If you've ever experienced reduced mobility, or being dependent on someone else to prepare meals, shop, or run errands, you may have some idea as to how debilitating being bedridden and immobile can be. A full 70 percent of all hip fractures are a direct result of osteoporosis. Roughly twenty-five percent of those suffering hip fractures will die of resulting complications; 50 percent will be disabled. In fact, more women die each year as a result of osteoporosis-related fractures than from breast and ovarian cancer combined.

Osteoporosis literally means "porous bones." Normally, in the life of the average healthy woman, by her late thirties and forties her bones become less dense. By the time she reaches her fifties, she may begin to experience bone loss in her teeth and become more susceptible to wrist fractures. Gradually, the bones in her spine may weaken, fracture, and compress, causing upper back curvature and loss of height, known as *kyphosis*, or sometimes, *dowager's hump*. There are many ways to maintain bone mass after menopause, however, and prevent the disfiguring effects of bone loss.

Osteoporosis is unfortunately more common in women because when a woman's skeletal growth is completed, she typically has 15 percent lower bone mineral density and 30 percent less bone mass than a man of the same age. Studies also show that women lose trabecular bone (the inner, spongy part making up the internal support of the bone) at a higher rate than men.

Three Types of Osteoporosis

There are three types of osteoporosis women are prone to: *postmenopausal*, *senile*, and *secondary*.

Postmenopausal Osteoporosis

Postmenopausal osteoporosis usually develops roughly ten to fifteen years after the onset of menopause. In this case, estrogen loss interferes with calcium absorption, and you begin to lose trabecular bone three times faster than the normal rate. You will also begin to lose parts of your *cortical* bone (the outer shell of the bone), but not as quickly as the trabecular bone.

Senile Osteoporosis

Senile osteoporosis affects men and women. Here, you lose cortical and trabecular bone because of a decrease in bone cell activity that results from aging. Hip fractures are seen most often with this kind of osteoporosis. The decrease in bone cell activity affects your capacity to rebuild bone, but is also aggravated by low calcium intake.

Secondary Osteoporosis

Secondary osteoporosis means that there is an underlying condition that has caused bone loss. These conditions include chronic renal disease, hypogonadism (overstimulation of the sex glands, or gonads), hyperthyroidism (an overactive thyroid gland), some forms of cancer, removal of parts of the intestine that interferes with calcium absorption, and the use of anticonvulsants.

Calcium

Everyone has at least four parathyroid glands that control the blood calcium level, or calcium balance. Your parathyroid glands stimulate the release of calcium from the bone to raise blood calcium levels. They also help your body convert vitamin D into calcium. These glands are located on the back of each lobe of your thyroid gland. The easiest way to grasp exactly where they're located is to imagine the capital letter H. At each tip of the H, imagine a circle. If the H is your thyroid gland, the circles at each tip are your parathyroid glands.

What Causes Bone Loss?

Our bones are always regenerating (known as *remodeling*). This process helps to maintain a constant level of calcium in the blood, essential for a healthy heart, blood circulation, and blood clotting. About 99 percent of all the body's calcium is in the bones and teeth; when blood calcium drops below a certain level, the body will take calcium from the bones to replenish it. But by the time we reach our late thirties, our bones lose calcium faster than it can be replaced. The pace of bone calcium loss speeds up for women who are three to seven years beyond menopause. But bones start absorbing calcium again when this *bone-pause* is past. And consumption of calcium-rich foods, combined with moderate exercise, can help to reverse osteoporosis.

The pace of bone loss then slows once again, but as we age, the body is less able to absorb calcium from food. One of the most influential factors on bone loss is estrogen; it slows or even halts the loss of bone mass by improving our absorption of calcium from the intestinal tract, which allows us to maintain a higher level of calcium in our blood. And, the higher the calcium levels in the blood, the less chance you have of losing calcium from your bones to replenish your calcium blood levels. In men, testosterone does the same thing regarding calcium absorption, but unlike women, men never reach a particular age when their testes stop producing testosterone. If they did, they would be just as prone to osteoporosis as women.

There is a long list of other factors that affect bone loss. One of the most obvious factors is calcium in our diet. Calcium is regularly lost to urine, feces, and dead skin. We need to continuously account for this loss in our diet. In fact, the less calcium we ingest, the more we force our body into taking it out of our bones. Exercise also greatly affects bone density; the more we exercise, the stronger we make our bones. In fact the bone mass we have in our late twenties and early thirties will affect our bone mass at menopause.

Finally, there are several physical conditions and external factors that help to weaken our bones and contribute to bone loss later in life. These include:

• Heavy caffeine and alcohol intake. Because caffeine and alcohol are diuretics, they cause you to lose more calcium in your urine. Heavy drinkers tend to suffer from more hip fractures. Since alcohol can also damage the liver, which could impair its ability to metabolize vitamin D, it can aggravate bone loss.

• Smoking. Research shows that smokers tend to go into earlier menopause, while older smokers have 20 to 30 percent less bone mass than nonsmokers. Several studies have shown that women who smoke have a greater risk of fractures than women who do not.

• Women in surgical menopause who are not on ERT. Losing estrogen earlier than you would have naturally increases your bone loss.

• Corticosteriods. These are used to eliminate or reduce allergic inflammation and they can affect absorption.

• Diseases of the small intestine, liver, and pancreas. These diseases prevent the body from absorbing adequate amounts of calcium from the intestine.

- Thyroid disease. Untreated thyroid disease can lead to faster bone loss.
- Lymphoma, leukemia, and multiple myeloma.
- Chronic diarrhea from ulcerative colitis or Crohn's disease. Causes calcium loss through feces.
- Surgical removal of part of the stomach or small intestine. Affects absorption.
- Hypercalciuria. A condition where one loses too much calcium in the urine.
- Early menopause (before age forty-five). The earlier you stop producing estrogen, the more likely you are to lose calcium.
- Lighter complexion. Women with darker pigments have roughly 10 percent more bone mass than fairer women because they produce more calcitonin, the hormone that strengthens bones.
- Low weight. Women with less body fat store less estrogen, which makes the bones less dense to begin with, and more vulnerable to calcium loss.
- Women with eating disorders (yo-yo dieting, starvation diets, binge/purge eaters). When there isn't enough calcium in the blood-stream through our diet, the body will go to the bones to get what it needs. These women also have lower weight.
- A family history of osteoporosis. Studies show that women born to mothers with spinal fractures have lower bone mineral density in the spine, neck, and midshaft.
- A high-protein diet. This contributes to a loss of calcium in urine.
- Women who have never been pregnant. They haven't experienced the same bursts of estrogen in their bodies as women who have been pregnant.
- Antacids with aluminum interfere with calcium absorption.
- Lactose intolerance. Since so much calcium is in dairy foods, this allergy is a significant risk factor.
- History of teenage pregnancy. When a woman is pregnant in her teens, her bones are not yet fully developed and she can lose as much as 10 percent of her bone mass unless she has an adequate calcium intake of roughly 2,000 milligrams during the pregnancy and 2,200 while breast-feeding.
- Scoliosis (curvature of the spine).

Fractures

One in four women over fifty has osteoporosis, and as the sixties generation begins turning fifty in record numbers, we'll be facing a "fractured generation" of sorts—the most debilitating of which are hip fractures. Your risk of a hip fracture is equal to your combined risk of breast, uterine, and ovarian cancer.

In general, all bones are vulnerable to fractures, including the ribs, ankles, and pelvis. Osteoporosis-related fractures are categorized as wrist fractures, vertebral fractures, and the most serious of all, hip fractures (fractures of the proximal femur).

Wrist Fractures

Wrist fractures start to occur in women fifty and over, and the incidence rises until age sixty-five, and then flattens out. You break your wrist usually by trying to break a fall. (Live in an icy area?) These heal fairly easily and don't lead to serious disability in the same way as hip fractures. But your wrist will still be stiff or sore, and if you use a computer or work with your hands, it will obviously cause discomfort and lost time.

Vertebral Fractures

Vertebral fractures are common within the first twenty postmenopausal years. Meaning, if your last period was at fifty-three, you can be vulnerable to these fractures until well into your seventies. This is when you may fall on the ice and fracture your tailbone. Women with bone loss in the teeth, or who have already suffered wrist fractures, which involve trabecular bone, are most at risk for vertebral fractures.

Hip Fractures

North American women have the highest rates of hip fractures in the world. At fifty-five, you have a 17 percent chance of sustaining a hip fracture, which compares to only 6 percent in men of the same age. And women who have had a hip fracture are four times more likely to have a second hip fracture than women without a history of fractures. Why are hip fractures so serious? Currently, about 25 percent of people with hip fractures die from complications, such as pneumonia. The problem begins with being bedridden. You're lying in bed, in pain, on a lot of pain medications. You just get sicker and sicker until one thing leads to another—actually the fate of many long-term, chronic illness sufferers. Fifteen to 25 percent are still in long-term care institutions a year after the injury.

Most hip fractures occur in Caucasian or Asian women who are in their seventies and eighties. White women sixty-five or older have twice the incidence of fractures as Black women. But by "boning up" on calcium now (see the following section "Preventing Bone Loss"), you can help to prevent this very debilitating fate. Researchers aren't sure whether the high rate of hip fractures in seventy- to eighty-year-olds is due to poor nutrition in younger years. The difference between you and your mother is huge from a nutritional standpoint. Mom grew up during the Depression; you grew up during abundant times—in the 1960s. That said, your mother probably wasn't much of a dieter. Anyone coming of age in the sixties was exposed to the Twiggy-like thinness that has remained in vogue (and in *Vogue*) ever since. And, your mother may not have smoked and may not—ultimately—have been as sedentary as you may be. So the fracture statistics may be similar for other reasons.

Preventing Bone Loss

There are a few routes you can take to prevent bone loss. Diet and lifestyle changes are the most natural route, and a route many women feel most comfortable with. When HRT is not advised, there are a few osteoporosis prevention drugs, discussed later in the chapter.

According to the National Institutes of Health Consensus Panel on Osteoporosis, premenopausal women require roughly 1,000 milligrams of calcium a day; perimenopausal or postmenopausal women already on HRT or ERT 1,000 milligrams; and perimenopausal and postmenopausal women not taking estrogen roughly 1,500 milligrams per day. For women who have already been diagnosed with osteoporosis, the panel recommends 2,500 milligrams of calcium a day. Foods that are rich in calcium include all dairy products (an eight-ounce glass of milk contains 300 milligrams calcium), fish, shellfish, oysters, shrimp, sardines, salmon, soybeans, tofu, broccoli, and dark green vegetables (except spinach, which contains oxalic acid and prevents calcium

Eight Ways to Avoid a Fall

If you have suffered some bone loss, here are some tips to fall-proof your home:

- Don't leave loose wires, cords, or slippery throw rugs lying around.
- Place a non-slip mat in the shower or bathtub.
- Install nightlights to avoid tripping in the middle of the night.
- Clean up spills on the floors to avoid slipping.
- Install treads, rails, or rugs on wooden stairs.
- Wear comfortable, sturdy shoes with rubber soles.
- Avoid activity when taking medications that can make you drowsy.
- Cut down on alcohol: you can become klutzy and fall more easily when you're under the influence of alcohol.

Risky Movements

If you have more severe bone loss, everyday movements can cause fractures. Watch out for the following:

- Lifting heavy objects (such as groceries) or excessive bending
- Forceful sneezing or coughing
- Reaching above your shoulders (as in reaching for something in closets or cupboards)
- A sudden twist or turn, which you may do when driving

You also have to be careful getting in and out of beds or chairs if you have severe bone loss. Stiffness can be quite severe if you have osteoporosis; sitting or lying down in one position for too long can make the normal movements of getting up hazardous. Go slowly. To lessen stiffness, use a pillow for back support, and avoid cold drafts.

absorption). It's crucial to determine how much calcium you're getting in your diet before you start any calcium supplements; too much calcium can cause kidney stones in people who are risk for them. In addition, not all supplements have been tested for absorbency. Dr. Robert Heaney, in his book *Calcium and Common Sense*, suggests that you test absorbency yourself by dropping your supplement into a glass of warm water, stirring occasionally. If the supplement doesn't dissolve completely, chances are it won't be absorbed by your body efficiently. It's crucial to remember that a calcium supplement is in fact a supplement and should not replace a high-calcium diet. So the dosage of your supplement would only need to be roughly 400 to 600 milligrams per day, while your diet should account for the remainder of your 1,000 to 1,500 milligrams daily intake of calcium. Discuss with your diabetes health-care provider how to incorporate enough calcium into your meal planning.

The most accurate way to measure your risk of osteoporosis is through bone densitometry (or DEXA), which measures bone mass and provides you with a fracture risk estimate. This test involves low-dose x-rays and takes about thirty minutes.

Selective Estrogen Receptor Modulators (SERMs)

SERMs are a new class of drugs originally designed to help treat estrogen-dependent breast cancers, but were instead shown to help prevent bone loss—particularly around the spine and hip—and even increase bone mass. The first drug from this family, approved for use in 1998, is raloxifene (Evista). Women who took raloxifene for three years reduced their risk of fractures by about 50 percent. Even better, raloxifene may help protect you from heart disease—good news since women with type 2 diabetes are at greater risk for heart disease. Raloxifene helps lower bad cholesterol. Some studies also suggest that raloxifene may also reduce the incidence of breast cancer in some women. Raloxifene and HRT are equally effective in protecting your bones. And of course, you can continue to take calcium and/or vitamin D with raloxifene.

The bad news is that raloxifene has some estrogen-like side effects, including hot flashes and the risk of blood clots. However, it doesn't cause breast tenderness or bloating. And unlike HRT, raloxifene does not help with the signs of menopause, and may even aggravate them. You cannot take raloxifene unless you are postmenopausal—you have been free from periods for at least one year. The drug has not been tested in women still having periods. If you are taking any type of blood thinner, such as warfarin, you also may not be able to take this drug, and should discuss it with your doctor.

Ideal raloxifene users are postmenopausal women at risk for osteoporosis and heart disease who are not taking HRT, or postmenopausal women at risk for osteoporosis and high-risk for breast cancer. Women with type 2 diabetes fall into this category. Women who should *not* take raloxifene include:

- Premenopausal women
- Pregnant women or women who are breast-feeding
- Women with a history of blood clots or leg cramps (signs of possible blood clots)
- Women on any form of estrogen or progestin therapy that comes as a pill, patch, or injection
- Women taking cholestyramine or colestipol
- Women with liver problems

Bisphosphonates: Bone-Forming Drugs

Osteoblasts are the cells responsible for building bone, while osteoclasts are cells that remove old bone so the new bone can be replaced. Bisphosphonates stop or slow down the osteoclasts, without interfering with osteoblasts, the bone-forming cells. So you wind up with greater bone density. In the past, these drugs were approved only for treating severe bone diseases, such as Paget's disease. Two bisphosphonates—etidronate (Didrocal/Didronel) and alendronate (Fosamax)—have been approved for use in women who are not on HRT, but who are at risk of osteoporosis. However, bisphosphonates do not relieve any menopausal signs, such as hot flashes, and offer no protection against heart disease.

Bisphosphonates are equally effective in reducing the risk of fractures as HRT and raloxifene (the rate is reduced by about 50 percent in women taking the drug for about three years). If you're taking bisphosphonates, however, you cannot take calcium supplements at the same time, because calcium prevents the body from absorbing the bisphosphonate.

If you're taking alendronate, you'll need to wait thirty minutes after taking it before you have food or take a calcium supplement. If you're taking etidronate, you'll need to take the drug in a cycle, which your doctor will discuss with you, so you can take calcium supplements. In general, alendronate is a more potent, more effective bisphosphonate.

The side effects of etidronate and alendronate may include nausea, abdominal pain, or loose bowel movements. In rare instances, some people develop skin rashes or esophageal ulcers.

Parathyroid Hormone (PTH)

There is also a new drug that can build bone density back to its original peak and sometimes can even surpass it. This drug is recombinant parathyroid hormone, simply known as PTH or parathyroid hormone, and the FDA approved one form of PTH, PTH-(1-34), known as Forteo, in 2003. As of this writing, there may be newer versions or brands of PTH available, so consult your doctor.

Type 2 Diabetes in Elderly Women

Ideally, the blood sugar, cholesterol, and blood sugar targets should not change with age. However, in elderly (people over seventy-five) or frail people with type 2 diabetes, looser blood sugar control may be necessary. This is especially true when there are a number of other diseases or conditions at work. The objective of the frail or dependent elderly person is to adjust blood sugar goals for a level of functioning that makes sense, given all the other health problems that person is managing. Sometimes, if there is limited life expectancy anyway, strict blood sugar monitoring and meal planning may interfere with what quality of life is possible. For example, if an elderly person has hypertension and/or high cholesterol, it may make more sense to bring these conditions under control first (and worry about blood sugar later) if death from a heart attack is imminent.

If someone receiving elder care is in good physical health, consult with a diabetes specialist or gerontologist about appropriate management for that individual.

Medications

Elderly people with diabetes can be managed with exercise and diet, but the use of thiazolidinediones (see Chapter 7) can be risky. These drugs are associated with an increased incidence of fluid retention in older patients so they must be used with caution in people with cardiovascular disease.

Sulfonylureas (see Chapter 7) should also be used with caution because *the risk of hypoglycemia increases exponentially with age.* In general, initial doses of sulfonylureas in the elderly should be half those used for younger people, and doses should be increased slowly. Gliclazide and glimepiride are the preferred sulfonylureas because they are associated with fewer incidents of hypoglycemia than glyburide. A new, long-acting formulation of gliclazide is recommended in the elderly, especially if the person is easily confused about taking medications. Nonsulfonylurea insulin secretagogues (repaglinide and nateglinide) may be associated with a lower frequency of hypoglycemia in the elderly, and is preferred for those with irregular eating habits.

Acarbose (see Chapter 7) can be used; however many elderly people can't tolerate the gastrointestinal side effects.

In lean elderly people with type 2 diabetes, impaired insulin secretion is usually the main problem, so an agent that stimulates insulin secretion (an insulin secretagogue; see Chapter 7) might be the first medication of choice. In obese elderly people with type 2 diabetes, the insulin resistance is more of a problem, so medications that improve insulin resistance would be required.

Premixed insulins and prefilled insulin pens are best. Avoid mixing insulins, to prevent errors and improve blood sugar control. It's best to use a rapid-acting insulin analogue that can be administered after meals—especially in elderly people with poor or irregular eating habits.

5

Lowering Fat and
Healthy Eating

THE KEY TO managing type 2 diabetes for most women is losing roughly twenty pounds, which is about 5 percent of body fat. Meal planning (see Chapter 6) is necessary to get you thinking about low-fat and healthy eating. Every day we are bombarded with information on low-fat products and diets, and it can get pretty confusing. This chapter offers the basics about lowering dietary fat and creating a healthy, balanced diet. Reducing your intake of certain fats and increasing your intake of others can dramatically reduce the risk of cardiovascular disease, which is one of the chief complications of type 2 diabetes. Studies show that reducing dietary fat may also prevent cancers, such as colorectal and estrogen-dependent cancers (like breast cancer).

Dietary guidelines from nutrition experts, government nutrition advisories and panels, and registered dieticians have not changed in fifty years. A good diet is a *balanced diet* representing all food groups, based largely on plant-based foods—carbohydrates—such as fruits, vegetables, legumes, and grains, with a balance of calories from animal-based foods—protein and fat—such as meats (red meat, poultry), fish, and dairy products. What has changed in fifty years is the terminology used to define a good diet, and the bombardment of information about which foods affect which physiological processes in the body, such as cholesterol levels or blood fats (triglycerides), blood sugar levels (blood glucose or glycemic load), and insulin. There are also different kinds of fats and carbohydrates, which has made eating seem so technical and scientific, ordinary people feel more like chemists when trying to plan for healthy meals and diets.

Confusing information about low-fat versus low-carb diets (see Chapter 6) has further distorted our perceptions about diet. But no matter how many properties in foods are dissected or what kind of diet program you buy into, healthy eating comes down to a balanced diet— something that actually means "balanced way of life" because the root word of *diet—diatta*—literally means "way of life."

Yet despite all the information you may read here, you may be unable to change your eating habits. That could be because you may not fully understand *why* you're eating. If this is the case, review Chapter 2 for some insights into eating behaviors and eating patterns.

Understanding Fat

Fat is technically known as *fatty acids*, which are crucial nutrients for our cells. We cannot live without fatty acids. Fat, therefore, is a good thing—in moderation. Like all good things, most of us want more than what we should have. Excess dietary fat is by far the most damaging element in the Western diet. A gram of fat contains twice the calories of the same amount of protein or carbohydrate. Decreasing the fat in your diet and replacing it with grain products, vegetables, and fruits is the best way to lower your risk of cardiovascular problems and many other diseases.

Fat in the diet comes from meats, dairy products, vegetable oils, and other sources such as coconuts (60 percent fat), peanuts (78 percent fat), and avocados (82 percent fat). There are three different kinds of fatty acids in these sources of fats: saturated, unsaturated, and transfatty acids (also called *transfat*), which are like a saturated fat in disguise. Some fats are harmful while others are beneficial to your health. The terms *good fats* and *bad fats* began to crystallize when research into diets high in monounsaturated fats were closely observed and found, in spite of containing these fats, to raise good cholesterol (HDL), which protects against heart disease.

Understanding fat is a complicated business. This section explains everything you need to know about fat, and a few things you probably don't *want* to know but should.

Saturated Fat

Saturated fat is solid at room temperature and stimulates cholesterol production in your body. Foods high in saturated fat include processed meats, fatty meats, lard, butter, margarine, solid vegetable shortening, chocolate, and tropical oils (coconut oil is more than 90 percent saturated). Saturated fat should be consumed only in very low amounts.

Unsaturated Fat

Unsaturated fat is partially solid or liquid at room temperature. These fats include monounsaturated fats, polyunsaturated fats, and omega-3 oils (fish oil), which protect you against heart disease. Sources of unsaturated fats include vegetable oils (canola, safflower, sunflower, corn), seeds, and nuts. To make it easy to remember, unsaturated fats, with the exception of tropical oils, such as coconut, come from plants. The more liquid the fat, the more polyunsaturated it is, which *lowers* your cholesterol levels. However, if you have familial hyperlipidemia or hypercholesterolemia (high cholesterol), which often occurs alongside diabetes, unsaturated fat may not make a difference in your cholesterol levels.

In Mediterranean diets, for example, which are considered among the healthiest diets, olive oil, herbs, and spices are routinely used in place of butter as spreads or dips for breads. Olive oil has been found to contain a host of protective factors and catalyst ingredients that allow phytochemicals from plant-based foods to work their magic in the body. The virtues of a Mediterranean diet, with its "good fats," became the basis for a revolution in dietary fat guidelines, which now recognize that healthy diets should have some monounsaturated fats, the best of which is olive oil (74 percent monounsaturated). Other monounsaturated oils are canola, peanut, sesame, soybean, corn, cottonseed, and safflower with canola (59 percent monounsaturated) being second to olive oil.

What Is a Triglyceride?

Each fat molecule is a chain made up of glycerol, carbon atoms, and hydrogen atoms. The higher the number of hydrogen atoms that are on that chain, the higher the saturation level of the fat. If you looked at each fat molecule carefully, you'd find three different kinds of fatty acids on it: *saturated* (solid), *monounsaturated* (less solid, with the exception of olive and peanut oils), and *polyunsaturated* (liquid) fatty acids, *or* three fatty acids plus glycerol, chemically known as *triglycerides*.

The liver breaks down fat molecules by secreting bile, which is stored in the gallbladder (the gallbladder's sole function). The liver also makes cholesterol. Too much saturated fat may cause your liver to overproduce cholesterol, which will increase the level of triglycerides in your bloodstream. This perpetuates the problem. Too much cholesterol can clog your blood vessels or get into the bile and crystallize, causing gallstones and gallbladder disease.

Fish Fat (Omega-3 Oils)

The fats naturally present in fish that swim in cold waters, known as *omega-3 fatty acids* or fish oils, are all polyunsaturated. Omega-3 fatty acids are crucial for brain tissue, and they lower your cholesterol levels and protect against heart disease. Coldwater fish have a layer of fat to keep them warm. Mackerel, albacore tuna, salmon, sardines, and lake trout are all rich in omega-3 fatty acids. Whale and seal meat, which were once the staples of the Inuit diet, are incredible sources of omega-3 fatty acids. Federal moratoriums on whale and seal hunting have taken away this once-vital source of Inuit food, which offered real protection against heart disease.

Artificial Fats

An assortment of artificial fats have been introduced into our diet, courtesy of food producers who are trying to give us the taste of fat without all the calories or harmful effects of saturated fats. Unfortunately, artificial fats offer their own bag of horrors.

Trans-Fatty Acids from Hydrogenated Oils

These are harmful fats that not only raise the level of bad cholesterol (LDL) in your bloodstream, but lower the amount of good cholesterol (HDL). Trans-fatty acids are what you get when you make a liquid oil, such as corn oil, into a more solid or spreadable substance, such as margarine. Trans-fatty acids, you might say, are the "road to hell, paved with good intentions." Someone, way back when, thought that if you could take the "good fat"—unsaturated fat—and solidify it so it could double as butter or lard, you could eat the same things without missing the spreadable fat. That sounds like a great idea. Unfortunately, to make an unsaturated liquid fat more solid, you have to add hydrogen to its molecules. This is known as *hydrogenation*. That ever-popular chocolate bar ingredient, hydrogenated palm oil, is a classic example of a fat containing trans-fatty acids. Hydrogenation also prolongs the shelf life of a fat, such as polyunsaturated fats, which can oxidize when exposed to air, causing rancid odors or flavors. Deep-frying oils used in the restaurant trade are generally hydrogenated.

Trans-fatty acid is sold as a polyunsaturated or monounsaturated fat with a line of copy such as "Made from polyunsaturated vegetable oil." In your body, however, it is treated as a saturated fat. This is why trans-fatty acids are a saturated fat in disguise. The advertiser may, in fact, say that the product contains "no saturated fat" or is "healthier" than the comparable animal or tropical oil product with saturated fat. So be careful: *read the labels*. The word you're looking for is *hydrogenated*. If the product lists a variety of unsaturated fats (monounsaturated X oil, polyunsaturated Y oil, and so on), keep reading. If the word *hydrogenated* appears, count that product as a saturated fat; your body will!

Margarine Versus Butter

There's an old tongue twister: "Betty Botter bought some butter that made the batter bitter; so Betty Botter bought more butter that made the batter better." Are we making our batters bitter or better with margarine? It depends.

Since the news of trans-fatty acids broke in the late 1980s, margarine manufacturers began to offer some margarines that contain no hydrogenated oils, while others have much smaller amounts of them. Margarines with less than 60 to 80 percent oil (nine to eleven grams of fat) will contain one to three grams of trans-fatty acids per serving, compared to butter, which is 53 percent saturated fat. You might say it's a choice between a bad fat and a *worse* fat.

It's also possible for a liquid vegetable oil to retain a high concentration of unsaturated fat when it's been partially hydrogenated. In this case, your body will metabolize this as some saturated fat and some unsaturated fat.

Fake Fat

We have artificial sweeteners; why not artificial fat? This question has led to the creation of an emerging yet highly suspicious ingredient: *fat substitutes*, designed to replace real fat and hence reduce the calories from real fat without compromising the taste. This is done by creating a fake fat that the body cannot absorb.

Thus, many foods have been created that contain "fat replacers," which simulate many of the properties of fat in food that make it "creamy" or "smooth." Carbohydrate-based gums and starches such as guar gum and modified food starch are common, including sugar-like compounds, fibers, and even fruit purees and applesauce. Carbohydrates can be used as thickeners, bulking agents, moisturizers, and stabilizers. For example, a new carbohydrates fat replacer, oatrim (marketed by Golden Jersey Products under the brand name Replace), is an oat-flour ingredient added to some brands of skim milk in the United States. Oatrim contains a type of fiber called *beta-glucan* that may help lower blood cholesterol in addition to providing fatlike creaminess. Unless they are new to the food supply, most carbohydrate-based fat replacers do not require government approval because they are already in use and are considered safe. In the United States, this is called "generally recognized as safe" (GRAS). A few, including carageenan (a seaweed derivative) and polydextrose, were submitted to the FDA for food additive approval because they were new to the food supply.

Protein-based fat replacers are made from milk, whey, egg, soy, or other types of protein that have been manipulated to create texture, appearance, and mouth feel (their texture and consistency in your mouth).

Types of Fat Replacers Available

Carbohydrate-Based Fat Replacers

Fat Replacer	Used in These Products
Maltodextrins	Baked goods
Starches	Baked goods, margarines, salad dressing, frozen desserts
Cellulose	Frozen desserts, sauces, salad dressings
Guar, xanthan, or other gums	Salad dressings
Polydextrose	Baked goods, cake mixes, puddings, frostings
Oatrim	Milk

Protein-Based Fat Replacers

Fat Replacer	Used in These Products
Protein concentrate (whey, egg white, soy)	Frozen desserts, reduced-fat dairy products, and salad dressings

Fat-Based Fat Replacers

Fat Replacer	Used in These Products
Caprenin	Chocolate
Salatrim	Chocolate
Olestra (not in Canada)	Snack chips, crackers

Then there are fat-based fat replacers. Salatrim and caprenin are such fat replacers and contain fatty acids that are partially but not completely digested, supplying 5 versus 9 calories per gram. These fat replacers cannot be used to fry or sauté foods, but are used in products such as reduced-fat chocolate chips.

Recommendations for Fat

Type of Fat	How Much to Eat
Total fat	No more than 30 percent of daily energy requirements
Saturated and polyunsaturated fat	No more than 10 percent of daily energy requirements
Monounsaturated fat	Substitute for other fat sources as much as possible
Fish fat	A serving at least once a week
Trans-fatty acids	Limit as much as possible

The calorie-free fat substitute olestra is another fat-based fat replacer. It was developed by Procter and Gamble, and approved for use in the United States by the FDA. Olestra required FDA approval because it is a new food ingredient, not a combination of ingredients that already were in the food supply. Olestra is the only fat replacer that entirely replicates fat, including for use in frying, which is why it can be used in salty snacks. A one-ounce portion of potato chips has no fat when made with olestra and ten grams of fat when made with oil. But olestra is a potentially dangerous ingredient that most experts feel can do more harm than good. Canada has not yet approved it.

Olestra is made from a combination of vegetable oils and sugar. It is known as a sucrose polyester. Therefore, it tastes just like the real thing, but the biochemical structure is a molecule too big for your liver to break down. So olestra just gets passed into the large intestine and is excreted. Olestra is more than an "empty" molecule, however. It causes diarrhea and cramps and may deplete your body of vital nutrients, including vitamins A, D, E, and K, which is necessary for blood to clot. Some nutrition experts fear a wider danger with olestra: instead of encouraging people to choose nutritious foods, such as fruits, grains, and vegetables, over high-fat foods, products like these encourage a high *fake*-fat diet that's still too low in fiber and other essential nutrients. And the no-fat icing on the cake is that these people could potentially wind up with a vitamin deficiency, to boot.

Health Canada is taking the same stance as many nutrition experts, who find that the long-term consequences of olestra in the food supply haven't been addressed. Many experts feel it is tantamount to springing an untested chemical on the public. Even people who add vitamins when using olestra will probably have the vitamins leached out of their intestine anyway.

The position of organizations such as the American Dietetic Association (ADA) is that fat-reduced or fat-replaced foods should only be part of a diet that includes plenty of fruits, vegetables, and grains. Fat replacers enable you to eat lower-fat versions of familiar foods without making major changes in the way that you eat. But they should not be eaten in excess.

Critics of olestra argue that people will make the mistake of thinking "no fat" is healthy and choose olestra-containing Twinkies over fruits and think they're eating well. Olestra is currently being used in snack foods only, but potential uses for olestra could include restaurant foods touted as fat-free: french fries, fried chicken, fish and chips, or onion rings. At home, olestra could be used as cooking oil for sautés, as a butter substitute for baking, or in fat-free cheese. Potentially, we could be facing a future of eating "polyester foods." In fact, Procter and Gamble filed for olestra to be approved as a fat substitute for up to 35 percent of the natural fats used in home cooking and up to 75 percent of the fats used in commercial foods. It did not ask for approval to use olestra in table spreads or ice creams, however.

The FDA did not approve olestra for use in the products Procter and Gamble requested. A new request, for olestra to be used only in salty snack foods, was submitted. In 1996, the FDA approved olestra for use in savory snacks; Procter and Gamble proceeded to market the trade name for olestra, *Olean*. By 1998, Frito-Lay and Procter and Gamble announced the release of Olean products in dozens of snack foods, and the FDA approves this under the proviso that a warning label about olestra's health consequences be carried with each Olean product. (Current warnings about the product, when eaten in large

amounts, causing fecal leakage are affixed to all Olean products.)
When the 1999 sales of Olean were disappointing, Procter and Gamble sought to have the warning removed; the FDA agreed to revise, but not remove the label.

The Center for Science in the Public Interest has been opposed to the approval of olestra because of safety concerns. Studies have not found that olestra substantially reduces fat intake, however, for the same reasons many low- or no-fat products have failed: people just eat more, a problem discussed at length in Chapter 2. Although olestra-made snacks taste identical to their originals, they still have plenty of calories from carbohydrates. People's behavior with olestra mirrors that of other low-fat snacks. They see olestra as a license to eat more, rather than less, and ultimately, unless they practice the types of healthy eating strategies discussed in this book, do not lose weight on olestra.

Increasing Fiber

For every action, there is an equal and opposite reaction. When you decrease your fat intake, you should increase your bulk intake, or fiber. Complex carbohydrates are foods that are high in fiber. Fiber is the part of a plant your body can't digest; it comes in the form of both water-soluble fiber (which dissolves in water) and water-insoluble fiber (which does not dissolve in water but instead absorbs water).

Soluble Versus Insoluble Fiber

Soluble and insoluble fiber do differ, but they are equally good things. Soluble fiber somehow lowers bad cholesterol, or LDL, in your body. Experts aren't entirely sure how soluble fiber works its magic, but one popular theory is that it gets mixed into the bile the liver secretes and forms a gel that traps the building blocks of cholesterol, thus lowering your LDL levels. It's akin to a spider web trapping smaller insects. Sources of soluble fiber include oats or oat bran, legumes (dried beans and peas), some seeds, carrots, oranges, bananas, and other fruits. Soybeans are also high sources of soluble fiber. Studies show that people with very high cholesterol have the most to gain by eating soybeans.

Soybean is also a *phytoestrogen* (plant estrogen) that is believed to lower the risks of estrogen-related cancers (for example, breast cancer), as well as lower the incidence of estrogen-loss symptoms associated with menopause.

Insoluble fiber doesn't affect your cholesterol levels at all, but it regulates your bowel movements. How does it do this? As the insoluble fiber moves through your digestive tract, it absorbs water like a sponge and helps to form your waste into a solid form faster, making the stools larger, softer, and easier to pass. Without insoluble fiber, solid waste just gets pushed down to the colon or lower intestine, where it is stored and dried out until you're ready to have a bowel movement. High-starch foods are associated with drier stools. This is exacerbated when you "ignore the urge," as the colon will dehydrate the waste even more until it becomes harder and difficult to pass, a condition known as *constipation*. Insoluble fiber will help to regulate your bowel movements by speeding things along. It is also linked to lower rates of colorectal cancer. Good sources of insoluble fiber are wheat bran and whole grains, skins from various fruits and vegetables, seeds, leafy greens, and cruciferous vegetables (cauliflower, broccoli, and brussels sprouts).

Fiber and Diabetes

Soluble fiber helps delay glucose from being absorbed into your bloodstream, which not only improves blood sugar control but helps to control postmeal peaks in blood sugar. This stimulates the pancreas to produce more insulin.

Fiber in the form of all colors of vegetables will also ensure that you're getting the right mix of nutrients. Experts suggest that you have several different colors of vegetables daily—for example, carrots, beets, and spinach. An easy way to remember what nutrients are in which vegetable is to remember that all green vegetables are for cellular repair; the darker the green, the more nutrients the vegetable contains. All red, orange, and purplish vegetables contain antioxidants (vitamins A, C, and E), which boost the immune system and fight off toxins. Studies suggest that vitamin C, for example, is crucial for people with type 2 diabetes because it helps to prevent complications, as well as rid the body of sorbitol, which can increase blood sugar. Another study suggests that vitamin E helps to prevent heart disease in people with type 2 diabetes by lowering levels of bad cholesterol, but this isn't yet conclusive. Other minerals, such as zinc and copper, are essential for wound healing. The recommendation is to eat all colors of vegetables in ample amounts to get your vitamins, minerals, and dietary fiber. It makes sense when you understand diabetes as a disease of starvation. In starvation, there are naturally lower levels of nutrients in your body that can be replenished only through excellent sources of food.

Breaking Bread

For thousands of years, cooked whole grains were the dietary staple for all cultures—rice and millet in the Orient; wheat, oats, and rye in Europe; buckwheat in Russia; sorghum in Africa; barley in the Middle East; and corn in pre-European North America.

Whole-grain breads are good sources of insoluble fiber (flax bread is particularly good because flaxseeds are a source of soluble fiber, too). The problem is understanding what is truly "whole grain." For example, there is an assumption that because bread is dark or brown, it's more nutritious; this isn't so. In fact, many brown breads are simply enriched white breads dyed with molasses. (*Enriched* means that nutrients lost during processing have been replaced.) High-fiber pita breads and bagels are available, but you have to search for them. A good rule is to simply look for the phrase *whole wheat*, which means that the wheat is, indeed, whole.

What's in a Grain?

Most of us will turn to grains and cereals to boost our fiber intake, which experts recommend should be twenty-five to thirty-five grams per day. Use Table 5.1 to help you gauge whether you're getting enough insoluble fiber. If you're a little under par, an easy way to boost your fiber intake is to simply add pure wheat bran to your foods. Wheat bran is available in health food stores or supermarkets. Three tablespoons of wheat bran are equal to 4.4 grams of fiber. Sprinkle one or two tablespoons onto cereals, rice, pasta, or meat dishes. You can also sprinkle it into orange juice or low-fat yogurt. It has virtually no calo-

Table 5.1 What's in a Grain?

Cereals	Grams of Insoluble Fiber
Fiber First (½ cup)	15.0
Fiber One (½ cup)	12.8
All-Bran (½ cup)	10.0
Oatmeal (1 cup)	5.0
Raisin Bran (¾ cup)	4.6
Bran Flakes (1 cup)	4.4
Shreddies (⅔ cup)	2.7
Cheerios (1 cup)	2.2
Cornflakes (1½ cups)	0.8
Special K (1½ cups)	0.4
Rice Krispies (1½ cups)	0.3

Breads	Grams of Insoluble Fiber (in 1 slice)
Rye	2.0
Pumpernickel	2.0
Twelve-grain	1 7
100% whole wheat	1.3
Raisin	1.0
Cracked-wheat	1.0
White	0.0

Keep in mind that some of the newer high-fiber breads on the market today have up to 7 grams of fiber per slice. This chart is based on what is normally found in typical grocery stores.

ries, but it's important to drink a glass of water with your wheat bran, as well as a glass of water after you've finished your wheat bran–enriched meal.

Fruits and Veggies

Another easy way of boosting fiber content is to know how much fiber your fruits and vegetables pack per serving. All fruits, beans (legumes), and vegetables listed in Table 5.2 show measurements for insoluble fiber, which is not only good for colon health, but for your heart. Some of these numbers may surprise you!

Food Supplements

Countries where high-fiber and plant-rich diets are the norm have far lower rates of cancer, heart disease, and diabetes. This fact has led to research into specific foods or food ingredients that you can now buy in pill or capsule form: garlic capsules, broccoli pills, and hundreds of other food supplements have sprung onto the health food market. Should you be taking supplements or simply eating a healthy diet? It depends on you. Ideally, by eating a variety of good foods that are high

How to Get More Fruits and Vegetables

Fruits and vegetables must be planned for in a diabetes meal plan.

- Go for one or two fruits at breakfast, one fruit and two vegetables at lunch and dinner, and a fruit or vegetable snack
- Consume many differently colored fruits and vegetables; at least three daily
- Put fruit and sliced veggies in an easy-to-use, easy-to-reach place (sliced vegetables in the fridge; fruit on the table)
- Keep frozen and canned fruit and vegetables on hand to add to soups, salads, or rice dishes

Table 5.2 What's in a Fruit or Vegetable?

Fruit	Grams of Insoluble Fiber
Raspberries (¾ cup)	6.4
Strawberries (1 cup)	4.0
Pear (1)	4.0
Blackberries (1 cup)	3.9
Orange (1)	3.0
Apple (1)	2.0
Grapefruit (½ cup)	1.1
Kiwi (1)	1.0

Beans	Grams of Insoluble Fiber (in ½ cup serving unless otherwise specified)
Green beans (1 cup)	4.0
White beans	3.6
Kidney beans	3.3
Pinto beans	3.3
Lima beans	3.2

Vegetables	Grams of Insoluble Fiber (in ½ cup serving unless otherwise specified)
Baked potato with skin (1 large)	4.0
Acorn squash	3.8
Peas	3.0
Brussels sprouts	2.3
Asparagus (¾ cup)	2.3
Corn kernels	2.1
Zucchini	1.4
Broccoli	1.1

in fiber and lower in fat, using the 40/30/30 system (see Chapter 6), supplementing is probably unnecessary. That said, fiber supplements are considered beneficial for most people with type 2 diabetes. If taken as a supplement, fiber must be ingested with an eight-ounce glass of water or other liquid.

Phytochemicals

Phytochemicals, or plant chemicals (phyto is Greek for "plant"), are the natural ingredients found in plant foods such as tomatoes, oats, soya, oranges, and broccoli. As researchers strive for some magic wellness ingredient, they're finding all kinds of disease-fighting chemicals inside common fruits and vegetables, which sometimes wind up as misleading claims on food labels. While phytochemicals, such as isoflavones (found in soybeans), allylic sulphides (found in garlic, onions, and chives), isothiocyanates (found in cruciferous vegetables like brussels sprouts, cabbage, and cauliflower), saponins (spinach, potatoes, tomatoes, and oats), and lignin and alphalinolenic acid (flaxseeds), sound exotic, you can easily get them by simply eating a variety of fruits, grains, and vegetables.

Another hot phytochemical right now is beta-glucans (found in legumes, oats, and other grains). Beta-glucans are believed to help prevent diabetes by delaying gastric emptying and by slowing down glucose absorption in the small intestine, so if you have diabetes, it can help to regulate your blood sugar.

Biologically engineered foods, which alter the natural genetic codes in vegetables, may interfere with these natural phytochemicals.

Functional Foods

Functional foods are foods that have significant levels of biologically active disease-preventing or health-promoting properties. Tomatoes, oatmeal, soy, and garlic are all examples of functional foods because they naturally contain beneficial phytochemicals. Functional foods are different from nutraceuticals (from the words nutrition and pharmaceutical), which are manufactured health foods, such as dietary fiber drinks.

Putting It All Together

When you look at all the government food guidelines, and the sound diet programs, they all say the same thing: eat largely plant-based foods because they're low in calories but high in vitamins, minerals, fiber, and phytochemicals. Cut down on saturated fat (or foods of animal origin); use unsaturated or fish fats instead, and cut down on refined sugars. The most important component to any diet, however, is activity: using more energy (calories) than you ingest will maintain your body weight or lead to weight loss. This is what dieticians of the 1950s and 1960s called a sensible or balanced diet. By 1990, it was called a low-fat diet. *But it's the same diet.*

Original food guidelines and serving suggestions were designed in the early twentieth century to prevent malnutrition from vitamin deficiencies. By 1950, the problem of overnutrition began to be evident, which is what led to a rise in obesity-related diseases such as type 2 diabetes. In a 1959 book on heart disease, *Eat Well and Stay Well*, which was written by a physician, Ancel Keys, and his wife, Margaret Keys, the guidelines for a healthy heart at that time were almost identical to today's dietary guidelines: maintaining normal body weight; restricting saturated fats and red meat; using polyunsaturated fats instead to a maximum of 30 percent of daily calories; eating plenty of fresh fruits and vegetables and nonfat milk products; and avoiding overly salted foods and refined sugar. The Keys's guidelines even stressed exercise, stopping smoking, and stress reduction!

Most people's diets do not come close to being balanced. Many North Americans eat nothing *but* the types of foods that have always been discouraged: saturated fats (thanks to fast food), sugar (thanks to the soft drink industry), refined carbohydrates (thanks to snack foods), and not enough fiber.

Again, losing weight means eating fewer calories and/or expending more calories than you eat. Fat has more calories per gram than carbohydrates (nine calories per gram versus four calories per gram). Saturated fats are the building blocks of clogged arteries and cardiovascular problems; unsaturated fats are heart-protective. We can therefore choose the right type of fat over the wrong type of fat. But overall weight loss, by *simply eating less*, will have more of an impact on reducing obesity and obesity-related health problems than "splitting fats" at the end of the day. Programs such as WeightWatchers, for example, which are based on calorie-counting, are considered terrific starting points for people with type 2 diabetes who need to lose weight. In Chapter 6, I explain some of the pitfalls of the very low fat diets versus the very low carb diets. In general, you can judge a good diet based on these four simple questions:

- Are all food groups included: plant-based; grains and complex carbs; proteins (lean meats); fats? If not, stay away.
- Are you encouraged to have the least number of calories from fats, and discouraged from junk foods and refined sugars? If so, this is sensible.
- Is promised weight loss averaging about one to two pounds per week, or is promised weight loss ten or more pounds per week? Anything more than one to two pounds a week is suspicious and likely faddish. Gradual weight loss is sustainable for life; speedy weight loss leads to yo-yo effects, where you gain as much back as you lost.
- Is it a diet that offers enough variety that you would feel good eating this way for life, and feeding your whole family with the foods encouraged? People on the Atkins diet, for example (see Chapter 6), have stated that they "can't take it" beyond a certain point, and cannot feed their children with the diet.

Nutrition experts suggest these components for a balanced meal:

- At least two kinds of vegetables (make them different colors, such as carrots and green beans, or beets and turnips)
- A starchy food, such as potato, rice, pasta, or bread
- A protein food such as fish, lean meat (any meat can be cut lean), fowl, beans, or lentils
- Milk and a fruit can be eaten after in the form of a dessert. Or you can make a dessert with milk or a milk product and fruit, eliminating extra sugars (plain yogurt and strawberries, for example).

- You can have alcohol, but plan for it with your dietitian: it's fattening! But it also helps to lower cholesterol. Do not have more than two glasses of wine per day.

In general, diabetes experts offer these tips for healthy eating:

- Eat three meals per day at regular times (this helps to keep your blood sugar stable throughout the day).
- Limit sugars and sweets such as sugar, regular pop, desserts, candies, jam, and honey (these are fattening without much nutritive value).
- Eat more high-fiber foods—whole grains, cereals, lentils, dried beans and peas, brown rice, fruits, and veggies. (These have more staying power and pack more nutrients.)
- Drink water instead of juice or sweet drinks. If you must have a soda, drink one with a sweetener. (Sugary liquids raise blood sugar.)
- Do something physical after eating, such as walking around the block. (This helps to improve blood sugar control.)

Milk Tips

In North America, we consume a lot of milk, and that has a big impact on our fat intake. Know what you're getting:

- Whole milk: 48 percent of calories from fat
- 2 percent milk: 37 percent of calories from fat
- 1 percent milk: 26 percent of calories from fat
- Skim milk: Fat-free
- Cheese: 50 percent of calories from fat, unless it's skim milk cheese
- Butter: 95 percent of calories from fat
- Yogurt: 15 percent of calories from fat

Adding Some Activity

In the first edition of this book, I included a chapter on active living and exercise. These days, women don't need me to tell them about the range of activities and forms of exercise available. You know what to do! It's important to note, though, that if you've been sedentary and are at risk for cardiovascular disease, diabetes experts suggest you have an exercise electrocardiogram (ECG) stress test if you want to begin a program more vigorous than brisk walking. Five to ten minutes of brisk walking per day is the suggested starting point for all sedentary people at risk for heart disease. Studies show that regular aerobic activity reduced heart attacks 45 to 70 percent over a twelve- to fourteen-year period in people with type 2 diabetes. For example, 150 minutes of moderate-intensity aerobic exercise each week spread over at least three nonconsecutive days of the week is considered enough to dramatically improve your cardiovascular health.

6

How Sweet: Counting Carbs and Planning Meals

THE DIABETES MEAL plan is not just for people with diabetes; it's healthy eating that everyone can follow. So when you begin to plan your meals, your entire family will benefit. Through what you eat, you'll be able to gain control of your condition while the rest of your family may be able to prevent or delay diabetes.

Only carbohydrates influence blood sugar levels, while fat- and cholesterol-containing foods increase blood fat levels—cholesterol and triglycerides. What lowers the sugar in your bloodstream is exercise and medications you may be taking, such as oral hypoglycemic pills or insulin. Ideally, by balancing your food with activity, you most likely will be able to control your diabetes. How do you know if you're balancing well? And how do you know what to eat so you can create this balance? That's what this chapter is all about.

A Few Good Foods

Before the discovery of insulin in 1921, people with diabetes went on the Allen Diet, a very low-calorie diet that required low quantities of carbohydrates, followed by exercise.

Dr. Frederick Madison Allen, a leading diabetologist who spent four years working with diabetic patients at the Rockefeller Institute in New York City, in 1919 published a six hundred–plus–page paper called "Total Dietary Regulation in the Treatment of Diabetes." Allen's work showed that diabetes was largely a problem of carbohydrate metabolism. He introduced a radical approach to diabetes, the traces of which are apparent in current meal planning. It was known as the starvation treatment, which consisted of fasting followed by a gradual building up of the diet. Allen's treatment also included exercise, which is now a vital aspect of diabetes treatment. The idea of emaciated patients fasting and exercising was controversial, but at the time it was the best treatment available without insulin. Although in some cases, Allen's patients did die of starvation, Allen ultimately prolonged the lives of many through his system of dietary regulation.

Allen's diet was found to be more tolerable than any of the fad diabetes diets that were popular in Allen's day. Doctors were doing everything from feeding patients with diabetes as much sugar as possible to compensate for the sugar lost in the blood to putting them on low-carbohydrate diets that were so unappetizing that most patients wouldn't stick to them. Oatmeal diets, milk diets, rice diets, and potato diets were also popular. The most logical diet, however, was the low-carbohydrate diet, which included recipes such as "Thrice-Boiled Vegetables." Although this diet was effective in eliminating sugar from the urine (it produced the same effects as food rationing, discussed in Chapter 2), it didn't work with patients who had insulin-dependent or type 1 diabetes.

Allen and his predecessors understood that *carbohydrates are key* to diabetes meal planning. Allen recognized the ability of carbohydrates to convert into glucose. The timing of this glucose conversion affects how quickly and how high the blood glucose level rises after eating. But what's changed drastically since the Allen Diet is that variety, quantity, and timing of meals are crucial, too.

What to Eat

To live, you need three basic types of foods: carbohydrates, protein, and fat. Carbohydrates are the main source of fuel for muscles. Protein is the "cell food" that helps cells grow and repair themselves. Fat is a crucial nutrient that can be burned as an alternative fuel in times of hunger or famine. Simple sugars that do not contain any fat will convert quickly into energy or be stored as fat.

Your body will change carbohydrates into glucose for energy. If you eat more carbohydrates than you can burn, your body will turn the extra into fat. The protein your body makes comes from the protein you eat. As for fats, they are not broken down into glucose and are usually stored as fat. The problem with fatty foods is that they have double the calories per gram compared with carbohydrates and protein, so you wind up gaining weight. Too much saturated fat, as discussed in Chapter 5, can increase your risk of developing cardiovascular problems. We also know that the rate at which glucose is absorbed by your body from starch and sugars is affected by other parts of your meal, such as the protein, fiber, and fat. If you're eating only carbohydrates and no protein or fat, for example, your blood sugar will go up faster.

Low-Fat Versus Low-Carb

A diet is considered low-fat when it restricts calories from fat to below 30 percent daily. There are dozens of established low-fat diets on the market, but they vary from extremely low-fat diets, which restrict calories from fat to about 10 percent, to more moderate low-fat diets, which restrict calories from fat to 15 to 30 percent. *Very low fat diets* (restricting calories from fat to 7 to 10 percent) are modeled after the originators of the very low fat diet as we know it today—Nathan Pritikin, who popularized low-fat eating in the 1950s, and Dean Ornish, who reframed the original Pritikin diet in the late 1970s. Ornish- and Pritikin-styled diets remain the most well-known and most effective diets for people who are extremely obese and at high risk of dying from an obesity-related health problem. *But they are generally too restrictive for people with type 2 diabetes.* The Center for Science in the Public Interest rated a number of diets for the masses in 2000. Very low fat diets such as Pritikin's and Ornish's were found to be acceptable, but also restricted some healthy foods, such as seafood, low-fat poultry, and calcium. For people with high triglycerides, it was suggested to cut out some carbohydrates and replace them with unsaturated fats.

The main problem with very low fat diets (7 to 10 percent of calories from fat) is that they are too restrictive for the general public because they are extremely difficult to stick to unless you are very knowledgeable about low-fat cuisine, and you are a creative chef. Also, new information about the benefits of monounsaturated fats and omega-3 fatty acids (the "good fats") have caused nutritionists to rethink the rules governing fat in the diet. In the 1970s and 1980s, the limitations of the very low fat diet (never intended for the masses, but as a heart disease therapy), led people to gorge on "bad carbs" (those high on the glycemic index, explained later in this chapter) because they believed that if a food was "fat free" it was healthy. Also, too few calories from fat left people hungry and craving food. Unfortunately, the gorging on carbs, which peaked in the1980s and early 1990s, led to a sharp increase in insulin resistance from carbohydrate overload in the diet.

Then came the diet backlash: *the low-carb diet*, or Atkins diet. Low-carbohydrate diets are the opposite of low-fat diets; they restrict carbohydrates (which a healthy diet ought to be based on) to about 5 percent, and encourage mostly high-fat foods—the more saturated fat, the better. These diets are also known as high-protein diets. In clinical circles, they are *ketogenic diets*; they trigger ketosis, which in the nondiabetic population occurs when the insulin hormone is shut down, forcing the liver to produce ketone bodies. People without diabetes certainly lose weight while in ketosis, but living in a state of ketosis is not exactly what nature intended for a healthy human body. When you have type 2 diabetes, however, living in a state of ketosis is dangerous and life-threatening, because it puts tremendous strain on your kidneys.

In addition to the dangers of ketosis, the Atkins diet can cause terrible constipation in the first phase, while consuming high levels of saturated fat spells disaster for people with type 2 diabetes, especially for those with high levels of LDL. Many people have a genetic condition that causes high triglycerides as well, which cannot be controlled through diet alone. In these people, the Atkins diet can be life-threatening (while a very low fat diet has been shown, since the 1950s, to be lifesaving)—even in people without type 2 diabetes. Anyone who suffers from any disease that puts a strain on the kidneys: hypertension, cardiovascular disease, or bladder infections or conditions should consult their doctor before attempting the Atkins diet. Of course, anyone who is pregnant should absolutely stay away from this diet.

The Center for Science in the Public Interest rates the low-carb diets, such as Atkins, Protein Power, and Sugar Busters, unacceptable in the nondiabetic population because of the high quantities of saturated fat and low quantities of fiber and essential nutrients. People become constipated and may burn fat due to ketosis, but at the same time, they are depriving their bodies of essential nutrients, many of which are known to decrease incidences of diseases such as certain cancers. People who load their bodies with saturated fats known to be associated with higher rates of cancers are putting themselves at risk for these cancers.

Nutritional experts maintain that carbohydrates do not make us fat; it is *overindulgence* in carbohydrates, protein, or fat that makes us fat. Eating fewer carbs, protein, and fat—*eating everything in moderation and expending more energy than is eaten—is the key to weight loss*. Eating whole-grain breads, pasta, rice, potatoes, vegetables, whole-grain cereals, beans, and fruit does not make us fat; eating candy, chocolate, cookies, biscuits, sweets, and cakes—all of which are refined carbohydrates—makes us fat. And that is discouraged on any balanced diet that does not force your body into ketosis. Any balanced diet will result in weight loss with the added benefit of no health risks. Even an extreme Ornish- or Pritikin-styled diet is fine for everyone, when followed correctly, and there are absolutely no health consequences other than improved health.

Carbohydrate Counting

All diabetes associations now encourage people with diabetes to "count carbs" in order to follow meal plans or specific types of diets in the 40/30/30 range (40 percent carbs, 30 percent protein, 30 percent fat). Foods that are mostly protein or fat do not have many carbohydrates, but as discussed earlier, carbohydrates are found in starches, fruits, vegetables, legumes, milk, and sugary or prepared foods. Your dietician or nutritionist will give you a carb goal per meal and snack. This may be the same amount or may vary depending on the day and your needs.

You should aim to meet your target carb count per meal within about five grams. Keep a record of the carbs you're having per meal and adjust the target depending on your blood glucose readings (see Chapter 7).

In the United States and Canada, a "Nutrition Facts" label appears on all packaged foods, with trivial differences in each country. (This does not include foods you buy in restaurants, or freshly made foods that are packaged, such as sandwiches you pick up in a convenience store.) These food labels now list the number of total carbohydrates *per serving size*. The carbohydrates panel lists the total amount of carbohydrates in grams first. This number includes starch, sugars, and fiber. Then fiber and sugars are listed separately (starch is not). Since fiber does not raise blood sugar, you should subtract the grams of fiber from the total grams of carbs listed for an accurate count.

Serving sizes are expressed in grams (for solids or net weight) or milliliters (for liquids or net volume). For example, if you were buying bread, the serving size would be expressed in this way: "serving size 1 slice (40 g)." In other cases, the serving size may indicate a fraction of the package contents. A box of pudding that makes six servings may list nutrition facts based on one-sixth of a box; an eight-slice pizza may list nutrition facts based on one-eighth of the pizza. Individually packaged foods, such as granola bars, will usually list serving sizes based on the whole bar. (But be careful: a "king size" candy bar, for example, can be considered two and a half servings, and give nutrition information based on two-fifths of the bar rather than the whole thing.) Serving sizes can be listed in metric units, cups, tablespoons, or pieces per unit (for example, one muffin, two cookies). For all nonmetric quantities listed such as "per stick," the metric unit will be in parentheses, such as "per stick (2.7 grams)."

To adequately count carbs, you need to count based on the serving size you are actually ingesting. Let's say you're planning to have a box, rather than a "serving," of macaroni and cheese dinner (as many people do). In this case, you need to multiply the amount of carbohydrates listed by the number of serving sizes you're planning to eat. If the box says "serves 4," and the carbohydrates per serving are listed as 25 grams, then you would be eating about 100 grams (25 × 4). In this case, you should also check the box to make sure that the serving size is based on the prepared meal, rather than just the dry macaroni! Frequently, packaged foods are calculated without the extras you have to use to *make* the food, such as butter, margarine, or milk. You have to separately count the carbs in a tablespoon of butter and/or milk if the box indicates the carbs for the unprepared mix. If you're planning to have a sandwich, the bread may list one slice of bread as a serving size. If the carbs listed per slice are 15 grams, then you would count the two slices of bread in a sandwich as 30 grams, as well as anything else containing carbs in the sandwich (tomato slices, mustard, and so on).

It's a good idea to purchase a basic carbohydrate reference book so you can count carbs for nonlabeled food items such as fresh foods you purchase or prepare yourself. The American Diabetes Association has good books on carb counting and converting foods into carbs for counting.

The Glycemic Index

The glycemic index (GI) shows the rise in blood sugar from various carbohydrates; therefore, planning your diet using the GI can help you control your blood sugar by using more foods with a low GI and fewer foods with a high GI. People with impaired fasting glucose (IFG), impaired glucose tolerance (IGT), or type 2 diabetes are now encouraged by diabetes experts to use the GI.

The Exchange Lists

The first thing you need to learn before you shop for food is the exchange system, developed by the American Diabetes Association, which tells you how various foods can be incorporated into your meal plan. There are seven exchange list categories:

- *Starches:* cereals, grains, pasta, breads, crackers, snacks, and starchy vegetables, such as legumes (peas and beans), potatoes, corn, and squash
- *Meat and Meat Substitutes:* poultry, fish, shellfish, game, beef, pork, lamb, cheese, tofu, tempeh, low-fat cheeses, egg whites, and soy milk
- *Fruit:* fresh fruit, frozen fruit, canned fruit, dried fruit, and juice (Remember: fruit is any produce that grows on trees/vines/plants, such as tomatoes!)

The Glycemic Index at a Glance

The glycemic index, developed at the University of Toronto, measures the rate at which various foods convert to glucose, which is assigned a value of 100. Higher numbers indicate a more rapid absorption of glucose. This is not an exhaustive list and should be used as a sample only. It is not an index of food energy values or calories; some low GI foods are high in fat, while some high GI foods are low in fat. Keep in mind, too, that these values differ depending on what else you're eating with that food and how the food is prepared.

Sugars

Glucose	100
Honey	87
Table sugar	59
Fructose	20

Snacks

Mars bar	68
Potato chips	51
Sponge cake	46
Peanuts	13

Cereals

Cornflakes	80
Shredded wheat	67
Muesli	66
All-Bran	51
Oatmeal	49

Breads

Whole wheat	72
White	69
Buckwheat	51

Fruits

Raisins	64
Banana	62
Orange juice	46
Orange	40
Apple	39

Dairy Products

Ice cream	36
Yogurt	36
Milk	34
Skim milk	32

Root Vegetables

Parsnips	97
Carrots	92
Instant mashed potatoes	80
New boiled potato	70
Beets	64
Yam	51
Sweet potato	48

Pasta and Rice

White rice	72
Brown rice	66
Spaghetti (white)	50
Spaghetti (whole wheat)	42

Legumes

Frozen peas	51
Baked beans	40
Chickpeas	36
Lima beans	36
Butter beans	36
Black-eyed peas	33
Green beans	31
Kidney beans	29
Lentils	29
Dried soybeans	15

Miscellaneous

Fish sticks	38
Tomato soup	38
Sausages	28

Source: Adapted from David Drum and Terry Zierenberg, R.N., C.D.E., *The Type 2 Diabetes Sourcebook* (Los Angeles: Lowell House,1998), p. 130. Used with permission.

- *Dairy:* most milk products
- *Vegetables:* most vegetables from A (for artichoke) to Z (for zucchini), but does not include starchy vegetables, which are under Starches
- *Fats:* monounsaturated, polyunsaturated, and saturated fats, based on the primary type of fat in the food
- *Other Carbohydrates:* cakes, pies, puddings, granola bars, gelatin, and any food that contains more fats and sugars than vitamins and minerals

Your dietitian or diabetes educator will work with you to create an individual meal plan built around the exchange lists. One person, for example, may eat for breakfast two items from list 1, three items from list 2, and two items from list 6; another person may require a completely different plan. Your individual meal plan will specify how many items from the above lists you can have at each meal, based on your unique circumstances.

The best advice regarding exchange lists is to purchase the American Diabetes Association's *Exchange Lists for Meal Planning* (the exchange list bible). It can be ordered directly from the American Diabetes Association at diabetes.org. For questions about the exchange lists, just call the ADA at 1-800-232-3472. A registered dietitian in your area can be found by calling the American Dietetic Association hotline at 1-800-366-1655.

Your dietitian or diabetes educator should also teach you how to incorporate carb counting into meal planning, which can be done by learning to read labels properly, setting goals for a certain number of carbohydrates per day, and keeping accurate records of your blood sugar levels.

How Much to Eat

Meal plans recommended by registered dietitians are tailored to your individual goals and medication regimen. Men and women will usually require different quantities of food. The goal is to keep the supply of glucose consistent by spacing out your meals, snacks, and activity levels accordingly. If you lose weight, your body will use insulin more effectively, but not all people with type 2 diabetes need to lose weight.

If you're on insulin, meals will have to be timed to match your insulin's peak. A dietitian can help by prescribing an individualized meal plan that addresses your specific needs (taking into account such things as weight control, shift work, and travel).

Anatomy of a Carbohydrate

Carbohydrates are like people; they can be simple or complex. Simple carbohydrates are found in any food that has natural sugar (honey, fruits, juices, vegetables, milk) and anything that contains table sugar, or sucrose.

Complex carbohydrates are more sophisticated foods that are made up of larger molecules, such as grain foods, starches, and foods high in fiber. The foods containing fiber, both soluble and insoluble (an important distinction), such as cereals, oatmeal, or legumes, are discussed in Chapter 5.

Sugars

Sugars are found naturally in many foods. Sucrose and glucose (found in table sugar), fructose (found in fruits and vegetables), lactose (found in milk products), and maltose (found in flours and cereals) are all naturally occurring sugars. What you have to watch out for is *added sugar*; these are sugars that manufacturers add to foods during processing or packaging. Foods containing fruit juice concentrates, invert sugar, regular corn syrup, honey, molasses, hydrolyzed lactose syrup, or high fructose corn syrup (highly concentrated fructose made through the hydrolysis of starch) all have added sugars. Many people don't realize that pure, *unsweetened* fruit juice is still a potent source of sugar, even when it contains no added sugar. Extra lactose, dextrose, and maltose are also contained in many foods. The products may have naturally occurring sugars, and then *more* sugar is added to enhance consistency, taste, and so on. With the exception of lactose, which breaks down into glucose and galactose, all of these added sugars break down into fructose and glucose during digestion. See the upcoming sidebar, "What's in a Sugar?" for the complete sugar breakdown. The best way to know how much sugar is in a product is to look at the nutritional label for carbohydrates.

However, *how fast* that sugar is ultimately broken down and enters the bloodstream greatly depends on the amount of fiber in your food, how much protein you've eaten, and how much fat accompanies the sugar in your meal.

As far as your body is concerned, all sugars are nutritionally equal. Honey and table sugar, for instance, are nutritionally comparable. Ultimately, all the sugars from the foods you eat wind up as glucose; your body doesn't know whether the sugar started out as maltose from whole-grain breads or lactose from milk products. Glucose then travels through your bloodstream to provide energy. If you have enough energy already, the glucose is stored as fat for later use. Sugars and starches affect blood sugar differently because of the time frame involved in glucose conversion. Sugars are converted faster than starches, so it's important to discuss sugar conversion with your dietitian.

Why Is Sugar Added?

Sugar is added to food because it can change the consistency of foods and, in some instances, act as a preservative, as in jams and jellies. Sugar can increase the boiling point or reduce the freezing point in foods; sugar can add bulk and density; it can make baked goods do wonderful things, including helping yeast to ferment. Sugar can also add moisture to dry foods, make foods crisp, or balance acidic tastes found in foods like tomato sauce or salad dressing. Invert sugar or corn syrup is used to prevent sucrose from crystallizing in candy.

Since the 1950s, a popular natural sugar in North America has been fructose, which has replaced sucrose in many food products in the form of high fructose syrup (HFS) made from corn. HFS was developed in response to high sucrose prices and is very cheap to make. In other parts of the world, the equivalent of high fructose syrup is made from whatever starches are local, such as rice, tapioca, wheat, or cassava. According to the International Food Information Council in Washington, D.C., the average North American consumes about thirty-seven grams of fructose daily.

Grocery Shopping

Food shopping can be daunting because most foods are not purely carbohydrate, protein, fat, or sugar, but often a mixture of two or three. That's where carb counting comes in, and the American Diabetes

Exchange lists. If you can count, you can plan a meal that has everything you need. A good meal plan will ensure that you are getting enough nutrients to meet your energy needs, and that your food is spread out over the course of the day. For example, if your meal plan allots for three meals with one or two snacks, meals should be spaced four to six hours apart so your body isn't overwhelmed. If you are obese, snacks will likely be discouraged because snacks can cause you to oversecrete insulin and increase your appetite. A meal plan should also help you to eat consistently rather than bingeing one day and starving the next.

Your dietitian or diabetes educator will work with you to create an individual meal plan using food choices within the exchange lists.

The Outside Aisles

What you need to live is usually found on the outside aisles of any supermarket or grocery store. Outside aisles stock the foods you can

Golden Rules of Diabetes Meal Plans

- Eat three meals a day at fairly regular times (spaced four to six hours apart).
- Ask your dietitian to help you plan your snacks.
- Try to eat a variety of foods each day from all food groups.
- Learn how to gauge serving sizes, volume of bowls and glasses, and so on.
- Ask your dietitian or diabetes educator about how to adjust your diet if you're traveling. (This depends on such things as whether or not you are on medication, where you're going, and what foods will be available.)
- Draw up a sick days plan with your dietitian. This special plan will be based on your regular meal plan.
- Ask about any meal supplements, such as breakfast bars, sports bars, or meal-replacement drinks. How will these figure into your meal plan?
- Choose lower-fat foods more often. (See Chapter 5.)

buy at outdoor markets: fruits, vegetables, meat, eggs, fish, breads, and dairy products. Natural fiber (both soluble and insoluble), discussed in Chapter 5, is also found in the outside aisles. But remember: foods you buy in the outside aisles can also be high in fat unless you select wisely, also discussed in Chapter 5.

The Inside Aisles

The inside aisles are not only the aisles of temptation, they may have complicated food labels.

What You Need to Know About Labels

- *Low fat:* the product has three grams of fat or less per serving, which is about six potato chips
- *Low-calorie:* 40 calories or less per serving
- *Reduced:* must have 25 percent less of the particular nutrient, such as carbs
- *Less and fewer:* must be reduced by 25 percent from regular product
- *High (for example, "high fiber"):* must have 20 percent or more of percent daily value (PDV) for the nutrient
- *Good source:* must contain 10 to 19 percent of PDV for the nutrient
- *Light:* must have half the fat, one-third the calories, or half the salt of regular product
- *Free, no,* or *zero (as in "cholesterol-free," "no fat," "zero fat"):* must have no more than half a gram per serving

"Sugar Free"

Sugar-free in the language of labels simply means "sucrose-free." That doesn't mean the product is *carbohydrate-free,* as in dextrose-free, lactose-free, glucose-free, or fructose-free. Check the labels for all ingredients ending in *-ose* to find out the sugar content; you're not just looking for sucrose. Watch out for "no added sugar," "without added sugar," or "no sugar added." This simply means, "We didn't put the sugar in, God did." Again, reading the nutrition information label is the most accurate way to find out the amount of sugar in the product. Nutrition claims in big, bold statements can be misleading.

Labels on food produced in the United States that say "sugar-free" contain less than half a gram of sugar per serving, while a "reduced-sugar" food contains at least 25 percent less sugar per serving than the regular product. If the label also states that the product is not a reduced- or low-calorie food, or if it is not for weight control, it's got enough sugar in there to make you think twice.

Serving sizes in the United States are defined by the U.S. FDA. That means that five cereals that all weigh the same amount per cup will share the same serving size.

Calories (how much energy) and calories from fat are also listed per serving of food in the United States. Total carbohydrate, dietary fiber, sugars, other carbohydrates (starches), total fat, saturated fat, cholesterol, sodium, potassium, and vitamins and minerals are given in percent daily values (PDV), based on the 2,000-calorie diet recommended by the U.S. government.

Artificial Sweeteners

A product can be sweet without containing a bit of sugar, thanks to the invention of artificial sugars and sweeteners. Artificial sweeteners will not affect your blood sugar levels because they do not contain sugar; they may contain a very few calories, however. It depends on whether that sweetener is classified as nutritive or nonnutritive.

Nutritive sweeteners have calories or contain natural sugar. White or brown table sugar, molasses, honey, and syrup are all considered nutritive sweeteners. *Sugar alcohols* are also nutritive sweeteners because they are made from fruits or produced commercially from dextrose. Sorbitol, mannitol, xylitol, and maltitol are all sugar alcohols. Sugar alcohols contain only four calories per gram, like ordinary sugar, and will affect your blood sugar levels. How much sugar alcohols affect your blood sugar levels depends on how much is consumed and the degree of absorption from your digestive tract.

What's in a Sugar?

- *Fructose:* a monosaccharide or single sugar. It combines with glucose to form sucrose and is one and a half times sweeter than sucrose. Sixty grams of fructose per day is acceptable for a 2,000-calorie per day diet.
- *Glucose:* a monosaccharide or single sugar. It combines with fructose to form sucrose. It can also combine with glucose to form maltose, and with galactose to form lactose. It is slightly less sweet than sucrose. Fifty grams of sucrose per day is acceptable for a 2,000-calorie per day diet.
- *High fructose corn syrup (HFCS):* a liquid mixture of about equal parts glucose and fructose from cornstarch. It has the same sweetness as sucrose.
- *Sucrose:* a disaccharide or double sugar made of equal parts of glucose and fructose. Known as table or white sugar, sucrose is found naturally in sugarcane and sugar beets.

Nonnutritive sweeteners are sugar substitutes or artificial sweeteners; they do not have any calories and will not affect your blood sugar levels. Examples of nonnutritive sweeteners are saccharin, cyclamate, aspartame, sucralose, and acesulfame potassium.

Stevia

Stevia is a natural, low-calorie sweetener that is thirty to one hundred times sweeter than sugar, without the aftertaste that is common in many sugar substitutes. Stevia is a herb that has been used in Paraguay and Brazil as a natural sweetener for centuries. It is declared safe to use Japan and is commonly found in soy sauce, chewing gum, and mouthwash. Stevia also is high in chromium (a mineral that helps to regulate blood sugar); is a high source of manganese, potassium, selenium, silicon, sodium, and vitamin A; and contains iron, niacin, phosphorus, riboflavin, thiamine, vitamin C, and zinc.

There has been an explosion of interest in stevia because it is a natural alternative to sugar that contains many nutrients to boot. Stevia is not approved as a sweetener by the U.S. FDA; instead it is legal only as a "dietary supplement." It also remains unapproved as a food additive in the United States. Stevia is available in Canada as an herbal product but is not officially approved as a sweetener or food additive by Health Canada, Agrafood Canada, or the Canadian Diabetes Association. Please consult with your diabetes educator about the safety of stevia in your meal planning.

Sugar Alcohols

Not to be confused with alcoholic beverages, sugar alcohols are nutritive sweeteners, like regular sugar. They are found naturally in fruits or are manufactured from carbohydrates. Sorbitol, mannitol, xylitol, maltitol, maltitol syrup, lactitol, isomalt, and hydrogenated starch hydrolysates are all sugar alcohols. In your body, these types of sugars are absorbed lower down in the digestive tract than regular sugar and will cause gastrointestinal symptoms if you use too much. Because sugar alcohols are absorbed more slowly, they were once touted as ideal for people with diabetes, but since they are carbohydrates, they still increase your blood sugar, just like regular sugar. Now that artificial sweeteners are on the market in abundance, the only real advantage of sugar alcohols is that they don't cause cavities. The bacteria in your mouth don't like sugar alcohols as much as real sugar.

Acceptable Daily Intake for Sweeteners

Sweetener	Intake (mg/pound)
Aspartame	18
Ace-K	7
Cyclamate	5
Saccharin	2
Sucralose	7*

*In Canada, the acceptable daily intake is 4 mg/pound for sucralose.
Source: Canadian Diabetes Association, "Guidelines for the Nutritional Management of Diabetes Mellitus in the New Millennium. A Position Statement." Reprinted from *Canadian Journal Diabetes Care* 23 (3): 56–69.

According to the FDA, foods that contain sugar alcohols can be labeled "sugar free." Sugar alcohol products can also be labeled "Does not promote tooth decay," which is often confused with "low calorie." Ten grams of sugar alcohol per day is acceptable for a 2,000-calorie per day diet.

At the Liquor Store

One alcoholic beverage delivers about 7 calories per gram or 150 calories per drink. A glass of dry red wine is about 100 calories; if it is sweet, it is more. Beer is roughly 150 calories per bottle, and hard liquors (such as vodka or gin) are about 100 calories per shot glass.

Many people with diabetes think they have to avoid alcohol completely. This is not so. Alcohol alone doesn't increase blood sugar because alcohol cannot be turned into glucose. It's the *sugar* in that alcoholic beverage that can affect your blood sugar level. The problem with alcohol is that it's so darned fattening, something people with type 2 diabetes may need to watch for. That said, red wine, in particular, has been proven to raise your good cholesterol (HDL). Red wine is believed to have a heart-healthy effect in three ways: it is an antioxidant, vasodilating, and antithrombotic. The two most studied compounds in wine are resveratrol and quercitin. Resveratrol apparently increases HDL cholesterol. The tannins in red wine, which are not as present in white wine or other liquor, seem to help blood flow and declog arteries. Grape juice or dealcoholized red wine apparently confer some of the same benefits as the alcoholic version. In general, a maximum of two glasses of red wine per day is the recommendation for people with type 2 diabetes.

It's crucial to note, however, that alcohol can cause hypoglycemia (low blood sugar) if you're on medication or insulin. Please discuss the effects of alcohol and hypoglycemia with your health-care team.

ADA Meal Planning Exchange Lists

Complex Carbs (Digest More Slowly)	ADA List
Fruits	Fruit
Vegetables	Vegetables or Starches
Grains (breads, pastas, and cereals)	Starches
Legumes (dried beans, peas, and lentils)	Starches

Simple Carbs (Digest Quickly)	ADA List
Fruits/fruit juices	Fruit
Sugars (sucrose, fructose, honey, corn syrup, sorghum, date sugar, molasses)	Fruit/Other Carbohydrates/ Starches
Lactose	Dairy

Proteins (Digest Slowly)	ADA List
Lean meats	Meat and Meat Substitutes
Fatty meats	Meat and Meat Substitutes/Fats
Poultry	Meat and Meat Substitutes
Fish	Meat and Meat Substitutes
Eggs	Meat and Meat Substitutes
Low-fat cheese	Meat and Meat Substitutes
High-fat cheese	Dairy or Fats
Legumes	Starches
Grains	Starches

Fats (Digest Slowly)	ADA List
High-fat dairy products (butter/cream)	Dairy/Fats
Oils (canola/corn/olive/ safflower/sunflower)	Fats

Lard	Fats
Avocados	Fats/Vegetables
Olives	Fats/Vegetables
Nuts	Fats/Vegetables
Fatty meats	Fats/Meat and Meat Substitutes
Fiber (Soluble and Insoluble)	**ADA List**
Whole-grain breads	Starches
Cereals (for example, oatmeal)	Starches
All fruits	Fruit
Legumes (beans and lentils)	Starches
Leafy greens	Vegetables
Cruciferous vegetables	Vegetables

7

Self-Care and Medications

DIABETES SELF-CARE is all about eliminating your diabetes symptoms, and then remaining as symptom-free as possible. Meal planning (Chapter 6) combined with exercise is the best way to remain symptom-free. This will help you lose weight if you need to, as well as distribute an even amount of calories to your body throughout the day. By not putting any unusual strain on your body's metabolism, you will likely not experience any surprises when it comes to your blood sugar levels. Exercise makes insulin much more available to your cells, while your muscles use sugar as fuel.

If you can't keep your blood sugar levels below 140 mg/dl, you are probably a candidate for diabetes medications, such as an oral hypoglycemic agent, discussed later in this chapter.

Testing Your Own Blood Sugar

In order to plan your meals and activities properly, you have to know what your blood sugar levels are throughout the day. One of the most important research projects ever undertaken was the Diabetes Control and Complications Trial (DCCT). This trial proved beyond a doubt that when people with type 1 diabetes kept their blood sugar levels as normal as possible, as often as possible, they could dramatically reduce the odds of developing small blood-vessel diseases related to diabetes, such as kidney disease, eye problems, and nerve disease, all discussed in later chapters.

In 1998, the results of a landmark British study, the United Kingdom Prospective Diabetes Study (UKPDS), showed that frequent blood sugar testing (meaning about three or four times a day) in people with type 2 diabetes also helped reduce eye, kidney, and nerve damage, as well as high blood pressure. Studies have also shown that people with type 2 diabetes on medication or insulin can lower their A1C results (a test of average blood sugar level, explained later in this chapter) by 0.6 percent if they test their blood sugar just once a day. Since the DCCT and UKPDS, many more studies have confirmed these results, showing that the key to preventing complications is to keep blood sugar levels, cholesterol, and blood pressure levels at the targets discussed in Chapter 1, as well as aiming to keep the A1C at the recommended targets. The closer the A1C reading is to the recommended target, the fewer complications develop down the diabetes road.

Glucose meters were first introduced in 1982. They allow people with diabetes to test their own blood sugar at any time without having to rely on doctors. When your parents or grandparents struggled with diabetes in the past, there was no such thing as a glucose meter. They had to go to the doctor to get their blood sugar tested regularly. Amazingly enough, through interviews with individual diabetes patients and several doctors, my research shows that there are still people who rely on the doctor to test their blood sugar. If you are still going to your doctor for a blood sugar test, purchase a glucose meter before your next doctor's visit and ask your doctor to show you how it works. There is no good reason to rely on a doctor to test your blood sugar. That said, you should have laboratory blood tests done at least once a year to make sure your meter results are accurate.

How Frequently Should You Test?

A healthy pancreas measures its owner's blood sugar levels once a second, or 3,600 times an hour. It produces exactly the right amount of insulin for that second. In light of this, testing your blood sugar frequently makes sense.

There is no official rule regarding how frequently you should test your blood sugar. As a result, two management philosophies have emerged regarding frequent self-testing of blood sugar and type 2 diabetes. Most physicians feel that the more involved you become in managing your blood sugar, the better off you'll be in the long run, and therefore, they support frequent self-testing of blood sugar in their type 2 patients. Diabetes experts also recommend that people with type 2 diabetes frequently self-test their blood sugar. In a newly diagnosed person with type 2 diabetes, frequent testing will show individual patterns of glucose rises and dips, which may help your health-care team tailor your meal plans, exercise routines, and medication regimens. And if you do have to take insulin in the future, you will need to get into the habit of testing your own blood sugar anyway.

Not all physicians agree with this policy, however. Some physicians have told me that for some of their patients with type 2 diabetes, the struggle to make necessary diet and activity changes is hard enough, and the frequent blood sugar testing can complicate that goal. For some people, the blood sugar testing interferes with more crucial goals, such as losing weight.

You have to find a plan that works for you and set realistic goals with your diabetes health-care team. Regardless of your doctor's approach to frequent self-testing of blood sugar, there are a host of easy-to-use home blood sugar meters that give you more choices in diabetes self-care than ever before, so take advantage of them. Your doctor, pharmacist, or diabetes educator can recommend the right glucose meter for you. When you get your glucose meter, experts suggest you compare your results to one regular laboratory test to make sure you've purchased a reliable and accurate machine.

Use the information in the sidebar "When to Test Your Blood Sugar" as a general guideline for testing times, and take it to your health-care provider to help design your plan. You should have an individualized testing schedule.

Choosing and Using Your Glucose Meter

As in the computer industry, glucose meter manufacturers tend to come out with technological upgrades every year. Some blood sugar monitors allow blood to be tested from the forearm or other parts in place of the fingertip. Diabetes experts state that fingertip blood appears to

When to Test Your Blood Sugar

In the days when diabetes patients went to their doctors' offices for blood sugar testing, they were usually tested first thing in the morning before eating (called a *fasting blood sugar level*) or immediately after eating (known as a *postprandial* or *postmeal blood sugar level*). It was believed that if either the fasting or postprandial levels were normal, the patient's blood sugar level was stable. This is now known to be completely false. In fact, your blood sugar levels can bounce around all day long. Because your blood sugar is constantly changing, a blood sugar test in a doctor's office is pretty useless because it measures what your blood sugar is only for that nanosecond; what your blood sugar is at 2:15 P.M. is not what it might be at 3:05 P.M.

It makes the most sense to test yourself before each meal, so you know what your levels are before you eat anything, as well as about two hours after meals. Immediately after eating, blood sugar is normally high, so this is not the ideal time to test anybody. In a person without diabetes, blood sugar levels will drop about two hours after eating, in response to the natural insulin the body makes. Similarly, test yourself two hours after eating to make sure that you are able to mimic a normal blood sugar pattern, too. Ideally, this translates into at least four blood tests daily:

- When you wake up
- After breakfast/before lunch (two hours after breakfast)
- After lunch/before dinner (two hours after lunch)
- After dinner/at bedtime (two hours after dinner)

The most revealing information about your blood sugar control is in the answers to the following questions:

- What is your blood sugar level as soon as you wake up? (In people with type 2 diabetes, it is often at its highest point in the morning.)
- What is your blood sugar level two hours after a meal? (It should be much lower two hours after eating than one hour after eating.)
- What is your blood sugar level when you feel ill? (You need to avoid dipping too low or high since your routine is changing.)

Variations on the Theme

- Test yourself four times a day (at the times indicated above) two to three times a week, and then test yourself two times a day (before breakfast and before bedtime) for the remainder of the week.
- Test yourself twice a day three to four days a week in a rotating pattern (before breakfast and dinner one day; before lunch and bedtime the next).
- Test yourself once a day every day, but rotate your pattern (day 1 before breakfast; day 2 after dinner; day 3 before bedtime; and so on).
- Test yourself four times a day (at the times indicated above) two days a month.

result in more accurate readings overall, especially in people who have fluctuations in blood sugar or may be hypoglycemic.

Newer models allow you to download the time, date, and blood sugar values for as many as 250 tests onto your personal computer or personal organizer device. The information can help you gauge whether your diet and exercise routine is working, or whether you need to adjust your medications or insulin. If you've never purchased a glucose meter, keep in mind that even the lowest-tech glucose meters all provide the following:

- A battery-powered, pocket-sized device
- An LED or LCD screen (that is, a calculator-like screen)
- Accurate results in seconds
- At least a one-year warranty
- The opportunity to upgrade
- A toll-free customer service hotline
- Mailings and giveaways every so often
- A few free lancets with your purchase; you may have to separately purchase a lancing device, a dispenser for your lancets; eventually, you'll run out of lancets and have to buy those, too

The directions for using a glucose meter vary according to manufacturer. Be sure to read the directions carefully and ask your pharmacist for guidance if there's something you don't understand. It's a good idea to record your results in a logbook. *A target reading before meals ranges from 72 to 127 mg/dl; a normal reading after meals ranges from 90 to 180 mg/dl.* In nondiabetic people, blood sugar readings before meals range from 72 to 108 mg/dl, and after meals, 90 to 144 mg/dl.

Factors That Can Taint Your Results

Keep in mind that the following outside factors may interfere with your meter's performance.

- *Other medications you're taking.* Studies show that some meters can be inaccurate if you're taking acetaminophen, salicylate, ascorbic acid, dopamine, or levodopa. As a rule, if you're taking any medications, check with your doctor, pharmacist, and glucose meter manufacturer (call the toll-free number) about whether your medications can affect the meter's accuracy.
- *Humidity.* The worst place to keep your meter and strips is in the bathroom, where humidity can ruin your strips unless they're individually wrapped in foil. Keep your strips in a sealed container away

from extreme temperatures. Don't store your meter and strips, for example, in a hot glove compartment; don't keep them in the freezer either.

• *Bright light.* Ever tried to use a calculator or portable computer in bright sunlight? It's not possible because the light interferes with the screen. Some meters are photometric, which means they are affected by bright light. If you plan to test in sunlight, get a biosensor meter that is unaffected by bright light (there are several).

• *Touching the test strip.* Many glucose meters come with test strips that must not be touched with your fingers or a second drop of blood. If you're all thumbs, purchase a meter that is unaffected by touch and/or allows a second drop of blood.

• *Wet hands.* Before you test, thoroughly dry your hands. Water can dilute your blood sample.

• *Motion.* It's always best to test yourself when you're standing still. Testing on planes, trains, automobiles, buses, and subways may affect your results, depending on the brand of glucose meter.

• *Dirt, lint, and blood.* Particles of dirt, lint, and old blood can sometimes affect the accuracy of a meter, depending on the brand. Make sure you clean the meter regularly (follow the manufacturer's cleaning directions) to remove buildup. If your meter requires battery changes, make sure you change them! There are meters on the market that do not require cleaning and are unaffected by dirt, but they may cost a little more.

What the Doctor Orders

Throughout the year, your managing doctor (primary care physician or endocrinologist) should order a variety of blood tests to make sure that your blood sugar levels are as controlled as they can be and that no complications from diabetes are setting in.

The Hemoglobin A1C Test

The most important test is one that checks your glycolsylated hemoglobin levels, known as the *A1C test* (formerly the HbA1C) test. Hemoglobin is a large molecule that carries oxygen in your blood-

Know Your Drugs

If you take any of the following prescription drugs, make sure you let your doctor know which ones can raise or lower blood sugar levels. (Some doctors aren't aware of all of these drugs.)

Drugs That Can Affect Blood Sugar Levels (Raise or Lower)

Alpha-blockers
Angiotensin converting enzyme (ACE) inhibitors
  (used for high blood pressure)
Certain antipsychotics
Beta-blockers
Calcium channel blockers
Corticosteroids
Cyclosporine
Diazoxide
Diphenylhydantoin (for example, Dilantin, used for
  seizures)
Certain diuretics
Ethanol in any form of alcohol
Fibric acid derivatives (used to treat certain fat
  disorders)
High-dose estrogen-containing oral contraceptives
Interferon alfa
Minoxidil
Nicotinic acid and niacin (used to lower cholesterol)
Pentamidine
Phenothiazines
Phenytoin
Protease inhibitors
Salicylates and acetaminophen
Thyroid hormone

stream. When the glucose in your blood comes in contact with the hemoglobin molecule, it conveniently sticks to it. The more glucose is stuck to your hemoglobin, the higher your blood sugar is. The A1C test measures the amount of glucose stuck to hemoglobin. And since each hemoglobin molecule stays in your blood about three to four months before it is replaced, this test can show you the average blood sugar level over the last three to four months. Therefore this test is recommended at least every six months, but optimally, every three months. If you have cardiovascular problems, you will need to have the A1C test more often.

What's a Good A1C Result?

Just like your glucose monitor at home, the goal of the A1C test is to make sure that your blood sugar average is as close to normal as possible. Again, the closer to normal it is, the less likely you are to experience long-term diabetes complications.

This test result is slightly different from your glucose meter result. For example, an A1C level of 7.0 percent is equal to 144 mg/dl on your blood glucose meter. A result of 9.5 percent is equivalent to 234 mg/dl on your blood glucose meter. In a person without diabetes, an A1C ranges from 4 to 6 percent.

The 2004 guidelines stipulate that values of 6 percent or less are good results and mean that your blood sugar is perfectly under control. Anything higher than 8.4 percent is alarming; this would be a poor result and means that your diabetes is not under control. Studies show that when your A1C result is 8.4 percent or higher, you have a greater chance of developing long-term complications. In fact, for every 1 percent drop in your A1C average (that is, for example, 7.2 percent down from 8.2 percent), the risk of long-term complications falls by about 25 percent.

Problems with the A1C Test

If your child comes home with a report card showing a B average, it doesn't mean your child is getting a B in every course; it means that he or she could have received a D in one course and an A+ in another.

Interpreting A1C Results

A1C test results are interpreted as follows:

Target	Suboptimal	Poor Control	Alarming
4–6.0%	<7.0%	7.0–8.4%	>8.4%

Correlation between A1C result and blood glucose test:

$$6\% = 135 \text{ mg/dl}$$
$$7\% = 170 \text{ mg/dl}$$
$$8\% = 205 \text{ mg/dl}$$
$$9\% = 240 \text{ mg/dl}$$

Based on fasting blood glucose levels.
Sources: *Diabetes Care* 27, Supplement 1, January 2004; Canadian Diabetes Association.

Similarly, the A1C test is just an average. You could have a decent result, even though your blood sugar levels may be dangerously low one day and dangerously high the next.

If you suffer from sickle-cell anemia or other blood disorders, the A1C results will not be accurate either. In this case, you may wind up with either false high or low readings.

And at any time, if your home blood sugar tests (if you've opted for self-testing) over the past two or three months do not seem to match the results of the A1C test, be sure to check the accuracy of your meter, and perhaps show your doctor or certified diabetes educator how you are using the meter in case your technique needs some refining.

Other Important Tests

It's important to have the following routine tests done at least once a year, and more often if you are at high risk for complications:

- Blood pressure (Chapter 1)
- Cholesterol (Chapter 1)
- Eye exam (Chapter 11)
- Foot exam (Chapter 10)
- Kidney tests (Chapter 12)

When Your Doctor Tells You to Take a Pill

Less than 10 percent of people with type 2 diabetes are able to make the necessary lifestyle changes to keep their diabetes under control. First, the older we get, the harder it is for us to change our eating habits. Second, many of us are not able to incorporate enough exercise or physical activity into our routines.

Today there are pills to help you manage your diabetes if the lifestyle changes you've made aren't doing the trick. Going on diabetes medication is in no way a cure-all, but taking a pill will help you stay as healthy as possible in the event that you cannot or will not make the necessary lifestyle changes.

There are several kinds of medications that may be prescribed for you. It's crucial to note, however, that these medications can only be prescribed for people who still produce insulin. They have no effect on people with type 1 diabetes, or insulin-dependent diabetes.

Before you fill your prescription for oral diabetes medications, you should know that between 40 and 50 percent of all people with type 2 diabetes require insulin therapy after ten years. Continuing insulin resistance may cause you to stop responding to oral medications. Furthermore, these pills are meant to complement your meal plan, exercise routine, and glucose monitoring; they are not a substitute.

Bear in mind, too, that physicians who prescribe the medications discussed in this section without also working with you to modify your diet and lifestyle are not managing your diabetes properly. These medications should be prescribed only after you've been unsuccessful in managing your type 2 diabetes through lifestyle modification and frequent blood sugar testing.

If you cannot get down to a healthy body weight, you are probably a good candidate for antidiabetic medication. And anyone with type 2 diabetes who cannot control his or her blood sugar levels *despite* lifestyle changes is also a good candidate.

Oral Diabetes Medications

More accurately, oral diabetes medications are known as *oral antihyperglycemic agents*, which means "pills for high blood sugar." There are several different types of oral antihyperglycemic agents. This section provides a general description of each class of oral antihyperglycemic agent used as of this writing; they are described in the order they are usually prescribed. The terms *antidiabetic agents* or *antidiabetic pills* are also used by doctors to describe these medications.

Biguanides

Biguanides (metformin) are pills that help your insulin work better. This medication primarily stops your liver from producing glucose, thus helping to lower your blood sugar levels and increase glucose uptake by your muscle tissue. These pills also help your tissues respond better to your insulin. Ultimately, biguanides can lower premeal and postmeal blood sugar levels in approximately 80 percent of people with type 2 diabetes. This medication also seems to lower the bad cholesterol levels. These pills do not increase insulin levels and will not directly cause low blood sugar. A biguanide is appropriate for people who are obese and have milder levels of high blood sugar. That's because biguanides do not result in weight gain, which is typically associated with sulfonylureas and insulin therapy. Biguanides will lower blood sugar in approximately 80 percent of people with type 2 diabetes, but about 15 percent of all people treated with this class of drug fail to respond to it, while 3 to 5 percent of people on this drug could stop responding to it. If you're elderly, a lower dose will probably be prescribed. If you've had type 2 diabetes for longer than ten years, this may not be an appropriate medication. Biguanides should never be taken under the following conditions either:

- Alcoholism
- Pregnancy
- Kidney or liver failure

About one-third of all people taking this drug will experience gastrointestinal side effects (no appetite, nausea, abdominal discomfort, and diarrhea). Adjusting dosages and taking your pills with your meals or afterward often clears up these symptoms. Biguanides are frequently prescribed in combination with any of the following medications discussed further on, including insulin.

Insulin Sensitizers

This class of drug is comprised of thiazolidinediones (TZDs), which are pills that make your cells more sensitive to insulin, thereby improving insulin resistance. And when this happens, more glucose gets into your tissues, and less glucose hangs around in your blood. The result is that you'll have lower fasting blood glucose levels, without the need to increase insulin levels. Both rosiglitazone (Avandia) and pioglitazone (Actos) work by stimulating muscle tissue to "drink in" glucose. They also decrease glucose production from the liver and make fat tissue more receptive to glucose.

The first generation of this drug, troglitazone (Rezulin), was released in 1997, and withdrawn from the market in March 2000 by its makers, Warner-Lambert Company, because of liver damage in patients on the drug. Avandia and Actos, released in 2000, are very similar in chemical structure to troglitazone but seem to have a much lower risk of liver damage than troglitazone. Nevertheless, it's very important to ask your doctor about the risks of either drug if they are prescribed. If you've ever had hepatitis (A, B, or C), you should not take this drug. A number of other factors in your history may prevent you from being on the drug, which you must discuss with your doctor. Trials with troglitazone showed that people with cardiovascular problems or who were immune-suppressed for any reason should not be on it. Therefore, please discuss the risks of Avandia or Actos if you have cardiovascular problems or are immune-suppressed, since the chemical structure of these drugs is similar to that of troglitazone. This drug may be prescribed with either biguanides as a combination therapy, or with biguanides and a sulfonylurea in a "triple therapy" cocktail.

Combination therapy with biguanides is so popular, in fact, that a new pill has been designed that mixes rosiglitazone and metformin.

Insulin Secretagogues

Insulin secretagogues (formerly known as oral hypoglycemic agents or OHAs) are pills that help your pancreas release more insulin. The most commonly prescribed insulin secretagogues are sulfonylureas. The sulfonylureas most prescribed are glyburide, glipizide, and glimepiride. Older generations of sulfonylureas still available but rarely used include chlorpropamide and tolbutamide. Short-acting insulin secretagogues are called *nonsulfonylureas* and are available as repaglinide and nateglinide.

Initially, roughly 75 percent of people with type 2 diabetes will respond well to sulfonylureas, but about 15 percent of all people treated with these medications fail to respond to them, while 3 to 5 percent of all people on these medications may eventually stop responding to them.

Sixty percent of people taking these medications continue to have high blood sugar levels two hours after meals. These pills can also cause increased appetite and weight gain. However, the main side effect with this class of medication is hypoglycemia (low blood sugar), which occurs in one in five people on these drugs. If you're over age sixty, hypoglycemia may occur more often, which is why it's dangerous for anyone over age seventy to take certain insulin secretagogues. Gliclazide and glimepiride are associated with less hypoglycemia than glyburide. There are combination formulas of glyburide and metformin (Glucovance) and glipizide and metformin (Metaglip).

Alpha-Glucosidase Inhibitors

Introduced in 1996, alpha-glucosidase inhibitors delay the breakdown of sugar in your meal. Acarbose was the first oral diabetes medication to be introduced since the sulfonylureas and biguanides in the 1950s. It reduces high blood sugar levels after you eat. Acarbose is very similar in structure to the sugars found in foods. Glucose, the main sugar in blood, is a simple sugar that is made when starch and sucrose (table sugar) are digested by enzymes in the lining of the small intestine called alpha-glucosidase. Acarbose stalls this process by forcing the starch and sugar you eat to "take a number" before they're converted into glucose. This slows down the absorption of glucose by the intestine, preventing a rise in blood glucose after a meal. But in order to work, acarbose must be taken with the first bite of each main meal. You'll also need to test your blood sugar two hours after eating to see how well you're responding to the medication. Research is under way to determine if acarbose can be used worldwide as a preventive for people with impaired glucose tolerance (IGT).

Acarbose is prescribed for people who cannot seem to get their after-meal (that is, postmeal or postprandial) blood sugar levels down to acceptable levels. A major benefit of acarbose is that it may reduce the risk of hypoglycemic episodes during the night, particularly in insulin users. Investigators are studying whether acarbose may be used one day as a substitute for morning insulin. The usual rules apply here: acarbose should complement your meal plan and exercise routine; it is not a substitute or way out, and does not, by itself, cause hypoglycemia.

Who should take acarbose?

- Anyone who cannot control his or her blood sugar through diet and lifestyle modification alone
- Anyone who is on an insulin secretagogue but is still experiencing high blood sugar levels after meals
- Anyone who cannot take any other type of antihyperglycemic agent, and for whom diet and lifestyle modifications have failed
- Anyone not doing well on another antihyperglycemic medication, but who wants to avoid starting insulin treatment

Who should not take acarbose? Anyone with the following conditions should not take this drug:

- Inflammation or ulceration of the bowel (inflammatory bowel disease, ulcerative colitis, or Crohn's disease)
- Any kind of bowel obstruction
- Any gastrointestinal disease
- Kidney or liver disorders
- Hernias
- Pregnancy or lactation
- Type 1 diabetes

For best results, it's crucial that you take acarbose with the first bite of each main meal. In fact, if you swallow your pill even five to ten minutes before a meal, acarbose will pass through your digestive system and have no effect. It's also important that you take acarbose with a carbohydrate; the medication doesn't work if there are no carbohydrates in your meal. You shouldn't take acarbose between meals, either, because it won't work. Nor should acarbose be used as a weight-loss drug.

The good news is that acarbose doesn't cause hypoglycemia. However, since you may be taking this drug along with an insulin secretagogue, you may still experience hypoglycemia, as acarbose doesn't prevent it, either. (See Chapter 8 for warning signs and treatment for hypoglycemia.)

The only side effects that acarbose causes are gastrointestinal: gas, abdominal cramps, softer stools, or diarrhea. Acarbose combined with metformin can produce unacceptable gastrointestinal symptoms. You'll notice these side effects after you've consumed foods that contain lots of sugar. Avoid taking antacids; they won't be effective in this case. Adjusting the dosage and making sure you're taking acarbose correctly will usually take care of the side effects.

Another brand of alpha-glucosidase inhibitor is called miglitol, and it works similarly to acarbose.

Questions to Ask About Oral Diabetes Medications

Before you fill your prescription, it's important to ask your doctor or pharmacist the following questions:

- *What does this drug contain?* If you are allergic to particular ingredients, such as dyes, it's important to find out the drug's ingredients before you take it.
- *Are there any medications I shouldn't combine with this drug?* Be sure to ask about interactions with cholesterol or hypertension medications, as well as any antidepressants or antipsychotics.
- *If this drug doesn't work well, would insulin ever be prescribed along with this pill?* In cases where blood sugar remains too high in spite of medication, insulin is used in

combination with an antihyperglycemic agent. This has become the standard of care, but was once controversial.

- *How will you measure the effectiveness of my drug?* You should be testing your blood sugar with a glucose meter, particularly two hours after eating, to make sure that the lowest effective dose can be prescribed. Your doctor should also be doing a glycosylated hemoglobin or A1C test two or three times per year.
- *How should I store my drugs?* All pills should be kept in a dry place at a temperature between 59 and 77 degrees Fahrenheit. Keep these drugs away from children, don't give them out as samples, and don't use tablets beyond their expiration date.
- *What symptoms should I watch out for while on these drugs?* You'll definitely want to watch for signs of high or low blood sugar.

Natural Therapies

Keep in mind that "natural" is not necessarily "not harmful," and many conscientious physicians require a higher standard of scientific evidence before recommending complementary therapies. For these reasons, I present this information for you to discuss with your doctor. Since the nutraceutical industry is ripe with charlatans, I also encourage my readers to visit quackwatch.com, which is a watchdog site that guards against false credentials and claims.

Guar Gum

This is a high source of fiber made from the seeds of the Indian cluster bean. When you mix guar with water, it turns into a gummy gel, which slows down your digestive system and is similar in effect to acarbose. Guar has often been used as a natural substance to treat high blood sugar as well as high cholesterol. Guar can cause gas, some stomachache, nausea, and diarrhea. (These are also side effects of acarbose.) The problem with guar is that there are no scientific studies to date concluding that it improves blood sugar control. Nevertheless, most experts agree that it can certainly provide some marginal benefits.

Fiber

Delay glucose absorption by eating more fiber, avoiding table sugar (sucrose), and eating smaller meals more often to space out your calories. Meal planning is discussed in detail in Chapter 6.

Chromium

In the alternative medicine literature, chromium is considered a valuable trace mineral that apparently helps your body use insulin more effectively; it also benefits the entire circulatory system. Natural medicine practitioners use chromium to help maintain blood sugar levels, reduce arterial plaque, reduce cholesterol, curb sugar cravings, and even help with weight loss. None of this has been demonstrated to work in evidence-based studies, but the anecdotal literature is filled with success stories. Many people with type 2 diabetes report that chromium supplements led to a dramatic improvement in blood sugar control. In fact, natural medicine practitioners view type 2 diabetes as a sign that one is deficient in chromium. It is also very useful for people who suffer from hypoglycemia. Natural sources of chromium include black pepper, brewer's yeast, cheese, clams, corn oil, calves' liver, chicken, lean meat, whole-grain cereals, and thyme. Chromium supplements range from 25 to 200 micrograms daily for adults, but do not begin this supplement without consulting first with your diabetes practitioner. Many people with type 2 diabetes combine chromium with vanadium (discussed next) to manage their blood sugar levels without the use of other medications or insulin.

Vanadium

Also a trace mineral, vanadium is said to copy the biological action of insulin, which means it reportedly helps your body use insulin more effectively. It is stored in our fat, liver, kidneys, and bones, and its biologically active form is vanadyl sulfate. Vanadium can be used to control blood sugar levels for people with type 2 diabetes, and when used with chromium, can become an alternative therapy under the supervision of a diabetes practitioner. The action of vanadium is blocked by tobacco, so if you smoke, this mineral cannot be utilized by the body. Natural sources of vanadium are black pepper, dill seeds, olives, radishes, and whole grains. Vanadium reportedly aids bones and teeth and lowers cholesterol. Vanadium should not be taken as a supplement; instead vandyl sulfate, the absorbable, biologically active form, can be used solely under the supervision of a doctor. High levels of vanadium can be toxic, and it is not recommended if you are taking lithium for any reason.

Aromatherapy

Essential oils, comprised from plants (mostly herbs and flowers), are meant as a complementary therapy that has no real downside since it is at worst harmless but pleasant. Many essential oils are known for their medicinal effects. The easiest way to use essential oils is in a warm bath; you simply drop a few drops of the oil into the bath, and sit and relax in it for about ten minutes. The aroma can also be inhaled (put a few drops of the oil in a bowl of hot water, lean over with a towel over your head, and breathe); diffused (using a lamp ring or a ceramic diffuser—that thing that looks like a fondue pot); or sprayed into the air as a mist. You can also rub the oils onto the soles of your feet (where the largest pores are), which will get them working fast! If you have type 2 diabetes, the following essential oils are reported to help normalize blood sugar levels: dill (this supports pancreas functioning and helps normalize insulin levels); cinnamon, fennel, and geranium (these also help support the pancreas); and coriander, cypress, eucalyptus, ginger, hyssop, juniper, lavender, rosemary, and ylang-ylang.

When Your Doctor Prescribes Insulin

Let me dispel a common fear about insulin: since insulin is not a blood product, you don't have to worry about being infected with a blood-borne virus such as HIV or hepatitis when injecting insulin.

Many doctors delay insulin therapy for as long as possible by giving you maximum doses of the pills discussed earlier in this chapter. This isn't considered good diabetes management according to top diabetes experts. If you need insulin, you should take insulin. The goal is to get your disease under control. Therefore, anyone with type 2 diabetes with the following conditions is a candidate for insulin:

- High blood sugar levels, despite maximum doses of pills for diabetes
- High fasting glucose levels
- Illness or stress (insulin may be needed until you recover)
- Major surgery
- Complications of diabetes
- Pregnancy (insulin may be needed temporarily)

If going on insulin will affect your job security, you should discuss this issue with your doctor so that appropriate notes or letters can be drafted to whomever it may concern. You should also keep in mind that if insulin therapy does not bring your diabetes under control within six months of treatment, it may be necessary to return to your oral drug therapy.

You can walk into any pharmacy in the world, identify yourself as a person with diabetes, and get at least one dose of insulin over the counter. This policy is designed for emergencies, since people can damage or lose insulin while traveling, and so on. Insulin is not a patented drug, which is one reason it remains an over-the-counter product. It is also not the sort of product that people would want unless they had diabetes. By supplying it over the counter, it remains a life-giving product that is not withheld from those in need; that doesn't mean it's given out free, but it is given out *hassle-free*, without the need to reach your doctor for permission.

The Right Insulin

The goal of a good insulin program is to try to mimic what your pancreas would do if it were working properly. Blood sugar rises in a sort of wave pattern. The big waves come in after a big meal; the small waves come in after a small meal or snack. The insulin program needs to be matched to your own particular wave pattern. So what you eat—and when—has a lot to do with the right insulin program. Therefore, the right insulin for someone who eats three square meals a day may not be appropriate for someone who tends to "graze" all day. And the right insulin for an active forty-seven-year-old man in a stressful job may not be the right insulin for a sixty-seven-year-old woman who does not work and whose heart condition prevents her from exercising regularly.

You and your health-care team will also need to decide how much control you need over your blood sugar. Insulin "recipes" depend on whether you need tight control (72 to 108 mg/dl), medium control (72 to 180 mg/dl), or even loose control (198 to 234 mg/dl). Loose control is certainly not encouraged, but on rare occasions, when a person is perhaps quite elderly and suffering from a number of other health problems, it is still done. To determine the appropriate insulin recipe for you, your health-care team should look at who you are as a person—what you eat, where you work (do you work shifts?), your willingness to change your eating habits, and other lifestyle factors.

There are many kinds of insulins available. Every manufacturer has a different brand name of insulin and a separate letter code for the insulin action. To make things as easy to understand as possible, the upcoming sidebar "Breaking the Codes" provides a translation of all these codes. Once you and your diabetes health-care team choose the right insulin for you, you will need to have a minicourse on how to use and inject insulin. This is usually done by a certified diabetes educator (CDE).

Insulin Brands

As you can see, insulin is highly individualized. It's simply not possible for me to tell you in this book which insulin you need to be on any more than I can tell you what, exactly, you need to eat each day. This is why a diabetes health-care team is so crucial. Your meal plans, medications, and insulin (when needed) are tailored to suit you. And that has everything to do with who you are, not which brand of insulin is popular. The following is a description of what's available as of this writing.

Human Insulin

All human insulin is biosynthetic, which means that the biochemically created product normally made by the human pancreas has been re-created in a test tube through DNA technology.

Today, most manufacturers produce only these insulins, which are considered the purest form of insulin available. Human insulins come in four different actions: immediate-acting, short-acting (clear fluid), intermediate-acting (cloudy fluid), and long-acting (cloudy fluid). Short-acting means that it stays in your body for the shortest duration of time; long-acting means that it stays in your body for the longest duration of time. (See the upcoming section, "Getting to Know Your Insulin," for details.)

Insulin Analogues

An insulin analog is a synthetic insulin that does not have an animal or human source. With traditional human insulins, you need to be extremely good at calculating when you're going to eat, how much you're going to eat, and how much insulin to inject. Basically, you need to be in excellent control of your diabetes. The problem with traditional, longer-acting insulin is that you can wind up with too much of it in your system, which can cause insulin shock, or hypoglycemia (low blood sugar, see Chapter 8). Insulin lispro (Humalog) and insulin aspart (NovoLog) are immediate-acting insulins: you inject them about fifteen minutes before you eat (while cooking dinner or when ordering food). Therefore some experts consider an insulin analog an easier insulin to work with.

A slow-acting insulin analog, called glargine (Lantus), is available in the United States. The benefit of glargine over human long-acting insulin is that it starts working in two hours, but has no peak, and has a duration of eighteen to twenty-four hours. That means you can eat at anytime after injecting it.

Premixed Insulin

Premixed insulin is short-acting insulin and intermediate-acting insulin mixed together. These are extremely popular insulins for people with type 2 diabetes for reasons explained in the section "Getting to Know

Your Insulin." They work well for people who have a very set routine and don't want to take more than one or two insulin injections daily.

Premixed insulins are labeled as 10/90 (10 percent short-acting; 90 percent intermediate-acting), 20/80, 30/70, 40/60, and 50/50. Premixed insulin is always cloudy. It's also possible to mix together short-acting with long-acting, or long-acting with intermediate-acting.

Pork Insulin

Eli Lilly still makes pure pork insulin. For information about obtaining it, contact your doctor or pharmacist.

Learning to Use Insulin

Insulin must be injected. It cannot be taken orally because your stomach acids would digest the insulin before it has a chance to work. Your doctor or a registered nurse (frequently a CDE is a registered nurse, too) will teach you how to inject yourself painlessly. Don't inject insulin by yourself without a training session. One convenient way to use insulin is with an insulin pen, but not all insulin can be used with the pen. If you use the pen, your insulin (if human or biosynthetic) will come in a cartridge. If you are not using a pen, your insulin will come in a bottle and you will need a needle and syringe. Always know the answers to the following questions before you inject your insulin:

- How long does it take before the insulin starts to work? (Known as the *onset of action.*)
- When is this insulin working the hardest? (Known as the *peak.*)
- How long will my insulin continue to work? (Known as the *duration of action.*)

How Many Injections Will I Need?

This really depends on what kind of insulin you're taking and why you're taking it. A sample routine may be to take an injection in the morning, a second injection before supper, and a third before bed. What you want to prevent is low blood sugar while you're sleeping. You may need to adjust your insulin if there is a change in your food or exercise routine (which could happen if you're sick). Your insulin schedule is usually carefully matched to your mealtimes and exercise periods.

Where to Inject It

The good news is that you do not have to inject insulin into a vein. As long as it makes it under your skin (but *not* in your muscle), you're fine. This is called a *subcutaneous injection*. Thighs and tummies are popular injection sites. These areas are also large enough that you can vary your *injection site*. (You should space your injections about an inch apart.) Usually you establish a rotating pattern. Other injection sites are the upper outer area of the arms, the upper outer surfaces of the buttocks, and lower back areas.

Insulin injected in the abdomen is absorbed more quickly than insulin injected in the thigh. In addition, strenuous exercise will speed up the rate of absorption of insulin if the insulin is injected into a limb you've just worked out. Other factors that can affect insulin's action is the depth of injection, your dose, the temperature (it should be room temperature or body temperature), and what animal your insulin came from (human or pig). A hardening of skin due to overuse will affect the rate of absorption.

Your doctor or CDE will show you how to actually inject your insulin (angles, pinching folds of skin, and so on). There are lots of tricks of the trade to optimize comfort. With the fine needle points available today, injection doesn't have to be an uncomfortable ordeal. The needle length also affects the absorption rate; the longer the needle, the deeper it goes, and the faster it's absorbed. With shorter needle lengths, patient advocates with diabetes recommend leaving the needle in for about five seconds to increase the rate of absorption.

Side Effects

The main side effect of insulin therapy is low blood sugar, which means that you must eat or drink glucose to combat symptoms. This side effect is also known as *insulin shock*. Low blood sugar or hypoglycemia is discussed in Chapter 8.

A rare side effect is *lipodystrophy* (a change in the fatty tissue under the skin) or *hypertrophy* (an enlarged area on your skin). Rotating your injection sites will prevent these problems. A sunken area on your skin surface may also occur, but usually only when using animal insulin. Rashes can sometimes occur at injection sites, too. Less than 5 percent of all insulin users notice these problems.

Questions to Ask About Insulin

The answers to the following questions will depend on your insulin brand. Pharmacists and doctors should know the answers to all these questions, but if they don't, call the customer care toll-free number provided by your insulin manufacturer.

- How do I store this insulin?
- What are the characteristics of this insulin (that is, onset of action, peak, and duration of action)?
- When should I eat after injecting this insulin?
- When should I exercise after injecting this insulin?
- How long are opened insulin bottles or cartridges safe at room temperature?
- What about the effect of sunlight or extreme temperatures on this insulin?
- Should this insulin be shaken or rolled?
- What should I do if the insulin sticks to the inside of the vial or cartridge?
- Should this insulin be clear or cloudy? And what should I do if the appearance looks "off" or has changed?
- What happens if I accidentally inject out-of-date insulin?
- What other medications can interfere with this particular brand?
- Who should I see about switching insulin brands?
- If I've switched from animal to human insulin, what dose should I be on?

Your Insulin Gear

If you've graduated to insulin therapy, here's what you'll need to buy:

- A good glucose meter that is made for people who test frequently
- Lancets and a lancing device for testing your blood sugar
- Insulin pens and cartridges (this is far easier) or traditional needles and syringes (a diabetes educator will need to walk you through the types of products available)
- The right insulin brand for you

Traveling with Insulin Post 9/11

The realities of traveling with needles in your carry-on baggage is that you might wind up being searched, delayed, or even detained by security at various airports unless you take the following precautions. This is especially true if you're flying out of the United States.

First, make sure you pack identification in the form of a doctor's note that clearly states you have diabetes. In fact, many experts suggest that for a trip, you switch to an insulin pen, if you can. (Again, not all insulins work with the pen.) Transport authorities recommend that you should clearly state to all security personnel that you have diabetes and are carrying your supplies on board. Have your letter in hand, and Medic-Alert bracelet or card for security to inspect.

Next, organize your supplies in your carry-on luggage so that they are easy to get at for searching. *You must ensure that you have needle guards in place, and your needles must be accompanied by the insulin in order for you to pass through security.* Your insulin and other diabetes medications must be in a container with a professionally printed label from your pharmacy, clearly identifying what it is. If the pharmacy places its label on the outside of the box containing the insulin, the insulin must be carried in the original packaging. All lancets must be capped and must be accompanied by a glucose meter that has the manufacturer's name imprinted on the meter. Prior to traveling outside of the country, contact the airlines and find out what precautions they require in order for you to pass through security with your supplies. Medical experts further advise:

- Bring a day's supply of food to anticipate delays.
- Pack an extra sugar source, such as dextrose tablets.
- Carry a list of hospitals in your travel destination areas.
- Keep your insulin with you; never pack it in checked luggage.
- Drink lots of liquids prior to boarding, as well as one glass of nonalcoholic liquid for every hour of flight.
- Avoid ordering a special meal because if it doesn't come, you don't get a meal. Pick at the food they give you and supplement with your own food.
- Stroll up and down the cabin as much as possible to avoid high blood sugar. (This bit of exercise will use up some sugar.)
- Consult your doctor or diabetes educator about adjusting insulin injections to different time zones.

Getting to Know Your Insulin

Rapid-Acting Insulin

Rapid-acting insulin is the "roadrunner": it gets there fast, but disappears quickly.

- Starts working in five to fifteen minutes
- Peaks in thirty to ninety minutes (premixed Humalog: forty-five minutes to two and a half hours)
- Duration of action: three and a half to four and a half hours (premixed Humalog: eighteen to twenty-four hours)
- When to eat: within ten minutes of injecting
- Peak effect (maximum action): thirty to ninety minutes
- Exits body in five to eight hours
- Appearance: clear. Don't use if cloudy, slightly colored, or if solid chunks are visible.

Short-Acting Insulin

Short-acting insulin is the "hare": it gets there fast but tires easily.

- Starts working in thirty minutes (insulin lispro or insulin aspart in under five to fifteen minutes)
- Peaks in two to four hours (insulin lispro or insulin aspart peaks in thirty to ninety minutes, or up to two and a half hours)
- Duration of action: six to eight hours (insulin lispro or insulin aspart peaks in three and a half to four and a half hours)
- When to eat: within thirty minutes of injecting (insulin lispro or insulin aspart: within ten minutes of injecting)
- Peak effect (maximum action): an hour and a half to five hours
- Exits body in eight hours
- Appearance: clear. Don't use if cloudy, slightly colored, or if solid chunks are visible.

Intermediate-Acting Insulin

Intermediate-acting insulin is the "tortoise": it gets there at a slower pace, but it lasts longer.

- Starts working in one to two hours (premixed any combination: thirty to sixty minutes)
- Peaks in four to twelve hours (usually around eight or less; premixed any combination: two to twelve hours)
- Duration of action: twenty-four hours or less (premixed any combination: eighteen to twenty-four hours)
- When to eat: within two hours
- Exits body in twenty-four hours
- Appearance: cloudy. Do not use if the white material remains at the bottom of the bottle after mixing, leaving a clear liquid above; or if clumps are floating in the insulin after mixing; or if it has a "frosted" appearance. (To learn the

Breaking the Codes

Here is a translation of the brand names and letter codes for insulins from various manufacturers:

- *Insulin Lispro or Insulin Aspart.* These are rapid-acting insulin analogs, which start to work in five to fifteen minutes. Lispro goes by the brand name *Humalog* and Aspart goes by the brand name *NovoLog* in the United States.
- *R or Toronto.* These are both short-acting insulins, or regular biosynthetic human insulins. *R* stands for "regular." Toronto is simply the regular insulin made by Connaught-Novo, which was developed in Toronto, hence its name.
- *N, NPH, Lente, L.* These are intermediate-acting insulins. *NPH* (shortened to *N* sometimes) stands for *neutral protamine Hagadorn* (the man who invented this insulin). *Lente* (shortened to *L* sometimes) is very similar to NPH except it has a more "lumbering" peak. NPH is said to have an "abrupt" peak.
- *Novolin Ultra or Ultra Lente.* These are both long-acting insulin. Both start acting in four hours, but Novolin peaks within eight to twenty-four hours, and exits in twenty-eight; Ultra Lente peaks in ten to thirty hours and exits in thirty-six hours.
- *Beef/Pork.* This was animal insulin made from cows or pigs. Beef is no longer available. Pure pork is still available through Eli Lilly.
- *Premixed Insulin (%R%N).* This is a premixed insulin, meaning that it is a mixture of some percentage of regular and some percentage of NPH. The combinations available are 10 percent regular and 90 percent NPH; and in the same order: 20/80, 30/70, 40/60, and 50/50. (Note: Many people with type 2 diabetes do well on 30/70.)
- *ge.* Sometimes you may see these letters, which stand for *genetically engineered.*

correct appearance of a premixed insulin, any combination, please ask your pharmacist.)

Long-Acting Insulin

Long-acting insulin is the "two-legged turtle": it's very slow, and it hangs around for a long time.

- Starts working in eight hours (glargine: two hours)
- Peaks in eighteen hours (glargine: no peak)
- Duration of action: thirty-six hours (glargine: eighteen to twenty-four hours)
- When to eat: within eight hours (glargine: anytime)
- Exits body in thirty-six hours or more (glargine: twenty-four hours)
- Appearance: cloudy. Do not use if the white material remains at the bottom of the bottle after mixing, leaving a clear liquid above; or if clumps are floating in the insulin after mixing; or if it has a "frosted" appearance. (To learn the correct appearance of glargine, ask your pharmacist or doctor.)

8

Preventing
Hypoglycemia

WHEN YOU'RE DIAGNOSED with type 2 diabetes, whether your treatment revolves around lifestyle modification, oral hypoglycemic therapy, or insulin therapy, you may experience an episode of low blood sugar. This is clinically known as *hypoglycemia*. Hypoglycemia can sometimes come on suddenly, particularly overnight. If left untreated, it can result in coma, brain damage, and death. Hypoglycemia is considered the official cause of death in about 5 percent of the type 1 diabetes population. In the past, hypoglycemia was a more common problem among people with type 1 diabetes. But since 40 to 50 percent of all people with type 2 diabetes will eventually graduate to insulin therapy, the incidence of hypoglycemia has increased by 300 percent in this group. Moreover, hypoglycemia is a common side effect of oral hypoglycemic pills, the medication the majority of people with type 2 diabetes take when they are first diagnosed.

This chapter will explain exactly what happens when you have low blood sugar, who's at risk, how to treat hypoglycemia, and how to avoid it.

The Lowdown on Low Blood Sugar

Any blood sugar reading below 72 mg/dl is considered too low. (Some literature states that blood sugar readings below 70 mg/dl are too low.) A hypoglycemic episode is characterized by two stages: the warning stage and what I call the actual hypoglycemic episode. The warning stage occurs when your blood sugar levels *begin* to drop and can occur as early as a blood sugar reading of 108 mg/dl in people with typically higher than normal blood sugar levels. When your blood sugar drops to 72 mg/dl or less, you are officially hypoglycemic.

During the warning stage, your body responds by piping adrenaline into your bloodstream. This causes symptoms such as trembling, irritability, hunger, and weakness, some of which mimic drunkenness. The irritability can simulate the rantings of someone who is drunk, while the weakness and shakiness can lead to the lack of coordination seen in someone who is drunk. For this reason, it's crucial that you carry a card or wear a bracelet that identifies that you have diabetes. Your liver will also release any glucose it has stored for you, but if it doesn't have enough glucose to get you back to normal, there won't be enough glucose for your brain to function normally and you will feel confused, irritable, or aggressive. When the brain is deprived of glucose, it begins to starve, a condition known as *neuroglycopenia*.

Once your blood sugar is 72 mg/dl and falling, you'll notice a more rapid heartbeat, trembling, and sweating. As the levels become lower, your pupils will begin to dilate, you will begin to lose consciousness, and you could perhaps experience a seizure. No one with diabetes is immune to hypoglycemia; it can occur in someone with long-standing diabetes just as much as in someone newly diagnosed. The important thing is to be alert to the warning signs, be prepared, and try to avoid future episodes.

Who's at Risk?

Since hypoglycemia can be the result of too high an insulin dose, it is often called *insulin shock* (or *insulin reaction*). This is a misleading term, however, because it implies that only people who take insulin can become hypoglycemic. For the record, all people with type 1 or type

2 diabetes can become hypoglycemic. If you are taking more than one insulin injection a day, you are at greater risk of developing hypoglycemia. Hypoglycemia can be triggered just as easily by

- Delaying or missing a meal or snack (see Chapter 6)
- Drinking alcohol (see Chapter 6)
- Exercising too long or too strenuously (without compensating with extra food)
- Taking too high a dose of a biguanide, such as a sulphonylurea, which can happen if you lose weight but are not put on a lower dose of your pill (see Chapter 7)

If You Take Pills

All people taking sulfonylureas (see Chapter 7) are vulnerable to hypoglycemia because this drug stimulates the pancreas to produce insulin. It is synonymous with taking an insulin injection. Furthermore, if you lose weight after you begin taking sulfonylureas, but don't lower your pill dosage, you could also experience hypoglycemic episodes. That's because losing weight will make your body more responsive to insulin.

Yet biguanides do not typically cause hypoglycemic episodes, since they work by preventing the liver from making glucose rather than stimulating insulin production. Similarly, acarbose does not, by itself, cause hypoglycemia. It works by delaying the breakdown of starch and sucrose into glucose. That's not to say, however, that hypoglycemia can't happen to you if you're taking biguanides or acarbose; you can still develop it if you miss meals or snacks or overexercise without compensating for it, although this is rare.

As discussed in Chapter 7, your diabetes pills may also react with other medications. For example, some of the older agents may work less or more effectively when combined with certain medications including blood thinners (anticoagulants), oral contraceptives, diuretics, steroids, aspirin, and various anticonvulsive and antihypertensive medications.

Another factor is the "half-life"—how long it remains in your body—of your oral medication. By knowing when the drug peaks in your body, you'll be able to prevent hypoglycemia from occurring.

Combination Therapy

Roughly 40 percent of all people taking a combination of insulin secretagogues experience hypoglycemic episodes, while 33 to 47 percent of people who combine insulin with sulfonylureas experience hypoglycemic episodes. These are higher odds than if you were taking only one oral hypoglycemic agent.

Recognizing the Symptoms

If you can begin to recognize the warning signs of hypoglycemia, you may be able to stabilize your blood sugar before you lose consciousness. Watch out for the adrenaline symptoms: initially hungry and headachy, then sweaty, nervous, and dizzy. Those who live with you or spend a lot of time with you should learn to notice sudden mood changes (usually extreme irritability, drunk-like aggression, and confusion) as a warning that you are "low."

One of the best examples of hypoglycemia symptoms on film is in the movie *Steel Magnolias*, in which Julia Roberts portrays a woman with type 1 diabetes opposite Sally Fields, who plays her mother. At the local beauty parlor, amidst happy chatter over Roberts's upcoming wedding, her character suddenly becomes aggressive and begins to verbally attack her mother, shaking all the while. The other customers look alarmed. Sally Fields realizes at once that Roberts is "low" and calmly takes over the situation. She grabs Roberts and calms people down. "It's all right, it's all right, she's just low. With all the excitement that's gone on, it's only natural. Get me some juice."

"I have a candy in my purse," pipes up a customer.

"No," insists Fields. "Juice is better, juice is better." Roberts becomes even more upset. Her reaction is sheer confusion and fright. Fields takes the juice and starts to feed her; Roberts, in confusion, spits it out and puts up a fight every step of the way. After Fields force-feeds her a little longer, Roberts starts to drink on her own and finally utters an intelligible sentence. "Oh, she's making some sense now," coos Fields. "Yes, she is. She's starting to make sense." In other words, Roberts's blood sugar is beginning to rise and the hypoglycemic symptoms that appeared out of nowhere are starting to dissipate. In this scene, Fields says "juice is better" because it is a more immediate source of glucose. But in fact, juice is *not* a good idea when someone is resist-

Symptoms of Hypoglycemia

Symptoms from Adrenaline	Starved-Brain Symptoms
Trembling	Difficulty concentrating
Palpitations (racing heart)	Confusion
Anxiety	Weakness
Hunger	Drowsiness
Nausea	Vision changes
Tingling	Dizziness
Tiredness	

- *Mild hypoglycemia.* You feel only the adrenaline symptoms (in left column) and can still help yourself or self-treat.
- *Moderate hypoglycemia.* You feel symptoms from both columns but can still think clearly enough and function enough to self-treat.
- *Severe hypoglycemia (blood sugar is below 51 mg/dl).* You feel symptoms from both columns and cannot think clearly enough or function properly to self-treat and need help from another person. Unconsciousness may also occur.

ing it; in this case, it is better to use glucose gel rather than risk someone aspirating or inhaling the juice when it is force-fed.

Whether you notice your own mood changes or not, you, too, will feel suddenly unwell. This is a warning that your blood sugar is low. Reach for your snack pack (see the section "A Snack Pack" later in this chapter). Not everyone experiences the same warning symptoms, but here are some signs to watch for:

- Pounding, racing heart
- Fast breathing
- Skin turning white
- Sweating (cold sweat in big drops)

- Trembling, tremors, or shaking
- Goosebumps or pale, cool skin
- Extreme hunger pangs
- Lightheadedness (feeling dizzy or that the room is spinning)
- Nervousness, extreme irritability, or a sudden mood change
- Confusion
- Feeling weak or faint
- Headache
- Vision changes (seeing double or blurry vision)

Some people will experience no symptoms at all. If you've had a hypoglycemic episode without any warning symptoms, it's important for you to eat regularly and to test your blood sugar. If you're experiencing frequent hypoglycemic episodes, it's important to find out why it keeps happening so you can adjust meal plans and activities accordingly. In some cases of long-standing diabetes and repeated hypoglycemic episodes, experts note that the warning symptoms may not always occur. It's believed that in some people, the body eventually loses its ability to detect hypoglycemia and send adrenaline. Furthermore, if you've switched from an animal to human insulin, warning symptoms may not be as pronounced.

Juice Is Better

If you start to feel symptoms of hypoglycemia, stop what you're doing (especially if it's active) and have some sugar. Next, test your blood sugar to see what it reads. Eating some regular food will usually do the trick. If your blood sugar is below 72 mg/dl, ingest some glucose. If you can drink and swallow, Sally Fields was right: real fruit juice is better when your blood sugar is low. The best way to get your levels back up to normal is to ingest simple sugar; that is, sugar that gets into your bloodstream fast. Half a cup of any fruit juice or one-third of a can of a sugary soft drink is a good source of simple sugar. Artificially sweetened soft drinks are useless. *It must contain fifteen grams of simple carbs or real sugar.* If you don't have fruit juice or soft drinks handy, here are some other sources high in simple sugar:

- Two or three tablets of commercial dextrose, sold in pharmacies. If you're taking acarbose or combining it with an oral hypoglycemic agent or insulin, the only sugar you can have is dextrose (Dextrosol or Monoject), due to the rate of absorption.
- Three to five hard candies (or about six Life Savers)
- Two teaspoons of white or brown sugar (or two sugar cubes)
- One tablespoon of honey

Once you've ingested enough simple sugar, your hypoglycemic symptoms should disappear within ten to fifteen minutes. Test your blood sugar ten minutes after having the sugar to see if your blood sugar levels are coming back up. If your symptoms don't go away, have more simple sugars until they do.

After a Low

If you've had a close call to the point where you experienced those adrenaline symptoms, be sure to have a snack or meal as soon as possible. If your next meal or snack is more than an hour away, eat half a sandwich or some cheese and crackers. That will ensure that your blood sugar levels don't fall again. Then check your blood sugar levels after you eat to make sure your levels are where they should be. Try to investigate the cause of your episode by asking yourself the following:

- Did you miss a meal or eat late? (Were you at one of those dinner parties where you came on time but everybody else arrived an hour later?)
- Did you eat less than normal? (Are you sick or upset over something?)
- Did you give yourself the right amount of pills or insulin?
- Did you do anything physically active that you didn't plan in the last hour or so? (For instance, did someone ask you to help move some heavy object from one side of the room to the other?)
- Did you remember to compensate for any exercising you did with the appropriate amount of carbohydrates?

Glucagon

Most people will be able to treat their low blood sugar without becoming unconscious, but on rare occasions, it can happen. And if that's the case, it's too late for juice, soft drinks, or any other kind of sugar. That's when something known as a *glucagon kit* comes in. Glucagon is particularly useful for people who have little or no warning symptoms of low blood sugar and have previously lost consciousness from low blood sugar.

Glucagon is a hormone injected under the skin. Like insulin, glucagon is destroyed by the digestive system when it's taken orally. Glucagon causes an increase in blood glucose concentration; it basically stimulates the body to make glucose. It does this by forcing the liver to convert all its glycogen stores into glucose almost immediately after it's injected. You'll need about one milligram of glucagon to do the trick. Injected under the skin, glucagon takes eight to ten minutes to work its wonders.

Glucagon will make you nauseous when you come to, so if glucagon is injected, it's crucial to ingest simple sugars as soon as you wake. The simple sugar will replace the glycogen your liver releases and will get rid of the nausea. Once you feel normal again, you should consume regular food. Get a prescription for a glucagon kit through your doctor; then purchase the kit at any pharmacy.

If you do not respond to glucagon, glucose will be administered intravenously in a hospital or ambulance.

People in a state of starvation (for example, anorexics) or who have chronic hypoglycemia will not benefit from glucagon because in those cases, there will be no glycogen stores in the liver ready for conversion into glucose.

The Third Person

The glucagon kit is for another person to use, someone who has been shown how to administer the drug to revive you. This may be someone close to you who is likely to be with you when you lose consciousness. The kit should have all the necessary instructions regarding giving injections. But here are the instructions just in case. Photocopy these instructions and post them in a safe place:

1. Inject one milligram of glucagon anywhere under the skin. (The abdomen or thighs are good spots.) For children five and under, half a milligram of glucagon is recommended.
2. Call 911, he or she will likely regain consciousness in fifteen minutes.
3. After the person wakes up, immediately give her or him about half a cup of fruit juice or a third of a can of a sugary soft drink. The drink must contain sugar; artificially sweetened drinks will not work.
4. Continue feeding the drink to this person until he or she feels well enough to eat regular food.

Recipe for Prevention

The recipe for preventing hypoglycemia or low blood sugar is the same as for preventing high blood sugar: frequent blood sugar monitoring (Chapter 7), following your meal plan (Chapter 6), following an exercise plan, and taking your medication as prescribed (Chapter 7). Any changes in your routine, diet, exercise habits, or medication dosages should be followed by a period of very close blood sugar monitoring until your routine is more established.

Frequent episodes of hypoglycemia may also be a sign that your body is changing: You may be losing weight, thanks to those lifestyle changes you've made, and the dosage of pills that was prescribed to you when you weighed 190 pounds may be too strong now that you're down to 145 pounds. Or you may be taking too high an insulin dose.

A Snack Pack

People with type 1 or 2 diabetes should have a snack pack with them for emergencies or for unplanned physical activity. The pack should contain all of the following:

- Juice (two or three boxes or cans)—in a pinch, you can substitute two cans of a soft drink sweetened with real sugar
- One package of dextrose tablets (alternatively, a bag of hard candies)

- Protein and carbohydrates (for example, packaged cheese and crackers)
- A card that says "I have diabetes"
- Glucagon, if you suffer from repeated episodes

Tell People You Have Diabetes

A crucial word about dealing with hypoglycemia: tell people close to you, or who work closely with you, that you have diabetes. You never know when you might experience symptoms: at a family function (weddings are notorious for delaying meals), at work, and so on. If you tell people about the symptoms of hypoglycemia and instruct them on what to do, you'll have more bases covered in case you experience an episode.

9

A Woman's Heart
and Diabetes

THE MOST IMPORTANT thing to grasp about diabetes complications is
that there are two kinds of problems that can lead to similar diseases.
The first kind of problem is known as a *macrovascular complication*.
The prefix *macro* means "large"; the word *vascular* means "blood vessels"—the veins and arteries that carry the blood back and forth
throughout your body. Put it together and you have "large blood vessel complications." A plain-language interpretation of *macrovascular
complications* would be "big problems with your blood vessels."

If you think of your body as a planet, a macrovascular disease
would be a disease that affects the whole planet; it is body-wide, or
systemic. Cardiovascular disease is a macrovascular complication that
can cause heart attack, stroke, high blood pressure, and body-wide
circulation problems, clinically known as *peripheral vascular disease*
(PVD). Peripheral vascular disease refers to "fringe" blood-flow problems and is part of the heart disease story. PVD occurs when blood
flow to the limbs (arms, legs, and feet) is blocked, creating cramp-
ing, pain, or numbness. *Pain and numbing in your arms or legs may*
be signs of heart disease or even an imminent heart attack.

Macrovascular complications are caused by too much blood sugar
and preexisting health problems. People with type 2 diabetes are far

more vulnerable to macrovascular complications because they usually have contributing risk factors, such as high cholesterol and high blood pressure (see Chapter 1). Obesity, smoking, and inactivity can aggravate these problems, resulting in major cardiovascular disease and leaving the individual at risk for heart attack or stroke. *When the terms* heart disease *or* cardiovascular disease *are used, they refer to your risk of heart attack and stroke.* Specifically, the term *atherosclerotic cardiovascular disease (ASCVD)* refers to fatty blockages of blood vessels anywhere in the body. When they occur in the coronary arteries that feed the heart muscle, they put you at risk for a heart attack. When ASCVD occurs in blood vessels in the brain, they put you at risk for having a *stroke*, in which part of the brain fed by the blocked blood vessel dies. When ASCVD affects arteries that feed your arms or your legs, it causes *peripheral vascular disease.* In addition, some people have heart disease that may not be related to ASCVD that affects the way the heart beats. The health problems that increase the risk of heart failure are the same problems that cause other heart problems: hypertension and clogged arteries from atherosclerotic cardiovascular disease (ASCVD), which are worsened by obesity, smoking, and diets high in saturated fat. Heart valve defects, caused by infections, also can result in heart failure. Some unfortunate people catch a virus infection of their heart that weakens it to the point of causing heart failure. In the absence of a heart valve problem, most people with heart failure already have underlying significant heart disease and hypertension, and may also have diabetes or chronic lung disease (from smoking).

Understanding Heart Attacks

A heart attack is clinically known as a *myocardial infarction (MI)*. *Myocardium* is the heart muscle. An MI occurs when there is not enough, or any, blood supply to the myocardium, such as when one of the coronary arteries that supply blood to the heart muscle is blocked. Roughly 90 percent of heart attacks are due to a blood clot. A variety of symptoms can occur during a heart attack, and women have different symptoms than men.

Heart disease is currently the number one cause of death in postmenopausal women; more women die of heart disease than of lung cancer or breast cancer. Half of all North Americans who die from heart attacks each year are women. In women with type 2 diabetes, that risk is at least doubled, if not tripled. Preventing heart disease after menopause may require taking cholesterol-lowering or blood pressure–lowering medication.

One of the reasons for such high death rates from heart attacks among women is medical ignorance: most early studies of heart disease excluded women. This led to a myth that more men than women die of heart disease. In fact: more men die of heart attacks before age fifty, while more women die of heart attacks after age fifty—as a direct result of estrogen loss. Moreover, women who have had oophorectomies (removal of the ovaries) prior to natural menopause are eight times more likely to have a heart attack than those who don't. Since more women work outside the home than ever before, a number of experts cite stress as a huge contributing factor to increased rates of heart disease in women.

Women also have different symptoms than men when it comes to heart disease, and the "typical" warning signs we know about in men—angina or chest pains—are often never present in women. In fact, chest pains in women are almost never related to heart disease. For women, the symptoms of heart disease and heart attack can be much more vague, seemingly unrelated to heart problems. Signs of heart disease in women can be surprising. Some of the symptoms are the same as in men, but some are completely different:

- Shortness of breath and/or fatigue
- Jaw pain (often masked by arthritis and joint pain)
- Pain in the back of the neck (often masked by arthritis or joint pain)
- Pain down the right or left arm
- Back pain (often masked by arthritis and joint pain)
- Sweating (this is also a classic sign of an overactive thyroid gland, so get your thyroid checked and test your blood sugar as it may be low)
- Fainting
- Palpitations (also a classic symptom of an overactive thyroid)
- Bloating (after menopause, this is a sign of coronary artery blockage)

- Heartburn, belching, or other gastrointestinal pain (this is often a sign of an actual heart attack in women)
- Chest "heaviness" between the breasts (this is how women experience "chest pain"; some describe it as a "sinking feeling" or burning sensation; also described as an "aching, throbbing, or squeezing sensation," "hot poker stab between the chest," or feeling like your heart jumps into your throat)
- Sudden swings in blood sugar
- Vomiting
- Confusion

Clearly, there are many other causes for the symptoms on this list, including low blood sugar. But it's important that your doctor includes heart disease as a possible cause, rather than dismissing it because your symptoms are not "male" (which your doctor may use as a point of reference). Bear in mind that if you're suffering from nerve damage, you may not feel a lot of these symptoms. Therefore, you should be suspicious of anything that feels out of the ordinary.

If you're diagnosed with heart disease, the "cure" is prevention through diet and exercise. Estrogen no longer is believed to protect women from heart disease.

Recovering from a Heart Attack

You can recover from a heart attack, but the damage resulting from the heart attack greatly depends on how long the blood supply to the heart muscle was cut off. The longer the blood supply was cut off, the more damage you will suffer. We all know that a heart attack is a major cause of death, but it can also leave you with varying degrees of disability depending upon the severity of the attack. For example, roughly half of all heart attack survivors will continue to have heart-related problems, which include reduced blood flow to the heart, called *ischemia*, and chest pains. As a result, the lifestyle you once enjoyed will need to change: your diet will need to be restricted to a "heart smart" diet (see Chapter 5), and you will need to reduce lifestyle stress and incorporate more activity into your routine. If you don't make these changes, the risk of repeated heart attacks is higher and can greatly affect your quality of life.

You may also feel more fatigued and winded after normal activities when recovering from a heart attack. Successful recovery greatly depends on the severity of the attack and lifestyle changes you make after the episode. The same medical strategies designed to prevent a first heart attack can also be used to avoid recurrent episodes.

Preventing Cardiovascular Disease

The way to prevent heart disease and peripheral vascular disease is by modifying your lifestyle: stop smoking, improve your diet, and exercise. Smoking, high blood pressure, high blood sugar, and high cholesterol (called the "catastrophic quartet" by one diabetes specialist) will greatly increase your risk of heart disease.

Heart Surgery

You also can reduce your risk of a heart attack or stroke by undergoing heart surgery, which ranges from minor surgical procedures such as angioplasty to major heart bypass surgery.

Angioplasty, also known as coronary balloon surgery, was developed in Zurich in 1977. This operation involves inserting a catheter through your skin into the coronary artery. The catheter has a balloon on the end, which is inflated once inside. The inflated balloon squashes the plaque that is blocking the artery, easing blood flow. The balloon also widens the artery by stretching it. Several inflations may be necessary, but it is successful about 70 percent of the time. As your blood flow improves, so does your overall health. There is about a 5 percent risk of having a heart attack during the procedure. About 25 percent of the time, the artery is too narrow for the catheter to fit or too clogged for angioplasty to work.

Laser angioplasty is the same procedure, except a laser is passed through the catheter and dissolves the plaque. This is a good way to handle very narrowed arteries or arteries that are too hardened with plaque for balloon angioplasty to work.

The first successful coronary artery bypass surgery was performed by a heart surgeon in 1967 in Cleveland. Since then, it has become a fairly standard surgery. Here, a vein from your leg is removed and connected to the aorta as it leaves the heart; the other end is connected to the coronary artery, just before the blockage. The vein acts as a bridge between the two, enabling the blood to flow, thus fixing the blood flow problem. The risk of a heart attack during this procedure is about 10 percent higher than with angioplasty, but after five years, 70 percent of bypass patients still enjoy an active life and are free from any symptoms of heart disease. Not everyone is a good candidate for this surgery; you'll need to discuss the risks of undergoing the surgery in light of your overall health with your health-care team.

Lower Your Blood Pressure

High blood pressure, or *hypertension*, is discussed in Chapter 1, along with blood pressure–lowering drugs (also called antihypertensive medications).

Lower Your Cholesterol

High cholesterol, or *hypercholesterolemia*, is also discussed in Chapter 1, along with cholesterol-lowering drugs.

Drugs That Prevent Platelet Clumping: Antiplatelet Therapy

Sometimes confused with anticoagulants (blood thinners), antiplatelet drugs prevent platelet clumping due to "stickiness." The best-known drug in this category is aspirin. Recent studies have shown that aspirin is just as effective in preventing heart attacks in women as it is in men. Other drugs reduce platelet clumping, too, but aspirin is available over the counter. *Anticoagulants*, also called blood thinners, are not as useful for preventing heart attack as they are for preventing strokes. Anticoagulants dissolve clots. Table 9.1 describes the various types of cardiovascular drugs.

Quit Smoking

This is discussed in Chapter 1.

Reduce Stress

There's no question about it: stress can lead to heart disease. Stress management is a complex topic, but the principles of stress management involve reorganizing your priorities so you can reduce chronic

Table 9.1 *Making Sense of Cardiovascular Drugs*

Drug Category	Also Called	Used for	Common Types
Antihypertensives	Blood pressure–lowering drugs	Lowering blood pressure	Diuretics
			*Beta-blockers
			Alpha-blockers
			Centrally acting agents
			*Calcium channel blockers
			ACE inhibitors
			Angiotensin receptor blockers (ARBs)
			*Vasodilators
Antihyperlipidemics	Cholesterol-lowering drugs	Lowering cholesterol/triglycerides	Niacin
			Statins
			Fibrates
			Resins
Anticoagulants	Blood thinners	Preventing stroke; dissolving clots	Warfarin
			Heparin
Thrombolytic agents	Clot busters	Dissolving clots	Plasminogen activators
Antiplatelet thereapy		Preventing heart attacks	ASA (aspirin)
			Clopidogrel (Plavix)

*Vasodilators are also used to relieve angina and palpitations.
Source: Compiled from the *Compendium of Pharmaceuticals and Specialties*, 2001.

stress as well as incorporating some healing strategies to help combat acute stress. Finding ways to downshift—work less, take more time off, reduce "e-stress," incorporate hands-on healing (get a massage!) eat better, exercise, and generally care for yourself through simple things such as getting enough sleep, for example—can dramatically reduce your current stress and improve your overall cardiovascular health.

Understanding Stroke

Cardiovascular disease also puts you at risk for a "brain attack" or stroke, which occurs when a blood clot (a clog in your blood vessels) travels to the brain and stops the flow of blood and oxygen to the nerve cells around the brain. When that happens, cells may die and vital brain functions can be temporarily or permanently damaged. Bleeding or a rupture from the affected blood vessel can lead to a very serious situation, including death. People with type 2 diabetes are two to three times more likely to suffer from a stroke than people without diabetes. About 80 percent of strokes are caused by the blockage of an artery in the neck or brain, known as an *ischemic stroke*; the remainder are caused by a burst blood vessel in the brain.

Since the 1960s, the death rate from stroke has dropped by 50 percent. This drop is largely due to public awareness campaigns regarding diet and lifestyle modification (quitting smoking, eating less fat, and exercising), as well as the introduction of blood pressure–lowering drugs and cholesterol-lowering drugs that help people maintain normal blood pressure and cholesterol levels (see Chapter 1).

Strokes can be mild, moderate, severe, or fatal. Mild strokes may affect speech or movement for a short period of time only; many people recover from mild strokes without any permanent damage. Moderate or severe strokes may result in loss of speech, memory loss, and paralysis; many people learn to speak again and learn to function with partial paralysis. How well you recover depends on how much damage was done.

Signs of a Stroke

If you can recognize the key warning signs of a stroke, it can make a difference by reducing the severity of a stroke. Call 911 or go to a hospital emergency room if you suddenly notice one or more of the following symptoms:

- Weakness, numbness, and/or tingling in your face, arms, or legs, especially on one side of the body; this may last only a few moments
- Loss of speech or difficulty understanding somebody else's speech; this may last only a short time
- Confusion
- Severe headaches that feel different from any headache you've had before
- Feeling unsteady, falling a lot
- Trouble seeing in one or both eyes

If you have any of these signs of stroke, it's important to get to the hospital as soon as possible. There are treatments that can reduce the severity of the damage caused by the stroke, making the difference between partial or severe disability and full recovery. For example, there are drugs that can dissolve clots, known as *tissue-type plasminogen activators* (TPA), such as reteplase or streptokinase, which are proteins derived from bacteria. Plasminogen activators made from recombinant DNA technology are alteplase and anistreplase. Anticoagulants, such as Coumadin, can also dissolve clots.

Common Disabilities Caused by Stroke

Stroke is responsible for a range of functional and physical disabilities, especially in people over forty-five. Depending on the severity of the stroke, your general health, and the rehabilitation process involved, the following impairments may dramatically improve over time:

- Weakness or paralysis on one side of the body. This may affect the whole side or just the arm or leg. The weakness or paralysis is always on the opposite side of the body from where the stroke occurred. So if the stroke affected the right side of the brain, you will experience the weakness or paralysis on the left side of your body. Paralysis may affect the face, an arm, a leg, or the entire side of the body. Walking, grasping objects, and the ability to swallow can be impaired as a consequence of one-sided paralysis.

- Muscle spasms or stiffness
- Problems with balance and/or coordination
- Problems understanding, speaking, and writing in your first language, which is called *aphasia*. This is a common problem, affecting about 25 percent of stroke survivors. At least one-fourth of all stroke survivors experience language impairments. It can take two forms: problems comprehending others, or problems articulating one's own words. Stroke survivors may be able to think clearly, but are unable to make the words "come out right," resulting in disconnected gibberish when they try to speak. The most severe form of aphasia is called *global aphasia*, which results in the loss of all language abilities: the person is not able to understand or communicate in any language. There is also a form of very mild aphasia, called *anomic aphasia*, where language is mostly unaffected, except for a few words that may be forgotten selectively, such as names of people or particular kinds of objects.
- Inability to respond to bodily sensations on one side of the body (called *bodily neglect*). This means that the ability to feel, touch, or sense pain or temperature can be lost. There may be no recognition of the person's own limb—an arm or leg may not be "noticeable" anymore.
- *Paresthesia*, (pain, numbness, or odd sensations) can be the result of damage to the nervous system, or *neuropathic* pain. Stroke survivors who have a paralyzed arm, for example, may feel as though the pain is radiating outward from the shoulder. The lack of movement causes the joint to be fixed or "frozen." Physical therapy can help to alleviate this. Pain can also result from a confused signal from the damaged brain, causing pain to be felt in the opposite side of the body.
- Difficulty remembering, thinking, focusing, or learning. Extremely short attention spans, combined with short-term memory loss, can make it difficult for stroke survivors to learn new tasks, make plans, or engage in a complex discussion. Often the ability to connect a thought to an action is lost.
- Unawareness of the stroke's effects. A stoke survivor may be paralyzed on one side, but not acknowledge the paralysis and have no awareness of the impairment, or the fact that a stroke has taken place.

- *Dysphagia* or difficulty swallowing
- Loss of bladder or bowel control. The ability to sense bladder or bowel urge may be lost, or simply the mobility required to go to the bathroom may be the obstacle. Incontinence becomes less severe with time. Physical therapists can help stroke survivors strengthen their pelvic muscles through special exercises. And by following a timed voiding schedule, incontinence may be solved. In other cases, people can learn to use catheters to prevent other incontinence-related health problems from developing.
- Fatigue
- Mood swings/personality changes. Natural feelings of anger, anxiety, and frustration can cause extreme mood swings or even personality changes in stroke survivors. Anger is frequently taken out on loved ones, family, or friends.
- Depression. A mild depression can become a major depression when the stroke survivor loses all engagement and interest in life, losing weight, not sleeping properly, and showing other physical manifestations. Sometimes antidepressants are necessary if counseling is not effective because of language difficulties.

Recovering from Stroke

According to the National Stroke Association in the United States, 40 percent of all stroke survivors experience moderate to severe impairments that require special care. Ten percent will need to be placed in a facility or nursing home, while 25 percent of stroke survivors have only minor disabilities that enable them to care for themselves. Ten percent will survive the stroke and completely recover with no long-term effects, and the remaining 15 percent of stroke sufferers die shortly after the stroke. Fourteen percent of all stroke survivors, regardless of their level of recovery, will have another stroke.

Stroke survivors may recover in long-term care facilities within hospitals or a separate rehabilitation hospital. Many receive home care through outpatient programs or various institutions. The crucial part of stroke rehabilitation is timing: it should begin as soon as a stroke survivor is stable, which is often within twenty-four to forty-eight hours after a stroke. Early stroke rehabilitation doesn't imply a rigorous physical therapy program. Because paralysis or weakness on one side is so often the result of the stroke, it's important to get stroke survivors moving again by helping them change positions frequently while lying in bed, or having a physical therapist move impaired limbs (called *passive range-of-motion exercises*). Helping survivors progress to sitting up in bed or transferring them to a chair from a bed are all part of rehabilitation. Eventually, many may be able to stand, bearing their own weight, or walk with or without assistance. Early rehabilitation also includes helping stroke survivors with bathing, dressing, and using a toilet.

The Recovery Team

There are many health-care providers who may become involved in stroke recovery. The recovery team can include your primary care physician, health-care specialists in physical medicine and rehabilitation, neurologists, internists, geriatricians (specialists in elder care), and rehabilitation nurses, who specialize in nursing care for people with disabilities.

One of the most important steps in stroke recovery is receiving good physical therapy. Physical therapists help survivors learn to use their impaired limbs by teaching them how to compensate for their disabilities with other ways to move, or by preventing the impaired parts of the body from wasting away further through disuse. An occupational therapist helps stroke survivors find new ways to complete self-directed tasks, such as dressing, cooking, cleaning, and gardening.

Another important recovery team member is the speech-language pathologist, who helps stroke survivors relearn language or develop new ways to communicate. They coach conversations by helping survivors develop prompts or cues to remember words; they may use sign language, symbol boards, or computers as language aids. (Voice-synthesizer products may be especially useful for people recovering from stroke.) Difficulties with swallowing can be improved through helping with swallowing reflexes, helping the stroke survivor to manipulate food with the tongue, finding better eating positions, or by encouraging different eating habits such as taking small bites and chewing slowly.

To help stroke survivors adjust to the emotional problems that may follow a stroke (such as despair or depression), social workers, psychologists, or psychiatrists may also be needed on your recovery team.

Preventing Another Stroke

Preventing another stroke involves the same strategies as preventing a heart attack recurrence. Obesity, inactivity, and especially smoking spell another stroke unless you make some lifestyle changes. You're also at greater risk for another stroke if you have:

- High blood pressure (hypertension)
- Restricted blood flow (ischemia)
- Heart disease
- Celebrated your sixty-fifth birthday
- High cholesterol

Cardiovascular disease, which leads to heart attack and stroke, is certainly the most common disease caused by macrovascular or large blood vessel complications. But most of the other notorious diabetes complications (eye disease, kidney problems, sexual dysfunction, foot problems) result when restricted blood flow from macrovascular complications results in nerve damage, known as diabetic neuropathy, discussed in the next chapter.

10

A Woman's Nerves and Diabetes

IN THE LAST chapter, we discussed one type of complication in type 2 diabetes called *macrovascular complications* (large blood vessel complications). A second type of complication is a *microvascular complication*. *Micro* means "tiny"; microvascular complications are problems with the smaller blood vessels (*capillaries*) that connect to various body parts. The problem is serious, but—if you think of your body as a planet—it's not going to affect the whole planet, just one region. Nerve damage (*neuropathy*) is a microvascular complication that targets body parts such as the feet, eyes, genitals, and skin. And, unlike macrovascular complications, you're not going to have a sudden life-threatening event such as heart attack or stroke from microvascular problems. For example, eye disease (see Chapter 11), clinically known as *retinopathy*, is a microvascular complication. Blindness is a serious problem, but you won't die from it.

People with type 1 diabetes are more vulnerable to microvascular complications, but many people with type 2 diabetes suffer from them, too. Microvascular complications are known as the sugar-related complications. The small blood vessel damage is caused by high blood sugar levels over long periods of time. The Diabetes Control and Complications Trial, referred to earlier in this book, showed that microvascular complications can be prevented by frequently self-testing to keep blood sugar levels as normal as possible.

Understanding Diabetic Neuropathy

When your blood sugar levels are too high for too long, you can develop *diabetic neuropathy* or *nerve disease*. Somehow, the cells that make up your nerves are altered in response to high blood sugar. Different groups of nerves are affected by high blood sugar; keeping your blood sugar levels as normal as possible is the best way to prevent many of the following problems. Drugs that help to prevent chemical changes in your nerve cells can also be used to treat nerve damage.

Types of Neuropathy

Polyneuropathy is a disease that affects the nerves in your feet and legs. The symptoms are burning, tingling, and numbness in the legs and feet. This, combined with poor circulation, is what can lead to amputations in extreme cases, as explained later in this chapter.

Autonomic neuropathy is a disease that affects the nerves you don't notice: the nerves that control your digestive tract, bladder, bowel, blood pressure, sweat glands, overall balance, and sexual functioning. Treatment varies depending on what's affected, but drugs can help individual parts of the body, such as the digestive tract.

Proximal motor neuropathy is a disease that affects the nerves that control your muscles. It can lead to weakness and burning sensations in the joints (hands, thighs, and ankles are the most common). These problems can be individually treated with physiotherapy and/or specific medication. When the nerves that control the muscles in the eyes are affected (see Chapter 11), you may experience problems with your vision, such as double vision. Finally, nerve damage can affect the spine, causing pain and loss of sensation to the back, buttocks, and legs.

Nerve Damage from Head to Toe

This section provides an overview of the body parts most commonly affected by diabetic neuropathy, listed in order from head to toe. This list is not exhaustive as there are hundreds of nerve-related problems that can occur. These are the major conditions that affect people with type 2 diabetes.

Eyes

For details on eye and vision problems caused by diabetes see Chapter 11.

Gastrointestinal Tract (GI Tract)

When high blood sugar levels affect your nerve cells, the nerves that control your entire gastrointestinal tract may be affected as well. In fact, 30 to 50 percent of people with diabetes suffer from *dysmotility*, a condition in which the muscles in the digestive tract become uncoordinated, causing bloating, abdominal pain, and reflux (heartburn). This is known as *gastroparesis*.

What Is Your GI Tract?

Imagine that your digestive tract is one long subway tunnel with different stops. If you were to look at the GI "subway map," the first stop is your mouth. The next stop is your pharynx, and the third stop is your esophagus. The esophagus is a major connecting stop. This is where the train stops for a while before switching tracks and moving on to the more active parts of your gut: the stomach, which connects to your duodenum, which connects to your small intestine, which connects to the last stop on the line, your large intestine.

Swallowing your food triggers all the muscles in your digestive tract to begin contracting in wavelike motions known as *peristalsis*. The act of swallowing is voluntary, but once the food is down the throat, the rest of the movement through the digestive tract is involuntary, or beyond our control. Our nervous system takes over. The food goes down the throat into the pharynx and into the esophagus. The esophagus connects your throat to your stomach.

In order for your food to get from the esophagus to the stomach, it must go through a crucial tunnel known as the *lower esophageal sphincter* (*LES*). When you swallow your food, the LES relaxes to allow your food to pass from the esophagus into the stomach. This is necessary in order to prevent your digested food from backing up into the esophagus.

The stomach is an accordion-like bag of muscle and other tissue near the center of the abdomen just below the rib cage. The bag expands to accommodate food and shrinks when it is empty. The stomach is a holding tank for your food until it can pass through to the rest of the gastrointestinal tract.

In the same way that the larger coffee grinds stay in the filter, the larger solid particles of food go from the stomach into the duodenum for further digestion, while the mushy, nicely worked over food remnants from the stomach will quickly pass from the duodenum into the next section of the small intestine (also called the *midgut*, or small bowel). The small intestine is usually called just that, but technically it has three parts: the duodenum, jejunum, and ileum.

The series of tubes that make up your GI tract empty food particles from one into the next. This process depends on continuous movement, known as *motility*, which is controlled by nerves, hormones, and muscles. If you're experiencing problems with other parts of your body, the motility can be slowed down (you'll be constipated and bloated) or speeded up (you'll have diarrhea).

By the time your food gets into the small intestine, the food is mushed up by the digestive secretions of your stomach, pancreas, and biliary tract. All this mush stays in the small intestine for a relatively long period of time, and all the usable nutrients are absorbed through the intestinal walls. These nutrients include digested molecules of food, water, and minerals from the diet. The waste products are sent to the large intestine (also called the colon or large bowel), where they sit around for about a day or two before they are expelled in the form of stools.

Diabetic nerve disease affects the GI tract above the colon—everything from the esophagus to the small intestine. A number of things can go wrong north of the colon because hundreds of nerves and secretions (hormones, enzymes, and chemicals that help to break down your food into usable nutrients) go to work for us whenever we eat. If even one hormone or enzyme is "off" in your system, there will be consequences. There are upper GI disorders and lower GI disorders. The upper GI disorders, which can be caused by diabetic nerve disease, can include heartburn/reflux, which is a symptom of a larger problem of dysmotility, also known as *gastroesophageal reflux disease (GERD)*. Diabetic nerve disease can also cause problems south of the colon, where muscles controlling the bowel become uncoordinated, causing them to open, leak stool, and allow bacteria to grow abnormally in the colon, resulting in bacterial-related diarrhea. This can be controlled with antibiotics.

Understanding Dysmotility

Dysmotility means "things not moving very well." Food travels from your esophagus into your stomach, which slowly releases it into the small intestine. There can be problems at any or all "stops" of this subway. Things can get stuck between the esophagus and stomach, causing symptoms of heartburn and reflux. In this case, the lower esophageal sphincter relaxes when it should be taut, allowing food to come back up. Or things can get stuck between the stomach and small intestine, which causes symptoms of bloating, early fullness, and gas. So when things aren't moving very well, you can have a lot of discomfort. This is known as a *motility disorder*.

Dysmotility, with all of its varying symptoms, is typically a very chronic condition. Symptoms keep coming back, and by the time dysmotility is finally diagnosed, most people have had these symptoms for a long time. The only way you can stop symptoms from recurring is by changing certain lifestyle habits (losing weight, quitting smoking, and staying in control of blood sugar levels may improve your condition) or taking a motility drug as a maintenance drug. If your dysmotility goes on for a long time, it could also lead to inflammation of the esophageal lining, a condition known as *esophagitis*. This can lead to a narrowing of the esophagus. (When your esophagus is inflamed, it narrows, just the way your shoes are suddenly too tight when your feet expand.)

Understanding Heartburn/Reflux

As described earlier, your food must pass from your esophagus into your stomach through the lower esophageal sphincter, which opens and closes through involuntary muscular contractions. If you have diabetic nerve disease, the sphincter may not shut completely after dumping the ingested food particles into the stomach. When that happens, the food, now bathed in your stomach acid, can actually come back up the sphincter, causing a burning sensation in your chest, and even a spreading pain throughout your neck and arms, which may even be mistaken for a heart attack. You can also experience nausea, belching, and regurgitation of that half-digested food. Thanks to the acid and enzymes it's been exposed to, the food will taste sour and bitter in your throat. The problem will be aggravated when you bend forward or lie down. You may even find that after an experience like this, you wake up with a sore throat. This problem is clinically called *acid reflux*, and in lay terms it is known as *heartburn* or *acid indigestion*.

Reflux usually lasts about two hours. Most people find that standing up relieves the burning; that's because gravity helps. You could also take an antacid to clear acid out of the esophagus. Not everyone will experience the same degree of heartburn. Reflux can be mild, moderate, or severe. It all depends on why it's occurring, how often it occurs, when it occurs, and how much food backup you have. But for the most part, chronic reflux is the first sign of a more serious underlying health problem such as dysmotility or GERD.

Skin

High blood sugar levels, combined with poor circulation, put the skin—on your whole body—at risk for infections ranging from yeast infections to open wound–related infections. You may form scar tissue or develop strange yellow pimples (a sign of high fat levels in the blood), boils, or a range of localized infections. Yeast infections, which typically plague women, can develop not just in the vagina (see the section "Genitals"), but in the mouth (called *thrush*), under the arms, or wherever there are warm, fatty folds. And all skin, whether on the feet or elsewhere, can become dry and cracked, requiring a daily regimen of cleaning, moisturizing, and protecting.

Kidneys

Diabetic kidney disease is very serious and requires a separate chapter, see Chapter 12.

Gallbladder

The gallbladder stores bile for the liver. But you don't really need the gallbladder because the liver is large enough to store as much bile as you'd ever want or need anyway. Nevertheless, we do come equipped with this extra storage space. Bile isn't a very reliable product to store because it can form into little stones inside the gallbladder, known as *gallstones* or *calculi*. When your gallbladder isn't emptying properly, a process controlled by nerves and one that can be impaired with diabetic nerve disease, you can form gallstones. Symptoms occur when the stones become large enough to obstruct the bile ducts. When this happens, you have *gallbladder disease*.

The symptoms of a gallbladder attack are quite severe; you'll feel sudden, intense pain in the upper abdominal region (which may shoot into your back), often after a fatty meal, but it may not be related to meals. Vomiting frequently brings relief, although nausea is not a symptom. The pain may then subside over several minutes or hours. Many people mistake gallstone symptoms with heartburn or a heart attack.

The obstruction can become infected or even gangrenous, which is a dire emergency (you don't want gangrene inside your abdominal cavity!). Usually gallbladder disease presents itself as a series of gallbladder attacks in which you'll feel the pain after a meal and, if there's infection, may even experience a fever. The attacks will become progressively worse until you decide to have the darned thing removed! As a rule, any abdominal pain accompanied by a fever means there is some sort of serious infection going on, which warrants emergency medical attention.

Because of other factors, such as estrogen, gallbladder problems are much more common in women than men (one in five women after age fifty versus one in twenty men), and is also common in women who are on hormone replacement therapy after menopause. Estrogen-containing oral contraceptives are also associated with gallstones.

Since the late 1980s, gastroenterologists have been able to widen the ducts with endoscopy to allow the gallstones to pass, avoiding major surgery in people who are not up to it or who do not want it. Removal of the gallbladder is called a *cholecystectomy*, one of the most common surgical procedures performed. Millions have their gallbladders removed annually for a variety of reasons, not all of which are related to diabetes.

Bladder

Nerves that control the bladder can be affected, which causes you to lose your sense of bladder urge and your ability to force a bladder contraction (to urinate voluntarily). Ultimately this can lead to incontinence as urine will start to leak out. Women can also suffer from repeated urinary tract infections caused by insufficient emptying of the bladder, resulting in bacteria overgrowth. Learning to go to the bathroom on a schedule (every four hours or so), instead of waiting for the urge, is one solution. Drugs can also increase the force of bladder contraction if your problem involves the inability to force bladder contraction.

When a bacterial bladder infection spreads to your kidneys, it is called *pyelonephritis*, causing inflammation. The symptoms of this are similar to a bladder infection (cystitis), but you may have a fever, pain in the flank, nausea, or vomiting in conjunction with your cystitis symptoms. A urine culture will be able to identify pyelonephritis, and this requires urgent referral to a urologist to prevent a serious kidney infection. Pyelonephritis is four to five times more common in women with diabetes.

Genitals

At least 30 percent of women with diabetes suffer from sexual dysfunction. Nerve damage can also affect arousal for women. Special nerve fibers and blood vessels that connect to the clitoris, vaginal wall, and vulva are necessary for achieving orgasm and lubrication. If you have sustained nerve damage, you may notice a loss of sensation in your genital area, which can be a frustrating experience. Estrogen therapy and lubricants may help, as well as trying different positions to increase arousal.

Vaginal dryness has a domino effect: the dryness itself can increase your vulnerability to yeast infections. Dry vaginas can be torn during intercourse, and the resultant wounds are vulnerable to yeast infection. High blood sugar levels also increase the amount of sugar in the vaginal walls, which can also cause yeast infections.

Sexual dysfunction in women is also related to nerve damage to the bladder. When the bladder is not emptied sufficiently, it leads to bacterial bladder infections, which make sex uncomfortable. Since type 2 diabetes often coincides with menopause, many women will notice a compromised libido anyway due to natural estrogen loss in menopause, which can be aggravated by nerve damage. Or vice versa. Antibiotics prescribed to women for the purposes of clearing up the bladder infection can predispose them to yeast infections, too, a classic side effect that all women can experience when they take antibiotics for any reason.

Yeast infections are caused by *Candida albicans*, a one-cell fungus. Under normal circumstances, candida is always in your vagina, mouth, and digestive tract. It is a friendly fungus. For a variety of reasons, candida will overgrow and reproduce too much of itself, changing from a harmless one-cell fungus into long branches of yeast cells, called *mycelia*. This is known as *candidiasis*.

Generally, any changes to your vagina's normal acidic environment can make you vulnerable to candidiasis. The list of factors that affect your vaginal environment is quite long. High blood sugar levels increase the amount of sugar stored in the vaginal cell walls, and yeast *loves* sugar. In fact, women who suffer from chronic yeast infections are encouraged to be screened for diabetes because yeast infections are so common in women with diabetes.

Anything that interferes with the immune system will make yeast thrive, too. Antibiotics, for example, not only kill the harmful bacteria, but also often the friendly bacteria that are always in the vagina and which are necessary to fend off infection.

Severe itching and a curdlike or cottage-cheesy discharge are classic symptoms of candidiasis. The discharge may smell like baking bread, fermenting yeast, or even brewing beer. If the discharge is foul-smelling or fishy, you can rule out yeast. The discharge may also be thinner and mucuslike, but it is always white. Other symptoms are swelling, redness, and irritation of the outer and inner vaginal lips, painful sex, and painful urination due to an irritation of the urethra.

When yeast is in the throat, it is called *thrush*. Thrush usually occurs in immune-deficient women (they may be HIV-positive or undergoing cancer treatments). Thrush is unsettling because the mouth and throat are coated with a milky-white goop. It can also be present in newborns, when yeast-infected mothers give birth. Thrush is treated orally with nystatin drops. Since yeast is present in the intestines, HIV-positive women can develop severe, life-threatening esophageal yeast infections.

Vaginal yeast infections are so common that over-the-counter anti-fungal agents in creams, suppositories, or pill form are available at all drugstores. A doctor will confirm yeast by taking a culture swab.

Plain yogurt, also an antifungal, is the best way to fend off yeast naturally. Simply eat a small container of any kind of yogurt daily; so long as it has active bacterial culture, any brand is fine. Alternatively, you can take *Lactobacillus acidophilus*, which is generally available in capsule form at any drugstore. If you find that you have thrush, citrus seed extract (Citricidal) and tea-tree oil can be used as a gargle.

Following an antiyeast diet may also be helpful. Certain foods interfere with the vagina's acidity, something you need to prevent yeast infections. The diet entails avoiding the following: sugar, honey, maple syrup, molasses, and any foods that contain them; alcoholic beverages; vinegars and foods containing vinegar such as pickled foods, salad dressings, mustard, ketchup, and mayonnaise; moldy nuts, such as peanuts, pistachios, and cashews; soy sauce, miso, and other fermented products; dairy food with the exception of butter, buttermilk, and yogurt; coffee, black tea, and sweetened soda; dried fruit; and processed foods.

Try to incorporate more of the following foods to compensate: whole grains such as rice, millet, barley, and buckwheat; breads, crackers, and muffins that are yeast-free and preferably wheat-free; raw or cooked fresh vegetables; fish, chicken, and lean meats (organically fed and hormone- and antibiotic-free); nuts and seeds that are not moldy; and fruit in moderation (limiting sweeter fruits).

There are some other ways to avoid yeast infections as well:

• Don't wear tight clothing around your vagina. Tight pants, panties, and nylon pantyhose prevent your vagina from breathing and make it warmer and moister for yeast. Wear looser pants that allow your vagina to breathe, switch to knee-highs or old-fashioned stockings (make sure these are not tight so they don't interfere with circulation), or wear pantyhose only for special occasions. And go bottomless to bed to let air into your vagina.

• Wear only 100 percent cotton clothing and/or natural fibers around your vagina. Synthetic underwear and polyester pants are not good ideas. All-cotton underwear and denim, wool, or rayon pants that are loose fitting are fine.

• Avoid vaginal deodorants or sprays. These products are unnecessary and disturb the vagina's natural environment, which is fully designed to self-clean.

• Don't douche unless it's for purely medicinal purposes. Douching can push harmful bacteria up higher into the vagina, disturb the vagina's natural ecosystem, or interfere with a pregnancy. Always a bad idea!

• Watch your toilet habits. Always wipe from front to back with toilet paper. When you do it the other way around, you can introduce fecal material and germs into your vagina. After a looser bowel movement, wet the toilet paper and clean your rectal area thoroughly so that fecal material doesn't stay on your underwear and wind up in your vagina.

• Don't insert anything into a dry vagina. Whether it's a penis or a tampon, make sure your vagina is well lubricated before insertion.

• Avoid using tampons.

• Avoid long car trips on vinyl seats. Vinyl seats increase a woman's risk of developing a yeast infection because the vinyl traps moisture and doesn't allow the crotch area to breathe.

Foot Complications

Your feet are the targets of both macrovascular (large blood vessel) complications and microvascular (small blood vessel) complications. In the first case, peripheral vascular disease affects blood circulation to your feet. In the second, the nerve cells to your feet, which control sensation, can be altered through microvascular complications. Nerve damage can also affect your feet's muscles and tendons, causing weakness and changes to your foot's shape.

What Happens to Your Feet

The combination of poor circulation and numbness in your feet means that you can sustain an injury to your feet and not know it. For example, you might step on a piece of glass or badly stub your toe and not realize it. If an open wound becomes infected and you have poor circulation, the wound will not heal properly, and infection could spread to the bone or gangrene could develop. In this situation, amputation may be the only treatment. Or, without sensation or proper circulation in them, your feet could be far more vulnerable to frostbite or exposure than they would be otherwise. Diabetes can also cause your feet to thicken as a result of poor circulation. In this case the skin on the foot becomes very thin and blood vessels are visible through the skin, which has a shiny appearance and looks red. Thinner skin can be more easily pierced and infected.

As if this weren't enough for your feet, they can also be damaged by bone loss: osteoporosis of the feet! Diabetes can cause your body to take more calcium from bones. Because there are twenty-six bones in your foot alone, bone loss in the foot can weaken it, and it can break more easily or become deformed with bigger arches and a clawlike toe. All of this can cause calluses that can get infected, leading to gangrene and amputation, too.

Diabetes accounts for approximately half of all nonemergency amputations, but all experts agree that doing a foot self-exam every day (described later in this chapter) can prevent most foot complications from becoming severe. Those most at risk for foot problems are people who smoke (smoking aggravates *all* diabetic complications) or who are overweight (overweight people with diabetes have a 5 to 15 percent risk of undergoing amputation during their lifetime). Roughly 80 percent of foot amputations could be prevented with proper foot care.

Signs of Foot Problems

The most common symptoms of foot complications are burning, tingling, or pain in the feet or legs. These are all signs of nerve damage. Numbness is another symptom that could mean nerve damage or circulation problems. If you experience pain from nerve damage, it usually gets worse with time (as new nerves and blood vessels grow), and many people find that it's worse at night. Bed linens can increase discomfort. Some people notice foot symptoms only after exercising or a short walk. But many people don't notice immediate symptoms until they've lost feeling in their feet.

Other symptoms are frequent infections (caused by blood vessel damage), hair loss on the toes or lower legs, and shiny skin on the lower legs and feet. Foot deformity or open wounds on the feet are also signs.

When You Knock Your Socks Off

When you take off your socks at the end of the day, get in the habit of doing a foot self-exam. This is the only way you can do damage control on your feet. You're looking for signs of infection or potential infection triggers. If you can avoid infection at all costs, you will be able to keep your feet. Look for the following signs:

- Reddened, discolored, or swollen areas (blue, bright red, or white areas mean that circulation is cut off)
- Pus
- Temperature changes in the feet or "hot spots"
- Corns, calluses, and warts (potential infections could be hiding under calluses; do not remove these yourself—see a podiatrist)
- Toenails that are too long, which can cut you
- Redness where your shoes or socks are rubbing due to a poor fit; when your sock is scrunched inside your shoe, the folds could rub against the skin and cause a blister.
- Toenail fungus under the nail
- Fungus between the toes, called *athlete's foot*, is common if you've been walking around barefoot in a public place.
- Breaks in the skin, especially between your toes, or cracks, such as in calluses on the heels; these open the door for bacteria.

If you find an infection, wash your feet carefully with soap and water; *don't use alcohol*. Then see your doctor or a podiatrist as soon as possible. If your foot is irritated but not yet infected (redness, for example, from poor-fitting shoes but no blister yet), simply avoid the irritant—the shoes—and it should clear up. If not, see your doctor. If you're overweight and have trouble inspecting your feet, get somebody else to check them for the signs listed above. In addition to doing a self-exam, see your doctor to have the circulation and reflexes in your feet checked four times a year.

Foot Steps

By following these "foot steps," you can prevent diabetes foot complications:

Do

- Walk a little bit every day; this is a good way to improve blood flow and get a little exercise!
- Check your shoes before you put them on: shake them out in case something such as your (grand)child's Lego piece, a piece of dry cat food, or a pebble is in there.
- Trim your toenails straight across to avoid ingrown nails. Don't pick off your nails. Use only a nail clipper, and be sure not to cut into the corners of the nails. Use a nail file or emery board to smooth or round rough edges.
- Place your feet flat on the floor when sitting down. Sitting cross-legged or in crossed-legged variations can cut off your circulation—even in people without diabetes.
- Wear comfortable, proper-fitting footwear.
- Avoid heat. Extreme heat, such as heating pads, very hot water, and even hot sun can cause swelling or burn your feet.
- If you're overweight, lose some weight; it puts less pressure on your feet.

Don't

- Don't walk around barefoot; wear proper-fitting, clean cotton socks with your shoes daily, and do wear slippers around the house. If it's cold out, wear woolen socks. At the beach, wear swim shoes, plastic "jellies," or canvas running shoes.
- Do not perform "bathroom surgery" on your feet, such as puncturing blisters or shaving calluses. Instead, see a podiatrist as needed.

- Do not wear clothing that restricts blood flow to your legs and feet, including girdles, garters, tight pantyhose, or socks that cut off the circulation.
- Do not use over-the-counter medications to treat corns and warts. These can be dangerous for people with diabetes.
- Do not soak your feet or take very hot baths; the heat can cause swelling or burns, especially if your feet are insensitive.
- Do not use lotion between your toes because the moistness can promote fungal infections.
- Do not wear tight socks, garters or elastics, or knee-highs that decrease circulation to your feet.
- Do not wear over-the-counter insoles; they can cause blisters if they're not right for your feet.
- Do not sit for long periods of time; check with your doctor if you have to take a long flight.
- Do not smoke.

Open Wounds

Open wounds on the feet are also called *foot ulcers* and affect millions with diabetes; about 20 percent of diabetes-related foot ulcers don't heal, leading to amputation to prevent gangrene. Any tear in the skin can lead to an open wound that becomes infected. Blisters, cracks in the feet from dryness, and stepping on something sharp are the most common causes of open wounds.

Healing Open Wounds

The first order of business is removing the source of irritation that caused the sore, such as bad shoes or poor hygiene (see "Foot Steps" earlier). In many cases antibiotics can heal the wound, as well as dressing the wound well (cleaning it, using proper bandages, and so on). Keeping pressure off the feet can also help to heal them. Often healing a foot ulcer requires home care; you may need to have a nurse or home health-care worker come into your home and dress your wound.

The Foot Self-Exam (FSE)

Ever heard of a breast self-exam? Well, this is a foot self-exam you can do, which I've compiled from different sources. Do this each day and you can prevent serious foot complications.

- Look for redness. Redness is a sign of irritation or pending breaks in the skin.
- Look for breaks in the skin, which include blisters or cracks, especially between the toes. They can become infected.
- Look for calluses, which can turn into sores or blisters.
- Look for changes in foot shape, such as deformity.
- Look for signs of swelling, which could also indicate fluid retention related to kidney disease (see Chapter 12).
- Wash your feet and lower legs every day in lukewarm water with mild soap. Dry them really well, especially between the toes.
- Baby your feet. When the skin seems too moist, use baby powder or a foot powder your doctor or pharmacist recommends (especially between the toes). When your feet are too dry, moisturize them with a lotion recommended by your doctor or pharmacist (avoid applying lotion between your toes). The reason is simple: breaks in the skin happen if feet are too moist (such as between the toes) or too dry (indicated by cracking). Use a gentle foot-buffing pad on your calluses after bathing.

When Wounds Don't Heal

Not all open wounds heal. To heal cuts, sores, or any open wound, your body normally manufactures *macrophages*, special white blood cells that fight infection, as well as special repair cells, called *fibro-*

blasts. These "ambulance cells" need oxygen to live. If you have poor circulation due to peripheral vascular disease (see Chapter 9), it's akin to an ambulance not making it to an accident scene in time because it gets caught in a long traffic jam.

When wounds don't heal, gangrene infections can set in. Until recently, amputating the infected limb was the only way to deal with gangrene. But *hyperbaric oxygen therapy (HBO)* may help. The procedure involves placing you in an oxygen chamber or tank and feeding you triple the amount of oxygen you'd find in the normal atmosphere. To heal gangrene on the feet, you'd need about thirty treatments—several per day for a week or so. The result is that your tissues become saturated with oxygen, enabling the body to heal itself. In a research trial in the 1990s, 89 percent of diabetics with foot gangrene were healed, compared to 1 percent of the control group. Not everybody is an HBO candidate, and not everybody has access to this therapy. But if you're being considered for surgical amputation, you should definitely ask about HBO first.

There are wound-healing products on the market. One is "replaceable skin" called Dermagraft, which is made of skin cells that are grown in a lab. Dermagraft is applied once a week to the wound and actually replenishes the skin. Another product, Regranex, contains natural growth factors found in our skin cells and comes in a gel applied once a day to jump-start healing. These products don't always work, but are a good option for wounds that won't heal.

When You Require an Amputation

When you require an amputation to stop a gangrene infection, there are a few ways you can maximize your health prior to surgery; they'll also help you heal after surgery.

First, quit smoking. Smoking restricts your blood vessels, as I've said many times in this book. You need your blood vessels to be as healthy as possible prior to surgery and after.

The next step is to review with your surgeon the risks of general anesthetic over what's called *continuous epidural anesthetic*, which has lower risks. Discuss whether the continuous epidural anesthetic

Shoe Shopping for Health

To save your feet, you may not be able to save on your next pair of shoes. These are good shoe-shopping rules:

- Shoe shop at the time of day when your feet are most swollen (such as afternoons). That way, you'll purchase a shoe that fits you in "bad times" as well as good times.
- Don't even think about high heels or any type of shoe that is not comfortable or that doesn't fit properly. Say goodbye to thong sandals. That strip between your toes can cause too much irritation.
- Buy leather; avoid shoes with the terms *man-made upper* or *man-made materials* on the label; this means the shoes are made of synthetic materials and your foot will not breathe. Cotton or canvas shoes are fine, as long as the insole is cotton, too. Man-made materials on the very bottom of the shoe are fine as long as the upper—the part of the shoe that touches your foot—is leather, cotton, canvas, or something breathable.
- Remember that leather does, indeed, stretch. When that happens, the shoe could become loose and cause blisters. On the other hand, if the shoe is too tight and the salesperson tells you the shoe will stretch, forget it. The shoe will destroy you in the first few hours of wear, which sort of "defeets" the purpose.
- If you lose all sensation and cannot feel whether the shoe is fitting, make sure you have a shoe salesperson fit you.
- Avoid shoes that have been on display. A variety of people try these shoes on; you never know what bacteria and fungi these previously tried-on shoes harbor.

can be continued for a few days after the procedure to decrease phantom sensations and pain. Ask whether the nerves will be anesthetized, too; they should be injected with a long-acting local anesthetic before they're severed during the procedure.

Find an amputee support group online. The Amputee Coalition of America networks with thousands of amputees across the United States.

Getting an Artificial Limb

Artificial limbs are also called *prosthetic limbs* or *prosthesis*. Insurance coverage for prosthetic limbs widely varies, and you may need to look into nonprofit agencies for help.

Prosthetic limbs are made by a special artisan known as an *orthotist* or *prosthetist*, a person who is trained in making artificial limbs and understands amputees' needs. The orthotist or prosthetist must have a doctor's prescription to make the limb. Some prosthetic companies have catalogs, allowing you to order direct, and sometimes bypassing the prescription, but it's best to be fitted for a limb in person and to work directly with a prosthetist. Amputees recommend shopping around for an orthotist or prosthetist; the limb prices vary wildly from manufacturer to manufacturer and prosthetist to prosthetist.

Most prosthetists are willing to work with you and answer the many questions you may have about how the limb is made, durability, ranges of motion, and so on.

Some Surprising Sexual Issues

When I was researching this section, it became apparent that new women amputees are unprepared for a surprising and sometimes disturbing issue—encountering someone with a "stump fetish." This is a type of sexual fetish that can be very disturbing for people who have just undergone amputation. A person with such a fetish is called an *acrotomophile*. On the amputee websites, they are also called *devotees*, a somewhat kinder label. Acrotomophiles tend to pose as fellow amputees in chat rooms on the Internet, inviting e-mail exchanges and so on. The e-mails can then develop into very solicitous and unpleasant sexual invitations. Some acrotomophiles are open and honest about their fetish, but many are covert about their fetishes and can be very manipulative. You may also be approached in public if you are on crutches or in a wheelchair. Stay alert and look this subject up on the Internet. The information on devotees is abundant.

Questions to Ask When Shopping for Artificial Limbs

- *What is the alignment of the limb?* This refers to the position of the prosthetic socket in relation to the foot and knee.
- *Is this assistive or adaptive equipment?* Refers to devices that assist in performance or mobility, including ramps and bars, changes in furniture heights, environmental control units, and specially designed devices.
- *Will you prepare a check socket, or test socket?* This is a trial socket, which is often transparent, made to evaluate comfort and fit prior to the final prosthesis design.
- *What is a control cable?* This is a steel cable used to move and lock mechanical joints and to operate body-powered prostheses.
- *What material will you use for the cosmetic cover?* This refers to the material from which the surface of the limb is made, giving it a more natural appearance. Materials used could be plastic, foam, rubber laminate, or stocking. An *endoskeletal* limb is one in which the prosthesis consists of a lightweight plastic or metal tube encased in a foam cover. An *exoskeletal* limb is a prosthesis made of plastic over wood or rigid foam.
- *Will it be made with energy-storing feet?* This refers to prosthetic feet with plastic springs or carbon fibers designed to help move the prosthesis forward.
- *Will it be designed with knee components?* This refers to devices designed to create a safe, smooth walking pattern.
- *Will it have a single axis?* This refers to a free-swinging knee with a small amount of friction.
- *Will it have stance control?* This refers to a friction device with an adjustable brake mechanism to add stability.
- *Will this limb be polycentric?* This refers to a multiple-axis joint, which is particularly useful with a very long residual limb.

- *Will it have manual locking?* This refers to a device that locks the knee in complete extension to prevent buckling and falls.
- *Will it have pneumatic or hydraulic controls?* This provides controlled changes in the speed of walking.
- *Will it have nudge control?* This is a mechanical switch that operates one or more joints of the prosthesis.
- *Will I see a preparatory prosthesis before the definitive prosthesis? Definitive* means the final product, which meets accepted clinical standards for comfort, fit, alignment, function, appearance, and durability. A *preparatory* prosthesis refers to a short-term prosthesis, generally without cosmetic finishing, which is provided in the early phase of fitting to expedite prosthetic wear and use; it also aids in the evaluation of amputee adjustment and component selection.
- *How is the socket constructed?* This refers to a portion of the prosthesis that fits around the residual limb or stump and to which prosthetic components are attached. A *hard socket* is a prosthetic socket made of rigid materials; a *soft socket* refers to the inner socket liner of foam, rubber, leather, or other material for cushioning the residual limb.
- *What materials will be designed to protect my residual limb (or stump)?* Ask about things such as a stockinette (a tubular open-ended cotton or nylon material); a stump sock (a wool or cotton sock worn over a residual limb to provide a cushion between the skin and socket interface); and a stump shrinker (an elastic wrap or compression sock worn on a residual limb to reduce swelling and shape the limb).

11

A Woman's Face and Diabetes: Eyes and Teeth

DIABETES IS THE leading cause of new blindness in adult women with diabetes. Seventy-eight percent of people with type 2 diabetes experience diabetes eye disease, clinically known as *diabetic retinopathy*. Microvascular complications, discussed in Chapter 10, damage the small blood vessels in the eyes. High blood pressure, associated with macrovascular complications, *also* damages the blood vessels in the eyes.

While 98 percent of people with type 1 diabetes will experience eye disease within fifteen years of being diagnosed, in type 2 diabetes eye disease is often diagnosed *before* the diabetes; in other words, many people don't realize they have diabetes until their eye doctors ask them if they have been screened for diabetes. In fact, 20 percent of people with type 2 diabetes already have diabetes eye disease before their diabetes is diagnosed. The longer you've had diabetes, the more at risk you are for diabetes eye disease. Because people are living longer with diabetes, it is now considered the most common cause of blindness under age sixty-five, and the most common cause of new blindness in North America.

Eighty percent of all eye disease is known as *nonproliferative* eye disease, meaning "no new blood vessel growth" eye disease. This is also called *background diabetic eye disease*. In this case, the blood vessels in the retina (the back of your eyeball) start to deteriorate, bleed, or hemorrhage (known as *microaneurysms*) and leak water and protein into the center of the retina, called the *macula*; this condition is known as *macular edema* and causes vision loss, which sometimes is only temporary. However, without treatment, more permanent vision loss will occur. Although nonproliferative eye disease rarely leads to total blindness, as many as 20 percent of those with nonproliferative eye disease can become legally blind within five years.

Proliferative eye disease means "new blood vessel growth" eye disease. In this case, your retina says, "Since all my blood vessels are being damaged, I'm just going to grow *new* blood vessels!" This process is known as *neovascularization*. The problem is that these new blood vessels are deformed or abnormal, which makes the problem worse, not better. These deformed blood vessels look a bit like Swiss cheese; they're full of holes and have a bad habit of suddenly bleeding, causing severe damage without warning. They can also lead to scar tissue in the retina, retinal detachment, and glaucoma, greatly increasing the risk of legal blindness. Diabetes can also cause cataracts, a clouding of the lens inside the eye that blurs vision.

This chapter will cover signs of eye disease and failing vision, laser treatment to slow vision loss, visual aids, and coping with low vision or blindness. But first, the best step is *prevention*.

Preventing Diabetes Eye Disease

The adage "Early detection is your best protection" is perhaps at its truest when it comes to diabetes eye disease! *It's crucial to have frequent eye exams.* The average person has an eye exam every five years. And if you're walking around with undiagnosed type 2 diabetes, you can also be walking around with early signs of diabetes eye disease. So, as soon as you're diagnosed with type 2 diabetes, get to an eye specialist for a complete exam every six months.

During an eye exam, an ophthalmologist will dilate your pupils with eye drops and then use a special instrument to check for:

- Tiny red dots (signs of bleeding)
- A thick or "milky" retina, with or without yellow clumps or spots (signs of macular edema)

- A "bathtub ring" on the retina—a ring shape that surrounds a leakage site on the retina (also a sign of macular edema)
- "Cottonwool spots" on the retina—small fluffy white patches in the retina (signs of new blood vessel growth or more advanced eye disease)

Today, it's estimated that if everyone with impaired glucose tolerance (see Chapter 1) went for an eye exam once a year, blindness from diabetes eye disease would drop from 8 percent in this group to 1 percent.

Stop Smoking

Since smoking also damages blood vessels, and diabetes eye disease is a blood vessel disease, smoking will certainly aggravate the problem. Quitting smoking may help to reduce eye complications.

Avoid Eye Infections

High blood sugar can predispose you to frequent bacterial infections, including conjunctivitis (pinkeye). Eye infections can also affect your vision. To prevent eye infections, make sure you wash your hands before you touch your eyes, especially before you handle contact lenses.

Control Your Blood Sugar

The Diabetes Complication and Control Trial showed that type 1 patients, who suffer most from diabetes eye disease, were able to delay the onset of eye damage by staying in tight blood sugar control. Also, by controlling your blood pressure and cholesterol (see Chapter 1), you can help to reduce the effects of swelling in the central part of the retina.

Signs of Eye Disease

Seventy-eight percent of people with type 2 diabetes will experience eye changes as a result of diabetes eye disease, and one-fifth will show signs of eye disease when they are first diagnosed. In the early stages of diabetes eye disease, there are no symptoms; this is why you need to have a thorough eye exam every six months. As the eye damage progresses, you may notice blurred vision, which is due to changes in the shape of the lens of the eye. During an eye exam, your ophthalmologist may notice yellow spots on your retina, signs that scar tissue has formed on the retina from bleeding. If the disease progresses to the point where new blood vessels have formed, vision problems may be quite severe as a result of spontaneous bleeding or detachment of the retina.

Vision can fail in two areas: central vision and peripheral vision. Central vision is identifying an object in focus. Peripheral vision is seeing out of the corner of your eye. When we lose our central vision, we lose the ability to focus on fine detail: print, television images, details of faces. When we lose our peripheral vision, we develop *tunnel vision* (a common sign of glaucoma). This restricts us from seeing obstructions, causing us to bump into corners of chairs and doors and trip on many objects. Diabetes eye disease affects both central and peripheral vision.

Vision loss is often very gradual. It may not be something you notice suddenly. Signs of failing vision are important clues that you may have diabetes eye disease that is progressing. The following are classic signs of failing or deteriorating vision:

- You sit closer and closer to the television.
- You're squinting in order to see.
- You need a stronger prescription for your glasses or contacts.
- You have difficulty reading the newspaper.
- You're bothered by bright lights.
- You're more accident-prone, bumping into chairs or doors; tripping over curbs and steps; and knocking things over all the time.
- You can't see well in the dark or at night; night driving is difficult.

If you have signs of failing vision, any of the following eye specialists can help:

- *Ophthalmologist*. This is a medical doctor who specializes in eye conditions. Ophthalmologists can be referred by your family doctor or an optometrist. Ophthalmologists perform eye surgery, prescribe glasses or contacts, and recommend visual aids.
- *Optometrist*. This is not a doctor, but a professional who is trained to correct vision problems with refraction, visual exercises, and visual aids. Optometrists can diagnose and recognize eye disease and can refer you to an ophthalmologist.
- *Optician*. This is the specialist who makes lenses for glasses and who is frequently on hand at optical stores to answer questions. He or she may be your first point of contact in finding help, particularly if you think you just need stronger glasses or contacts. Opticians often recognize more serious problems with the eyes and can recommend (but not formally refer you to) an ophthalmologist.

Much of the time, these specialists help you see better with what you've got. They can help you get around and complete daily tasks with visual aids such as enlarging images, assisting with lighting, and improving color contrasts (see the section "Visual Aids" later in this chapter).

Can Diabetes Eye Disease Be Treated?

Not completely. A procedure known as *laser photocoagulation* can burn and seal off the damaged blood vessels, which stops them from bleeding or leaking. In the earlier stages of eye disease, this procedure can restore your vision within about six months. In most cases, however, laser surgery only slows down vision loss, rather than restoring vision. In other words, without the treatment, your vision will get worse; with the treatment, it will stay the same.

If new blood vessels have already formed, a series of laser treatments are done to purposely scar the retina. Since a scarred retina needs less oxygen, blood vessels stop reforming, reducing the risk of further damage.

In more serious cases, surgery known as a *vitrectomy* is performed. In this procedure, blood and scar tissue on the retina is surgically removed.

After-Effects of Laser Treatment

While you're healing from laser surgery, you may notice blurred vision that lasts anywhere from a few weeks to a few months. You may also notice that it takes longer for your eyes to adapt to very bright or very dark lighting (called *night vision*). This may or may not improve and is a common side effect of all laser eye surgery, even in people who are having it done to improve astigmatism. Finally, you may notice "floaters," which are evidence that there is bleeding inside the eye.

Coping with Low Vision or Blindness

There are many misconceptions about what "blindness" means. Blindness is usually defined as total loss of sight, yet more than 80 percent of people who are considered blind can make out the outlines of objects, identify the sources of light, ascertain the direction of light, distinguish light from dark, and so on.

Registered Blind

There are degrees of blindness that go from low or impaired vision to profound vision loss. All these definitions can be classified as "registered blind," a category that allows you to be eligible for income tax and other government benefits. You are considered registered blind when you have visual acuity in your better eye, after correction, of 20/200 or less. That means that you can see at 20 feet what someone with perfect vision can see at 200 feet. (*Visual acuity* refers to the sharpness and clarity of "near vision"—how well you see close-up objects.) You can also be registered blind if your visual field changes (you lose peripheral vision) resulting in a narrowing of your central vision to 20 degrees or less (you may be able to read, but walking around is hazardous because you can't see what's around you).

So that means that most people who are registered blind see *something*. A lot of people who appear sighted in public and who seem to get around just fine with some visual aids are registered blind.

Visual Aids

If your vision is deteriorating, a range of visual aids are available that can make living and working far easier than it was for many of our parents and grandparents who suffered from partial or complete vision loss. This is, in part, due to a range of technologies that can enhance images through magnification, lighting, and color contrast. A number of tactile products exist as well using the Braille alphabet.

Visual aids are used by people with partial sight, also known as *low vision, reduced vision,* or *impaired vision.* Some people still refer to low vision as *legally blind* or *partial blindness.* These terms are slowly falling out of favor because of myths surrounding what blindness means in most cases (see further on). Of those who identify themselves as visually impaired, fewer than 20 percent are totally blind—without any usable vision. When you hear that diabetes causes blindness, it is not untrue, but it usually refers to a scenario in which you are visually impaired with *some usable vision left,* which makes you a candidate for visual aids (also called low-vision aids).

Making Things Larger

One of the most common visual aids involves products that can magnify an image, known as *magnification devices.* These devices can extend the image over a large enough area of the retina for it to be detected by the healthy cells at the edges, or periphery. Magnification devices typically magnify as much as twenty-two times the normal size. Even as I write these words now, my computer can magnify my screen so that the words I'm typing are 500 percent larger. Magnification aids commonly used can be telescopes, which make distant objects appear closer; binoculars, which many people can use for watching television, movies, or plays; monoculars, which can help you read distance objects such as street names, house numbers, or bus numbers; or pocket magnifiers, illuminated magnifiers, or stand-mounted magnifiers, which are frequently used for a wide assortment of tasks, from working to crafts and leisure activities.

Some people need different visual aids for different tasks. Typically one aid will be used for fine detail tasks, such as reading; another one for watching television; and another one for outdoor use. You can also buy many items with large print, including large-print books, telephones, and clocks.

High-Tech Magnification Devices

Magnification devices can be low-tech (magnifying reading glasses) or high-tech (computer software or hardware). Typically, high-tech devices work with desktop or laptop computers, palm devices, and so on. They may be sold as software or as an interface (a smaller piece of hardware you connect to something like a computer). There are literally hundreds of high-tech visual aids available. The best way to find them is through the Internet; if it's difficult for you to use a computer, a librarian at a public library can assist you with locating this information. Simply visit your favorite software/hardware manufacturer's website and search for "adaptive products," "products for the visually impaired," or "visual aids."

Making Things Brighter

Products that improve lighting are also visual aids. Direct light sources can dramatically improve the ability of people with low vision to complete tasks by reducing glare, improving background light, and so forth. Low-tech solutions you can try:

- A direct light source focused on the task, not on the person
- Increase the lightbulb wattage on lamps
- Use high-intensity lights that reduce glare but increase light
- Retrofit the home with adjustable indirect track lighting for flexibility
- Install fluorescent lighting under kitchen cabinets and near the sink and stove
- Keep a flashlight by the stove
- Equip the home with nightlights to ease the transition from darkness to light
- Place floor lamps or other nonglare light sources near the TV

- Install dimmer switches or three-way lightbulbs
- Sit with your back to the window to reduce glare (especially in public places)
- Wear a hat with a visor for light sensitivity outdoors
- Get ultraviolet-inhibitor sunglasses for outdoor glare (ask your optician)

Making Things Stand Out

You can make objects stand out by using color coding, another type of visual aid. The general rule is to contrast the background with the foreground; smoother textures tend to make colors appear light, while uneven surfaces tend to make colors appear darker.

In the home, for example, using color contrast can make it easier to find things or identify objects. You can buy markers that are brightly colored and that dry into a hard plastic. They can be used to mark appliances, such as the stove, washer, or dryer. Nail polish or colored tape can be used on keys or mailboxes. Brightly colored elastic bands can be used as markers for jars or tins. You can even use colored magnets for metal surfaces (such as colored alphabet letters). In the kitchen, dark pots against a white stove (or the reverse) can help, or you can put colored tape near the end of the pot handles. When you eat, color contrast between placemats or tablecloth and dishes makes it easier to distinguish between them than using table coverings with glossy finishes or patterns. Electrical outlets should also contrast with the surrounding walls; just buy colored wall plates for your outlets.

A little redecorating using color can work wonders: color-contrasting paint can be used around door frames or to paint cupboards. Color contrasting can also be used to separate your clothes (by color or texture). For the bathroom, you can use colored toothpaste that will contrast with white bristles on the toothbrush; a color-contrasted bathmat will help, as well as using a colored soap in the shower or bath. Using different colors for towels and washcloths can help you tell which you're using.

Making Things Touchy-Feely

Tactile products are "touchy-feely." Such products are designed with Braille lettering (the raised dots system invented by Louis Braille back in the nineteenth century and still used today). Essentially, Braille is another way to read and write printed information. It is equivalent, in every way, to print. You can read or write words, numbers, music notations, and any other symbols that appear in print. It works by arranging combinations of the six dots of the Braille "cell." Braille is read by touch and is therefore a tactile language. Most people use the first finger on one or both hands to read it. Braille can be used for any language, mathematics, scientific equations, and computer notations. The only people who can't use Braille are those who suffer from numbness in their fingers or hands, but most people with diabetes-related numbness will feel it in their legs or feet (see Chapter 10), not their fingers.

You can get hundreds of Braille-adapted products, including glucose meters, pill organizers, thermometers, and so on. Braille is actually all around us in modern architecture, but the sighted population doesn't always notice. (For example, most elevators and ATMs are equipped with Braille lettering on the buttons.) There are also computers with Braille keyboards and a refreshable Braille screen.

Braille as a Second Language

The problem with tactile products has to do with people's reluctance to learn Braille. Most people equate learning Braille with being totally blind, which is truly unfortunate. Braille is just as useful for people who have partial sight, and in many situations knowing Braille can make life a little easier. It's like knowing a second language to enhance your communications skills. For example, learning Spanish comes in handy in all kinds of situations, from being able to communicate and make friendships with Spanish-speaking people to ordering food in a Mexican restaurant. It's the same thing with Braille: It comes in handy and can enhance, rather than detract from, your life. People who lose their hearing are similarly reluctant to learn sign language, but in numerous situations, signing would make a hearing-impaired person's life easier.

When you know a different language, it allows you access to a new community of people, too, which is very important when you feel isolated or alone. You already know that when you can talk to someone else who has diabetes, you immediately "connect" with one another because you share a common struggle. It's the same thing with vision loss; meeting someone else who is coping with vision loss helps you feel less alone and allows you to talk to someone who knows what you're going through. Imagine Braille as a bridge to new friends and a new community. It can also keep you employed as it enables you to make notes on documents, read a spreadsheet, take minutes at a meeting, file materials, read label diskettes, and so on.

Braille also lessens your dependency on voice synthesizers for reading or writing, audiotape recordings, magnifiers, and other print enhancers. These are great visual aids, but are not convenient in all circumstances. At home, you can also use Braille to label CDs, clothing, spices, cans, and so on. You can also play games such as cards, Scrabble, backgammon, and chess.

Making Things Talk

An obvious visual aid is a product that talks. Before the popularity of voice synthesizers, audiotaped books were about the only talking product available. Today, voice synthesizers can be used with almost any information product, including small things such as thermometers. With scanners, you can scan printed material into a voice-synthesized computer that can tell you what something says, including labels or fine print. Voice-recognition software can be used to "type" on a computer. There is also a wealth of information on the Web.

Diabetes and Tooth Decay

High blood sugar levels get into your saliva and feed the bacteria in your mouth. The bacteria, in turn, break down the starches and sugars to form acids that eventually break down your tooth enamel. This is how cavities are formed.

Moreover, damage to the small blood vessels in your gums can lead to periodontal problems, while blood sugar levels naturally rise when you're fighting a gum infection (known as a *periodontal infection*) such as an abscess. Preventing dental problems means the usual mouth-care regimen. You're also advised to have your teeth cleaned and examined at least every six months or more depending on your periodontal health, and to avoid sugary foods (which you should be doing anyway). Unfortunately, this is just not enough information for most people with diabetes, especially if they already have gum disease.

Diabetes-Related Gum Disease

Gum disease, also called *periodontitis*, is often not noticeable until it's serious. It's caused by bacteria that are normally in the mouth, which can vary in aggressiveness. The bacteria settle around and under the gum line (where the gums and teeth meet); this is called *plaque*. Brushing and flossing can remove the plaque, preventing it from hardening into *tartar* (also called *calculus*). Bacterial infections can develop from tartar. At this stage, it's called *gingivitis*, but as the bacterial infection worsens, you're looking at full-blown periodontitis.

Healthy gums go around the tooth the way a cuff goes around your wrist. When the gums fit more loosely, the bacteria get high up, alongside the tooth, near the bone, where no toothbrush or floss can go (but a periodontist can with special cleaning instruments). The bacteria can cause an inflammatory reaction that erodes the bone supporting the teeth, making them loose. Eventually, you may have to have your teeth pulled and wear dentures.

Roughly 90 percent of all North Americans have gum disease at some point in their lives. Because people with diabetes have more frequent infections and are slower to heal due to inefficient white blood cells, this can also affect the gums. Second, any kind of infection, such as a urinary tract infection or even a cold or flu, will increase blood sugar levels. So when the gums become infected, it can have serious consequences for your overall health. Also, damage to small vessels (microvascular complication) can affect the support tissues in the gums, too.

Two things are going on with diabetes-related gum disease: high blood sugar can make you vulnerable to gum disease, and gum disease can increase your blood sugar levels even more because it is an active infection.

The Link to Heart Disease

Here is some news you don't want, but must have: gum disease increases your risk of heart disease. The link has been known for years, but very few people are aware of it. It's believed that inflamed gums can produce inflammatory by-products that affect the cardiovascular system. Also, the bacteria that spread in gum disease can produce damage to blood platelets, causing clots. Since people with type 2 diabetes are already at high risk for heart disease and stroke, this means that type 2 diabetes, combined with gum disease, puts you at extreme risk for heart disease. Treating or preventing gum disease can have a positive effect on your cardiovascular health!

The Smoking Gum

If you've read other chapters in this book, you know what a bad combination smoking and diabetes is. Unfortunately, smoking can predispose you to gum disease, making your already high risk from diabetes higher still. More smokers than nonsmokers have gum disease; at least half of all cases of gum disease are directly linked to smoking, and some studies show that as much as 75 percent of gum disease is smoking-related.

If you quit smoking, you can reduce the likelihood of developing gum disease; the longer you've not smoked, the greater the chances you will not suffer gum disease.

Preventing Gum Disease

The strategy is to try to prevent gum disease, if possible, by employing all of those "dentist" rules that have been drilled into you since you can remember: brushing after eating, flossing, rubber-tip massage, fluoride rinses, and so on, and, most of all, frequent checkups. Going for regular cleaning by your dentist or dental hygienist to remove built-up tartar is considered a first-line prevention strategy; however, it is what you do at home that can really make the difference. Ask your dentist or hygienist to show you how to brush and floss properly; it's amazing how many of us were taught the wrong way by our parents or dentists of yesteryear.

If you have diabetes, consider going for routine dental cleanings every three months instead of every six months, too. Extra cleaning can really help to reduce plaque, which is the building block of gum disease. A device called a tongue scraper can also help in reducing plaque and gum disease (it's sold as a tool to reduce bad breath).

Doing the Right Thing the Right Way

Whether you want to prevent gum disease or are being treated for gum disease, brushing and flossing are "doing the right thing," but many of us are doing the right thing *the wrong way*! The first thing most people do when their gums start to bleed from brushing or flossing is stop. This is the worst response. Keep at it; the bleeding should stop after a few days as you strengthen the gums.

Sometimes people use the wrong brushes. Use soft bristles; hard bristles can damage the gums, and you can "brush off" gum tissue, which can lead to recession and root exposure.

Next, people buy the wrong floss and assume that flossing doesn't work for them. If you're finding that your floss is shredding or breaking, get another brand. If your teeth are very close together, finer, unwaxed floss is better. If shredding is a problem, a thicker, waxed floss is better.

Take a long piece of floss and inch your way to the end with each tooth. Use a clean piece of floss for each tooth. If the plaque you remove is foul-smelling, by the way, that is a sign you have bad breath. You can recheck when you floss next; if the smell improves, so has your breath.

Brushing your teeth for five seconds is better than nothing, but the dental health experts recommend you need to brush for about three minutes, at least once a day. Again, use a soft instead of a hard brush. With a soft brush, you can also massage your gums and loosen plaque that is high up. Ask your dentist to show you how to do this and for a sample of a special brush you can use for hard-to-reach places; it can brush behind your front teeth, for example, an area often missed, or behind your side teeth.

Many years ago, the manufacturers of Close Up toothpaste used the line "How's your love life?" to sell their toothpaste. Well, they were onto something. Did you know that gum disease can be transmitted by kissing? If your lover has gum disease, chances are he or she has aggressive bacteria that can be transferred to your mouth, too. For more information about gum disease transmissibility, it's worth visiting the website periotrans.com.

A Gum-Smart Diet

A gum-smart diet can start with the right chewing gum! If you don't have the opportunity to brush after eating, chew some "dental gum." Several of these products have exploded onto the shelves "in the toothpaste section," as one commercial tells us. These gums may have tartar-fighting or whitening agents and are sugar free. When you chew a sugar-free gum after eating, you get the saliva activated, which can wash away bacteria that form plaque.

All that stuff you tell your kids about sugar and cavities still applies! Use the same rules for yourself. Avoid sticky sweets and sugary snacks—something you need to do anyway if you're managing diabetes and planning meals. Ask your dietitian about "gum-smart" snacks such as nuts, seeds, and raw fruits and vegetables.

If you plan to eat something sweet, have it with a meal so your saliva can wash it down. After meals, if you can't brush, rinse your mouth with water and chew some sugar-free or dental gum.

Signs of Gum Disease

Any of the following are signs that you have gum disease:

- Bleeding gums. This is often the first sign of gum disease. You may notice bleeding when you brush your teeth or floss. If your gums are bleeding, it's always a sign of gum disease (unless it occurs when you are just starting to floss regularly), but you can also have gum disease, but not have bleeding gums.
- Receding gums. This occurs when the gum is not covering as much tooth as it should, sometimes exposing the roots.
- New spaces between teeth. This is called *migration* and refers to two teeth that used to touch but that no longer do.

- Chronic bad breath (*halitosis*). Bad breath can be caused by poor digestion, or by insufficient cleaning and a buildup of plaque. And, of course, there are many foods that cause bad breath. But if bad breath persists after proper cleaning and a good oral hygiene routine (including brushing the tongue), gum disease is probably the reason.
- Red gums. Healthy gums should be the color of salmon or coral, not blood. If you breathe through your mouth, red gums are more common, too.
- Loose teeth.
- Less tapered gum coverage around the teeth. The gum should meet the tooth at a knife-edge margin. If this margin is rolled and swollen, it's a sign of gum disease.
- Shiny gums. Gums should have some stippling to them (little dots) so they don't shine; shiny red gums are not a good thing.

When you notice any of these signs of gum disease, have your dentist look for other signs that you can't see yourself, such as root cavities, pockets in the gums, and tooth decay under the gum line.

Seeing a Gum Specialist

If gum disease has progressed beyond the early stage gingivitis, you'll be referred to a *periodontist*—a dentist who has done a three-year "residency" of sorts in treating gum problems and gum disease. Periodontists can help to restore gum tissue or regenerate it. At your first visit, the periodontist will use a special probe that can measure gaps between the gums and teeth, as well as look for exposed roots, which need special care. Gaps between the gum and teeth are called *pockets* and normally shouldn't be deeper than one to three millimeters. Pockets deeper than this can be a sign of serious gum disease.

Periodontists may also do special cleanings called *root planing*, where the gum tissues are usually anaesthetized, and the roots of the teeth (these may be exposed or still covered by gums) are cleaned. The goal is to get rid of as much plaque and tartar as possible to prevent bacterial infections from developing or progressing once they have developed. Root planing may also involve using antibiotics to help kill off the bacteria high inside the gums. Gum surgery involves restoring the gumline to a more readily cleanable state by reducing the pockets and removing the diseased parts.

If you have gum disease, it must be treated. Doing so will lower your blood sugar levels and can improve your overall health and ability to control your diabetes. If gum disease has progressed to the point where your teeth are loose or keep becoming infected (such as forming root infections and abscesses), some teeth may need to be extracted and you may need dentures. For more information on dentures, contact the American Dental Association.

12

Women, Diabetes, and Kidney Disease

DIABETIC KIDNEY DISEASE, also known as *diabetic nephropathy*, is what happens when macrovascular and microvascular complications converge. The high blood pressure that is aggravated by macrovascular complications, combined with the small blood vessel damage caused by microvascular complications, can cause kidney failure—something you can die from unless you have *dialysis* (filtering out the body's waste products through a machine) or a kidney transplant. About 15 percent of people with type 2 diabetes will develop kidney disease, which often goes by the terms *renal disease* or *nephropathy*. When your kidneys have failed and you require dialysis, this is known as *end-stage renal disease* (*ESRD*); diabetes is considered to be the leading cause of kidney disease, responsible for roughly 45 percent of all cases of end-stage renal disease. Certain population groups, such as American Indians, Native Hawaiians, and Alaskan Natives, or people of African or Hispanic descent, are more at risk for kidney failure than Caucasians. The good news is that the risk of developing chronic kidney disease increases with the length of time you've had diabetes, so by getting your diabetes under control early in the game, you may be able to prevent kidney disease or kidney failure.

What Do Your Kidneys Do?

Kidneys are the public servants of the body; they're busy little bees! If they go on strike, you lose your water service, garbage pickup, and a few other services you don't even appreciate.

Kidneys regulate your body's water levels; when you have too much water, your kidneys remove it by dumping it into a large storage tank, your bladder. The excess water stays there until you're ready to urinate. If you don't have enough water in your body (you're dehydrated), your kidneys will retain water.

Kidneys also act as your body's sewage filtration plant. They filter out all the garbage and waste that your body doesn't need and dump it into the bladder; this waste is then excreted in your urine. The two waste products your kidneys regularly dump are *urea* (the waste product of protein) and *creatinine* (a waste product produced by the muscles). In people with high blood sugar levels, excess sugar will get sent to the kidneys, and the kidneys will dump it into the bladder, too, causing sugar to appear in the urine.

Kidneys also balance calcium and phosphate, needed to build bones. Kidneys operate two little side businesses on top of all this. They make hormones. One hormone, called *renin*, helps to regulate blood pressure. Another hormone, called *erythropoietin*, helps bone marrow make red blood cells.

What Affects Your Kidneys?

When you suffer from cardiovascular disease, you probably have high blood pressure. High blood pressure damages blood vessels in the kidneys, which interferes with their job performance. As a result, they won't be as efficient at removing waste or excess water from your body. And if you are experiencing poor circulation, which can also cause water retention, the problem is further aggravated.

Poor circulation may cause your kidneys to secrete too much renin, which is normally designed to regulate blood pressure, but in this case increases it. All the extra fluid and the high blood pressure place a heavy burden on your heart—and your kidneys. If this situation isn't brought under control, you'd likely suffer from a heart attack before kidney failure, but kidney failure is inevitable.

The Micro Problem

When high blood sugar levels affect the small blood vessels, this includes the small blood vessels in the kidney's filters, called the *nephrons*—hence the term *diabetic nephropathy*. In the early stages of nephropathy, good, usable protein is secreted in the urine. That's a sign that the kidneys were unable to distribute this usable protein to the body's tissues. Normally, they would excrete only the waste product of protein—urea—into the urine.

Another microvascular problem also affects the kidneys: nerve damage. The nerves you use to control your bladder can be affected, causing a sort of sewage backup in your body. The first place that sewage hits is your kidneys. Old urine floating around your kidneys isn't a healthy thing. The kidneys can become damaged as a result, aggravating all the conditions discussed in this section.

The Infection Problem

There's also a third problem at work. If you recall, frequent urination is a sign of high blood sugar. That's because your kidneys help to rid the body of too much sugar by dumping it into the bladder. Well, guess what? You're not the only one who likes sugar; bacteria, such as *E. coli* (the "hamburger bacteria"), like it, too. In fact, they thrive on it. So all that sugary urine sitting around in your bladder and passing through your ureters and urethra can cause this bacteria to overgrow, resulting in a urinary tract infection (UTI) such as cystitis (inflammation of the bladder lining). The longer your urethra, the more protection you have from UTIs. Men have long urethras; women have very short urethras, however, and at the best of times are prone to these infections—especially after a lot of sexual activity, explaining the term *honeymoon cystitis*. Sexual intercourse can introduce even more bacteria (from the vagina or rectum) into a woman's urethra due to the close space the vagina and urethra share. Wiping from back to front after a bowel movement can also introduce fecal matter into the urethra, causing a UTI.

Any bacterial infection in your bladder area can travel back up to your kidneys, causing infection, inflammation, and a big general mess, aggravating all the other problems!

The Smoking Problem

In the same way that smoking contributes to eye problems (see Chapter 11), it can also aggravate kidney problems. Smoking causes small vessel damage throughout your body.

Signs of Diabetic Kidney Disease

Obviously, there are a lot of different problems going on when it comes to diabetes and kidney disease. If you have any of the following early warning signs of kidney disease, see your doctor as soon as possible:

- Bad taste in the mouth (sign of toxins building up; see Chapter 11 on tooth decay)
- Blood or pus in the urine (a sign of a kidney infection)
- Burning or difficulty urinating (a sign of a urinary tract infection)
- Fever, chills, or vomiting (a sign of *any* infection)
- Foamy urine (a sign of kidney infection)
- Foul-smelling or cloudy urine (a sign of a urinary tract infection)
- Frequent urination (a sign of high blood sugar and/or urinary tract infection)
- High blood pressure (see Chapter 1)
- Itching skin or painful joints (a sign of high phosphorus levels)
- Leg swelling or leg cramps (a sign of fluid retention)
- Less need for insulin or oral diabetes medications
- Morning sickness, nausea, and vomiting
- Pain in the lower abdomen (a sign of a urinary tract infection)
- Protein in the urine (a sign of microvascular problems)
- Puffiness around eyes, swelling of hands and feet (sign of edema, or fluid retention)
- Weakness (a sign of anemia)

In the early stages of kidney disease, there are often no symptoms at all. Many of the symptoms in the preceding list are signs that your kidney function has deteriorated to the point where toxins and wastes have built up, causing, for example, nausea and vomiting, fluid retention, even chronic hiccups. Heart failure (not to be confused with a heart attack, discussed in Chapter 9) and fluid in the lungs are characteristic of very late stages of kidney failure.

When you experience any of these symptoms, it's crucial to have a blood test that looks for creatinine levels. Again, creatinine is a waste product removed from the blood by healthy kidneys. A creatinine blood test greater than 1.2 for women and 1.4 for men is a sign of kidney disease. Another test that looks for blood urea nitrogen (BUN) is also important; when the BUN rises (no pun intended) it's a sign of kidney disease, too. Other more sensitive tests that detect the level of kidney function include creatinine clearance, glomerular filtration rate (GFR), and urine albumin.

Treating Kidney Disease

If you have high blood pressure, getting it under control through diet, exercise, or blood pressure–lowering medication will help to save your kidneys. If you have high blood sugar, treating any urinary tract infection as quickly as possible with antibiotics is the best way to avert kidney infection, while drugs known as ACE inhibitors can help to control small blood vessel damage caused by microvascular complications. In general, slowing the progression of kidney disease can be done by:

- Controlling high blood pressure (see Chapter 1)
- Controlling blood sugar levels (see Chapter 1)
- Adopting a kidney-smart diet (see the next section)
- Avoiding medications that may damage the kidneys (sit down with your pharmacist or doctor and try to find substitutes for medications that can affect the kidneys; there are many substitutes for commonly prescribed medications)

- Treating urinary tract infections
- Exercise and weight loss

The Kidney-Smart Diet

To prolong the life of your kidneys when you experience signs of kidney disease or are in the early stages and perhaps have been alerted through blood test results, you can adjust your diet to cut down on the work your kidneys normally do as well as meet nutritional needs, such as increasing iron intake, which may be lower due to anemia. Diet can even control the buildup of food wastes and reduce fatigue, nausea, itching, and a bad taste in the mouth that can occur when toxins build up in the body. And, of course, diet will help to control high blood sugar. When you think about a kidney-smart diet, remember *3PS*, a term I've coined to remember protein, potassium, phosphorus, and sodium. The diet involves *cutting down on 3PS*. A dietitian or nutritionist can help you make the cuts necessary to save your kidneys, but keep you as healthy as possible.

Protein

Protein is a good thing normally; it builds, repairs, and maintains your body tissues, and also helps you fight infections or heal wounds. But as protein breaks down in the body, it forms urea as a waste product. The kidneys normally flush out urea; when they can't, it builds up in the blood, so it's necessary to cut down on protein. You need to eat enough for health, however. Meat, fish, poultry, eggs, tofu, and dairy products are high in protein.

Potassium

The nerves and muscles normally rely on the mineral potassium to work well. But without the filtering process of your kidneys, too much can build up in the blood, which can affect the heart. Normally the kidneys get rid of potassium excess, so most of us never think about it. But when your kidneys aren't functioning well, you can cut down on potassium-rich foods, such as potatoes, squash, bananas, oranges, tomatoes, dried peas, and beans.

Phosphorus

Your bones normally rely on the mineral phosphorus, also known as phosphate, to stay healthy and strong. When phosphorus levels rise, usually the kidneys just filter out excess phosphorus and we feel fine. But when the kidneys aren't working well, phosphorus levels rise until we get itchy skin or painful joints. Limiting foods with phosphorus will help reduce toxic levels of this mineral. These foods include anything with protein, seeds, nuts, dried peas, beans, and processed bran cereals. You'll need some phosphorus-containing foods for health. When you ingest them, you can also take a phosphate binder, a medication that binds with the phosphorus in your intestine so it can pass in your stool. Ask your doctor about prescribing the binder.

Sodium

As discussed previously, sodium affects your body fluids and blood pressure. Reducing sodium means cutting down on salt and packaged or canned products with sodium (canned soups, for example, are notorious for their sodium content). Start reading labels and stop salting your foods. Avoid foods with a high sodium content. Processed foods, such as deli meats, fast foods, salty snacks, and anything with salty seasonings, are high in sodium. There are many herbs you can use instead; lemon and vinegar are terrific substitutes, too.

A Word About Fluids

Kidneys produce urine, which eliminates many of our wastes. When kidneys are not functioning well, not as much urine is produced, and this can cause fluid retention—swelling in hands, legs, feet, and so on. Limiting your fluid intake may help, but it isn't necessary in all cases. Fluids include water, soup, juice, milk, Popsicles, and gelatin; you and your doctor should discuss how to limit your fluid intake.

From Kidney Disease to Kidney Failure

Kidney failure is also known as *chronic renal insufficiency (CRI)*; this term means your kidneys are operating at 50 percent or less of normal capacity. By this point, your kidneys are working with "half the staff" and are not able to remove the bodily wastes as efficiently. Again, you may not notice symptoms of kidney failure at all; the disease progresses slowly and as the kidneys continue to fail and waste products build up, you'll begin to feel sick. Because your kidneys stop making enough of the crucial hormone erythropoietin (EPO), you can suffer from low iron levels or anemia, as well as weakness. When the kidneys are functioning at less than 10 percent of their capacity, you'll need to consider dialysis or even a kidney transplant, if possible. By this point, you've progressed to end-stage renal disease.

When You Need Dialysis

Dialysis comes from the root word *dissolution*, which means to "set free." It is a lifesaving treatment that replaces many of your kidneys' functions, such as removing waste, salt, and extra water to prevent them from building up in the body; it keeps levels of potassium, sodium, and bicarbonate in check, and helps to control your blood pressure. Dialysis has been available since the mid-1940s and began to be used as a regular treatment for people with kidney failure in the 1960s. Dialysis allows people with kidney failure to live a long time, often as long as someone with functioning kidneys. In the United States, both Medicaid and Medicare cover dialysis for people who qualify for these programs but many have no health insurance to cover these costs. Your local Kidney Foundation office has information about the nearest dialysis units in your area and can give you some advice about making suitable arrangements for accommodations. Dialysis can be done at home, but it requires supervision by a trained health-care professional.

There are two types of dialysis: *hemodialysis* (*hemo* means "blood") and *peritoneal dialysis* (*peritoneal* means "abdominal").

Hemodialysis

Hemodialysis involves cleaning your blood through an artificial kidney machine called a *dialyzer*. The blood flows into the machine and goes back into your body nice and clean, free of waste products and excess buildup of chemicals and fluid.

You are connected to the artificial kidney through a blood vessel in your arm or leg. If there are problems finding a healthy blood vessel, a "bridge" can be created through a graft or catheter (a narrow plastic tube). The connection process can be uncomfortable, depending on how it's done.

The length of time a hemodialysis treatment lasts depends on the functioning capacity of your kidneys, how much waste has built up, how much fluid builds up between treatments, your overall size, and the type of artificial kidney used. Typical treatments last about four hours and are required three times per week. Only a small amount of your blood can be handled by the machine, so it takes a while. The blood has to circulate many times before it is clean. Hemodialysis can be done in a hospital, in an outpatient care center, or at home.

Peritoneal Dialysis

Peritoneal dialysis filters the blood from within the body. This treatment can involve using a machine (known as *continuous cycling peritoneal dialysis—CCPD*), or a catheter and bag, similar to an ostomy or ileostomy (known as *continuous ambulatory peritoneal dialysis—CAPD*), available since 1976. CAPD does *not* mean you have dialysis in an ambulance; it means that you can remain *ambulatory*—able to walk around.

CCPD is usually done at home; in this case the catheter is connected to a special machine called a *cycler*.

If you opt for CAPD, you do this procedure yourself, which is required about four or five times a day. The usual procedure is to put a bag of dialysate (about two and a half quarts) through your catheter and into your peritoneal cavity. The dialysate stays there for about four or five hours before it is drained back into your catheter bag. When the bag is full, toss it and exchange it for a new bag of dialysate and new catheter bag. This allows you to carry on with your normal activities without planning your life around a dialysis machine.

Lifestyle Adjustments for Dialysis

Dialysis treatments, unlike some other treatments such as chemotherapy, do not leave you feeling sick or weak afterward; they leave you feeling healthier. But during the procedure, you may feel muscle cramps, nausea, or dizziness because the waste products are removed more abruptly than they are when your kidneys are functioning. Low blood pressure can also occur, causing dizziness, headaches, and even vomiting. As you have more treatments, these side effects should pass.

Dialysis also means you have to stay on your 3PS diet (described earlier), cutting down on protein, potassium, phosphorus, and sodium.

You can travel while on dialysis; you just have to contact a dialysis center near your destination and make arrangements for a treatment. If you're using CAPD, don't worry about it. Just pack your equipment and luggage and go.

You can also continue to work if you're on dialysis; you just need to arrange your work schedule around your dialysis treatments. Physical jobs involving heavy lifting, digging, and so on do not mix well with kidney failure. You can't do hard labor when you're on dialysis.

Stopping Dialysis

Dialysis is a medical treatment that keeps you alive. As discussed in Chapter 9, when someone has no quality of life, lifesaving medical interventions can be withdrawn. This decision is legal and is not in any way the same thing as euthanasia, which means you use medical intervention to end a life. In the film *Whose Life Is It Anyway?* Richard Dreyfus plays a quadriplegic who is dependent on dialysis. Because he cannot move on his own, he feels his life does not have quality or value, and he asks for withdrawal of all medical treatment, including dialysis.

Stopping dialysis may be a decision you make yourself, or it may be a decision your surrogate makes (this is the person, such as a spouse or adult child, you appoint to make decisions on your behalf when you're not conscious or are incapacitated). There may be other health problems behind this choice; you may be experiencing failing health as a result of stroke or cancer, for example, or your age, level of mobility, and other circumstances in your life may be factors. In these cases, you may decide to stop your dialysis treatment and die a natural death of kidney failure. This is a choice that is yours to make and no one else's.

You may also decide to state the conditions under which dialysis should be stopped, such as in the event of a coma or stroke that leaves you with no quality of life. This is called an *advance directive* or *liv-*

ing will. In the same way that you can stipulate in an advance directive that you do not want to be resuscitated if your heart stops during
a heart attack, you can stipulate that dialysis be stopped in such an
event.

You may also decide that being on dialysis is not allowing you the
quality of life you want; if this is the case, you may be a candidate for
a kidney transplant, but that may involve dialysis until a donor comes
forward.

When You Want a Kidney Transplant

The good news is that you can get a new kidney when the one you have
stops working. Kidney transplants are an option for people with kidney failure. That's because people have two kidneys, but can live with
only one. As long as people are healthy, they can give away a kidney
to someone who needs it. (In fact, kidney donation is so doable, medical ethicists are worried that some people are selling their kidneys as
a way to make money, creating a scenario where the rich buy kidneys
from the poor!)

Living Donors

In the film *Steel Magnolias*, Sally Fields plays mother to Julia Roberts,
whose character has type 1 diabetes. When Julia Roberts's kidneys fail,
Sally Fields donates one kidney to her. The general rule is this: if you've
got a matching donor, you've got a new kidney! The person donating
the kidney is a *living donor*. Kidney donation is similar to bone marrow donation, in that the blood type and tissues should match as closely
as possible to avoid the kidney being rejected as foreign by your body.
Relatives are always good bets, but you can use anybody's kidney if
the match is there. With a living donor, transplant success rates are
greater than 90 percent in the first year.

Transplant Waiting Lists

If you don't know anyone willing to give you a kidney, you have to wait
for a kidney to become available through the death of someone who

has filled out a donor card on a driver's license. Many people die each day in car accidents and other types of accidents, but unless they specify that they *want* to donate their organs, their families may not be aware that they wish to be a donor. People who donate organs after they die are called *cadaver donors*. I prefer the term *posthumous donors*. The success rates with posthumous donors are not as high as those with living donors, but these transplants are still about 80 percent successful for the first year.

Without a living donor, you have to be on a transplant waiting list, and the wait can be long when you factor in the blood and tissue matching. When they don't have a donor, transplant patients receive kidneys according to need, rather than "first come, first served." But your overall health is also weighed. For example, if a person's kidneys are failing because the person is in terrible health as a result of out-of-control diabetes and a host of other complications, a new kidney may not fare very well in his or her body and may eventually fail, too. Someone in better health may get a kidney faster because he or she has a greater chance of being a successful recipient.

Generally, to be considered for a transplant from either a live or posthumous donor, you must be healthy enough to have the surgery and be free from infection or other diseases, such as cancer. You must also be willing to take antirejection drugs, which can have side effects.

Preparing for a Transplant

Obviously you don't just bring your sister to a hospital and say, "Give me her kidney." Preparing for a transplant is rather involved. First, you will need to meet with a transplant surgeon or a team of transplant specialists to find out whether the risks of the transplant surgery and antirejection medications outweigh the inconveniences of dialysis. In other words, is a new kidney going to give you a better quality of life than the one you have now? In many cases, the answer is yes, but in a significant number of cases, the answer is no because of health complications.

In most transplant units, you're provided with some names of recipients you can talk to about the process. You then have to prepare for major surgery, which can be planned in advance if you have a living donor. Numerous tests and workups determine your fitness for undergoing a transplant surgery. In a nutshell, if you're a good candidate for a kidney transplant and you can find a donor, you may have a better quality of life than you do on dialysis, if you can tolerate the antirejection drugs.

Appendix

Diabetes Resources

American Association of Diabetes Educators
500 North Michigan Avenue, Suite 1400
Chicago, IL 60611
1-800-388-DMED or (312) 661-1700
aadenet.org

The American Diabetes Association
ADA National Service Center
1660 Duke Street
Alexandria, VA 22314
(703) 549-1500
diabetes.org

American Foundation for the Blind
11 Penn Plaza, Suite 300
New York, NY 10001
(212) 502-7661
fax: (212) 502-7777
afb.org

American Heart Association
7320 Greenville Pike
Dallas, TX 75231
(214) 373-6300
americanheart.org

Canadian Diabetes Association
15 Toronto Street, Suite 800
Toronto, Ontario, Canada M5C 2E3
(416) 363-3373
fax: (416) 363-3393
diabetes.ca

The Diabetes Research and Wellness Foundation (provides free
    medical alert ID necklaces and diabetes self-management diaries)
P.O. Box 3837
Merrifield, VA 22116
(202) 298-9211
diabeteswellness.net

The International Diabetes Federation
Avenue Emile De Mot 19
B-1000 Brussels, Belgium
32-2-5431636
idf.org

International Diabetic Athletes Association
1647-B West Bethany Home Road
Phoenix, AZ 85015
(602) 433-2113
diabetes-exercise.org

Joslin Diabetes Center
1 Joslin Place
Boston, MA 02215
(617) 732-2415
joslin.org

MedicAlert Foundation
2323 Colorado Avenue
Turlock, CA 95382
1-800-825-3785
medicalert.org

National Diabetes Information Clearinghouse
Box NDIC
Bethesda, MD 20892
(301) 468-2162
diabetes.niddk.nih.gov

National Kidney Foundation
30 East 33rd Street
New York, NY 10016
(212) 889-2210
1-800-622-9010
kidney.org

National Federation of the Blind
1800 Johnston Street
Baltimore, MD 21230
(410) 659-9314
nfb.org

National Osteoporosis Foundation
1150 17th Street NW, Suite 500
Washington, DC 20036-4603
(202) 223-2226
1-800-223-9994
nof.org

North American Menopause Society (NAMS)
P.O. Box 94527
Cleveland, OH 44101
(216) 844-8748
menopause.org

Overeaters Anonymous
P.O. Box 44020
Rio Rancho, NM 87174-4402
(505) 891-2664
overeatersanonymous.org

The Smoking Quitline of the National Cancer Institute
1-877-44U-QUIT
smokefree.gov

Other Websites of Interest

Americans with Disabilities Act Information on the Web
  (covers individuals with diabetes)
usdoj.gov/crt/ada

The British Diabetic Association
diabetes.org.uk

The Diabetes Prevention Program
preventdiabetes.com

The Diabetic Retinopathy Foundation
retinopathy.org

The Indian Health Service Diabetes Program
tucson.ihs.gov/healthcare/professions/diabetes

The National Institute of Diabetes and Digestive and
  Kidney Disease
niddk.nih.gov/health/diabetes/diabetes.htm

Bibliography

American Association of Clinical Endocrinologists. *Achieving Glycemic Control in Diabetes Mellitus: Overview of the 2002 AACE Diabetes Guidelines.* March 2003.

American Board for Certification in Orthotics and Prosthetics Inc. Retrieved online from the Amputee Web Site, amputee-online.ca (accessed July 2001).

American Diabetes Association. "An Introduction to Oral Medications for Diabetes." Diabetes.com (accessed January 1999).

American Diabetes Association. "Carbohydrate Counting: A New Way to Plan Meals." Posted to diabetes.com (accessed January 1999).

"American Diabetes Association 2003 Clinical Practice Recommendations." *Diabetes Care* 27, suppl. 1, January 2004.

Amputation Prevention Global Resource Center. *Prevent Foot Ulcers and Amputations.* Booklet retrieved online from diabetesresource .com (accessed July 2001).

Antonucci, T., et al. "Impaired Glucose Tolerance Is Normalized by Treatment with Thiazolidinedione." *Diabetes Care* 20, no. 2 (February 1997): 188–193.

Avandia (Rosiglitazone). Product monograph. Smith-Kline Beecham, 2003.

Barud, S., and L. Murphey. "Osteoporosis: Options for Prevention and Treatment." *The Female Patient* 29, no. 8 (August 2004): 20–31.

Bell, S. J., and R. A. Forse. "Nutritional Management of Hypoglycemia." *Diabetes Education* 25, no. 1 (January–February 1999): 41–47.

Boctor, M. A., et al. "Gestational Diabetes Debate: Controversies in Screening and Management." *Canadian Diabetes* 10, no. 2 (June 1997): 5–7.

"Buying Your Prosthesis." Amputee Web Site, amputee-online.ca (accessed July 2001).

Canadian Diabetes Association. "Guidelines for the Nutritional Management of Diabetes Mellitus in the New Millennium." Reprinted from *Canadian Journal Diabetes Care* 23, no. 3 (2000): 56–69.

Canadian Diabetes Association. *2003 Clinical Practice Guidelines for the Prevention and Management of Diabetes in Canada.* Posted to diabetes.ca (accessed 2004).

Canadian Medical Association Journal and the Canadian Diabetes Association. "1998 Clinical Practice Guidelines for the Management of Diabetes in Canada." *Canadian Medical Association Journal* 159, no. 8, suppl. (1998): s1–s27.

Chakravarthy, M. V., and F. W. Booth. "Eating, Exercise, and 'Thrifty' Genotypes: Connecting the Dots Toward an Evolutionary Understanding of Modern Chronic Diseases." *Journal of Applied Physiology* 96, no. 1 (January 2004): 3–10.

Cheng, T. O. "The Mediterranean Diet Revisited." *Quarterly Journal of Medicine* 94, no. 3 (March 2001): 174–175.

"Complications: Your Eyes and Diabetic Retinopathy." Canadian Diabetes Association, diabetes.ca (accessed July 2001).

End Stage Renal Disease in the United States. Booklet retrieved online from kidney.org (accessed July 2001).

Enserink, Martin. "The Vanishing Promises of Hormone Replacement." *Science* 297, no. 5580 (July 19, 2002): 325–326.

Feig, Denice S. "The Fourth International Workshop Conference on Gestational Diabetes Mellitus." *Canadian Diabetes* 10, no. 2 (June 1997): 2.

First Nations Health Commission, Assembly of First Nations. "Report on the Second International Conference on Diabetes and Native Peoples." November 1993.

"Foot Care and Ulcer Prevention for People with Diabetes: Is Amputation the Only Answer?" University of Manitoba Diabetes Research and Treatment Centre, umanitoba.ca (accessed July 2001).

Friedman, Jeffrey M. "A War on Obesity, Not the Obese." *Science* 299, no. 5608 (2003): 856–858.

"The Genetics of Obesity." *Endocrinology and Metabolism Clinics of North America* 32, no. 4 (December 2003): 761–786.

"The Gum Disease Project." Retrieved from periodiabetes.com (accessed July 2001).

Guthrie, Diana, and Richard A. Guthrie. *The Diabetes Sourcebook.* Los Angeles: Lowell House, 1996.

Hill, James O., Holly R. Wyatt, George W. Reed, and John C. Peters. "Obesity and the Environment: Where Do We Go from Here?" *Science* 299, no. 5608 (2003): 853–855.

Hu, F. B., and W. C. Willett. "Optimal Diets for Prevention of Coronary Heart Disease." *Journal of the American Medical Association* 288, no. 20 (November 27, 2002): 2569–2578.

International Food Information Council. *IFIC Review: Intense Sweeteners: Effects on Appetite and Weight Management.* International Food Information Council, 1100 Connecticut Avenue NW, Suite 430, Washington, DC 20036, November 1995.

International Food Information Council. *IFIC Review: Uses and Nutritional Impact of Fat Reduction Ingredients.* International Food Information Council, 1100 Connecticut Avenue NW, Suite 430, Washington, DC 20036, October 1995.

International Food Information Council. "Q & A About Fatty Acids and Dietary Fats." International Food Information Council, 1100 Connecticut Avenue NW, Suite 430, Washington, DC 20036, 1997.

International Food Information Council. "What You Should Know About MSG." International Food Information Council, 1100 Connecticut Avenue NW, Suite 430, Washington, DC 20036, September 1991.

International Food Information Council. "What You Should Know About Sugars." International Food Information Council, 1100 Connecticut Avenue NW, Suite 430, Washington, DC 20036, May 1994.

"A Jelly Bean Glucose Test." *American Baby*, April 1996, 6.

"Jelly Beans Offer Sweet Relief." *Diabetes Dialogue* 44, no. 2 (Summer 1997): 52–53.

Jovanovic-Peterson, Lois, June Biermann, and Barbara Toohey. *The Diabetic Woman: All Your Questions Answered*. New York: G. P. Putnam's Sons, 1996.

Kelner, Katrina, and Laura Helmuth. "Obesity—What Is to Be Done?" *Science* 299, no. 5608 (2003): 845.

Kenshole, Anne. "To Be or Not to Be Pregnant." *Diabetes Dialogue* 44, no. 2 (Summer 1997): 6–8.

Kra, J. Siegfried. *What Every Woman Must Know About Heart Disease*. New York: Warner Books, 1996.

Liebman, Bonnie. "Syndrome X: The Risks of High Insulin." *Nutrition Action* 27, no. 2 (March 2000): 3–8.

Linden, Ron. "Hyperbaric Medicine." *Diabetes Dialogue* 43, no. 4 (Fall 1996): 24–26.

Lindesay, J. E. "Multiple Pain Complaints in Amputees." *Journal of Rehabilitation and Social Medicine* 78 (1985): 452–455.

Ludwig, Sora. "Gestational Diabetes." *Canadian Diabetes* 10, no. 2 (June 1997): 1, 8.

Macdonald, Jeanette. "The Facts About Menopause." *Diabetes Dialogue* 44, no. 2 (Summer 1997): 24–26.

Marx, Jean. "Cellular Warriors at the Battle of the Bulge." *Science* 299, no. 5608 (2003): 846–849.

McSweeney, J. C., et al. "Recognizing Prodromal Symptoms in Women at Risk for Coronary Heart Disease." *The Female Patient* 29, no. 8 (August 2004): 10–15.

MediSense Canada Inc. *Real World Factors That Interfere with Blood-Glucose Meter Accuracy*. Patient information, distributed 1996.

"Microalbuminuria in Diabetic Kidney Disease." Retrieved from kidney.org (accessed July 2001).

National Diabetes Information Clearinghouse, National Institute of Diabetes and Digestive and Kidney Diseases, U.S. Department of Health and Human Services, National Institutes of Health. Diabetes Prevention Program. *The Bigger Picture of Glucose Management*. NIH Publication no. 03-5099, January 2003.

National Diabetes Information Clearinghouse, National Institute of Diabetes and Digestive and Kidney Diseases, U.S. Department of

Health and Human Services, National Institutes of Health. Diabetes Prevention Program. *Insulin Resistance and Pre-Diabetes.* NIH Publication no. 03-4893, April 2004.

National Diabetes Information Clearinghouse, National Institute of Diabetes and Digestive and Kidney Diseases, U.S. Department of Health and Human Services, National Institutes of Health. Diabetes Prevention Program. *Hypoglycemia.* NIH Publication no. 02-3926, September 2002.

National Kidney Foundation. *Dialysis.* Booklet retrieved online from kidney.org (accessed July 2001).

Nestle, Marion. *Food Politics: How the Food Industry Influences Nutrition and Health.* (Berkeley: University of California Press, 2002).

Neuschwander-Tetri, B. A., et al. "Troglitazone-Induced Hepatic Failure Leading to Liver Transplantation. A Case Report." *Annals of Internal Medicine* 129 (July 1, 1998): 38–41.

"New Tool Allows Early Prediction of Patient's Stroke Outcome." Retrieved online from the National Institute of Neurological Disorders and Stroke, ninds.nih.gov (accessed June 28, 2001).

Pierce, J. G., Jr., and M. J. Iuorno. "Diabetes in Women." *The Female Patient* 28, no. 2 (February 2003): 26–31.

Poirier, Laurinda M., and Katharine M. Coburn. *Women and Diabetes: Life Planning for Health and Wellness.* New York: American Diabetes Association and Bantam Books, 1997.

"Position of the American Dietetic Association: Use of Nutritive and Nonnutritive Sweeteners." *Journal of the American Dietetic Association* 93 (1993): 816–822.

"Preventing Diabetic Kidney Disease." Retrieved online from kidney.org (accessed July 2001).

"Q & A on Low-Calorie Sweeteners." *Diabetes News* 1, no. 2 (Spring 1997): 3.

"Recovering After a Stroke." Agency for Healthcare Research and Quality, ahrq.gov (accessed July 2001).

Rosenthal, M. Sara. *The Canadian Type 2 Diabetes Sourcebook, Second Edition.* Mississauga, ONT: John Wiley & Sons, 2004.

Rosenthal, M. Sara. *50 Ways to Manage Type 2 Diabetes.* Chicago: Contemporary Books, 2001.

Rosenthal, M. Sara. *The Gynecological Sourcebook, Fourth Edition.* New York: McGraw-Hill. 2003.

Rosenthal, M. Sara. *Managing Diabetes for Women.* Toronto: Macmillan Canada, 1999.

Rosenthal, M. Sara. *The Skinny on Fat.* Toronto: McClelland and Stewart, 2004.

Sachiko T., St. Jeor, Barbara V. Howard, Elaine Prewitt, Vicki Bovee, Terry Bazzarre, and Robert H. Eckel for the AHA Nutrition Committee. "Dietary Protein and Weight Reduction. A Statement for Healthcare Professionals from the Nutrition Committee of the Council on Nutrition, Physical Activity, and Metabolism of the American Heart Association." *Circulation* 104 (2001): 1869–1874.

Schlosser, Eric. *Fast Food Nation: The Dark Side of the American Meal.* New York: Houghton Mifflin, 2001.

Schwartz, Carol. "An Eye-Opener." *Diabetes Dialogue* 43, no. 4 (Winter 1996): 20–22.

Soule Odegard, P., and S. L. Gray. "Diabetes: Treatment Considerations in Older Women." *The Female Patient* 28, no. 6 (June 2003): 21–25.

"Standards of Medical Care for Patients with Diabetes Mellitus." *Diabetes Care* 21, suppl. 1, *Clinical Practice Recommendations,* 1998.

"The United Kingdom Prospective Diabetes Study (UKPDS) for Type 2 Diabetes: What You Need to Know About the Results of a Long-Term Study." Posted to diabetes.org (accessed January 1999).

Utiger, Robert. "Restoring Fertility in Women with PCOS." *The New England Journal of Medicine* 335, no. 9 (August 29, 1996).

Weiss, P. M., et al. "Insulin Delivery System Options in Diabetes: Novel Approaches to an Old Disease." *The Female Patient* 28, no. 7 (July 2003): 14–24.

"When You Become an Amputee." Retrieved from the Amputee Web site, amputee-online.ca (accessed July 2001).

Willett, W. C., et al. "Intake of Trans Fatty Acids and Risk of Coronary Heart Disease Among Women." *Lancet* 341 (1993): 581–585.

Williamson, G. M., et al. "Social and Psychological Factors in Adjustment to Limb Amputation." *Journal of Social Behavior and Personality* 9 (1994): 249–268.

Williamson, Gail M. "Perceived Impact of Limb Amputation on Sexual Activity: A Study of Adult Amputees." *The Journal of Sex Research* 33, no. 3 (1996): 221–230.

Wu, J., and J. P. Levine. "Cardiovascular Disease." *The Female Patient* 29, no. 8 (August 2004): 34–43.

Zinman, Bernard. "Insulin Analogues." *Diabetes Dialogue* 43, no. 4 (Winter 1996): 14–15.

Index